STUDIES IN ENGLISH LITERATURES

Edited by Koray Melikoğlu

Pablo Armellino

Ob-scene Spaces
in Australian Narrative

An Account of the Socio-topographic
Construction of Space in Australian Literature

STUDIES IN ENGLISH LITERATURES

Edited by Koray Melikoğlu

ISSN 1614-4651

3   *Daniel M. Shea*
    James Joyce and the Mythology of Modernism
    ISBN 3-89821-574-1

4   *Paul Fox and Koray Melikoğlu (eds.)*
    Formal Investigations
    Aesthetic Style in Late-Victorian and Edwardian Detective Fiction
    ISBN 978-3-89821-593-0

5   *David Ellis*
    Writing Home
    Black Writing in Britain Since the War
    ISBN 978-3-89821-591-6

6   *Wei H. Kao*
    The Formation of an Irish Literary Canon in the Mid-Twentieth Century
    ISBN 978-3-89821-545-9

7   *Bianca Del Villano*
    Ghostly Alterities
    Spectrality and Contemporary Literatures in English
    2nd, revised editon
    ISBN 978-3-89821-714-9

8   *Melanie Ann Hanson*
    Decapitation and Disgorgement
    The Female Body's Text in Early Modern English Drama and Poetry
    ISBN 978-3-89821-605-5

9   *Shafquat Towheed (ed.)*
    New Readings in the Literature of British India, c.1780-1947
    ISBN 978-3-89821-673-9

10 *Paola Baseotto*
    "Disdeining life, desiring leaue to die"
    Spenser and the Psychology of Despair
    ISBN 978-3-89821-567-1

11 *Annie Gagiano*
    Dealing with Evils
    Essays on Writing from Africa
    ISBN 978-3-89821-867-2

12 *Thomas F. Halloran*
    James Joyce: Developing Irish Identity
    A Study of the Development of Postcolonial Irish Identity in the Novels of James Joyce
    ISBN 978-3-89821-571-8

Pablo Armellino

OB-SCENE SPACES IN AUSTRALIAN NARRATIVE

An Account of the Socio-topographic
Construction of Space in Australian Literature

ibidem-Verlag
Stuttgart

Bibliografische Information der Deutschen Nationalbibliothek
Die Deutsche Nationalbibliothek verzeichnet diese Publikation in der
Deutschen Nationalbibliografie; detaillierte bibliografische Daten sind im
Internet über http://dnb.d-nb.de abrufbar.

Bibliographic information published by the Deutsche Nationalbibliothek
Die Deutsche Nationalbibliothek lists this publication in the Deutsche Nationalbibliografie;
detailed bibliographic data are available in the Internet at http://dnb.d-nb.de.

Cover illustration: *Institute of Australian Values* (detail), David Disher, 2007. Copyright David Disher.

∞

Gedruckt auf alterungsbeständigem, säurefreien Papier
Printed on acid-free paper

ISSN: 1614-4651

ISBN-10: 3-89821-873-2
ISBN-13: 978-3-89821-873-3

© *ibidem*-Verlag
Stuttgart 2009

Alle Rechte vorbehalten

Das Werk einschließlich aller seiner Teile ist urheberrechtlich geschützt. Jede Verwertung
außerhalb der engen Grenzen des Urheberrechtsgesetzes ist ohne Zustimmung des Verlages
unzulässig und strafbar. Dies gilt insbesondere für Vervielfältigungen,
Übersetzungen, Mikroverfilmungen und elektronische Speicherformen sowie die
Einspeicherung und Verarbeitung in elektronischen Systemen.

All rights reserved. No part of this publication may be reproduced, stored in or introduced into a retrieval
system, or transmitted, in any form, or by any means (electronic, mechanical, photocopying, recording or
otherwise) without the prior written permission of the publisher. Any person who does any unauthorized act
in relation to this publication may be liable to criminal prosecution and civil claims for damages.

Printed in Germany

Contents

Acknowledgements

1 Introduction: Obscene Settings   1

2 The Establishment of the Antipodes   21

    2.1 The Carceral Archipelago   27
    2.2 True History: Squatters, Selectors and Bushrangers   46

3 The Outback   57

    3.1 Nineteenth Century Idealizations   57
       3.1.1 Lawson, Paterson and Baynton   58
       3.1.2 *Picnic at Hanging Rock*   77

    3.2 White Men in the Outback   87
       3.2.1 *Voss*   87
       3.2.2 *Remembering Babylon*   103
       3.2.3 *Coonardoo*   116
       3.2.4 *Capricornia*   129

    3.3 An Aboriginal Perspective   139
       3.3.1 *Doctor Wooreddy's Prescription*   141
       3.3.2 *Benang*   153
       3.3.3 *Plains of Promise*   169

4 The City: The Crumbling Bulwark   189

    4.1 The Ubiquitous Closet   196
    4.2 The Vanishing of the Scene   204
    4.3 From the Periphery to the Centre   214
    4.4 Ostracized from Society   220
    4.5 Gangs and the Significance of Subcultures   224
    4.6 Solving the Conflict   240

5 Back to the Outback   245

    5.1 An Ongoing Legacy   246
    5.2 Tumbling Skeletons from the Closet   257

Bibliography   267

Acknowledgements

This book originates from a doctoral thesis written for a PhD candidature at the University of Turin, Italy. I therefore wish to thank the English Department of the University of Turin for making the researching and writing of this work possible. In particular, I am grateful to Professor Carmen Concilio and Professor Pietro Deandrea for their friendship and enduring support.

I also wish to express my deepest gratitude to the English Department of La Trobe University for making me welcome for three years at the Bundoora Campus in Melbourne. Special thanks go to Professor Sue Thomas and Professor Gregory Kratzmann who offered important advice and assistance.

I would like to thank the PhD students from both institutions who, in innumerable conversations, provided hints and inspiration.

I would also like to thank my wife Stephanie and my dear friend Jen for their precious help and counsel.

Finally, one most deeply felt 'thank you' to my parents for their persistent support.

Pablo Armellino

1 Introduction:
Obscene Settings

'Obscene' is a word that evokes repugnance and is generally associated with deviance, violence and perverse sexuality. The unpleasantness of such material suggests an inherent difficulty in dealing with the subject: talking about obscenity implies voicing the unspeakable and uncovering undesirable truths. Using the *MLA International Bibliography* to run a search for the term 'obscene' (as 'subject' and using the wildcard '*') returns a large number of entries (347 as of the 23 of August 2006) ranging in topic from censorship to the linguistic use of coarse language and from violence to pornography. Yet, most of these studies are concerned with the mechanisms leading to the suppression of obscenity (censorship), not the obscene material itself. This suggests that obscenity has an intrinsic place in our culture: due to its alleged offensiveness, it is ostracized as far as possible beyond the reach of our daily life. Using simple logical inference, one might assume that if obscenity is actively displaced, it must also have a place. This is a very appealing idea, and only recently the *Oxford English Dictionary* proceeded to clarify the possible etymology and the meaning of 'obscene.' The second edition of the *OED* (1989) states:

> obscene, a.
> [...] [ad. L. *obscēnus, obscænus* adverse, inauspicious, ill-omened; transf. abominable, disgusting, filthy, indecent: of doubtful etymology. Perh. immed. after F. *obscène* (1560 in Godef. *Compl.*).]
> 1. Offensive to the senses, or to taste or refinement; disgusting, repulsive, filthy, foul, abominable, loathsome. [...]
> 2. Offensive to modesty or decency; expressing or suggesting unchaste or lustful ideas; impure, indecent, lewd. †*obscene parts*, privy parts (*obs.*). [...]
> 3. Ill-omened, inauspicious. (A Latinism.) *Obs.* [...] (*The Oxford English Dictionary*, 2nd ed., 656)

2   Obscene Spaces in Australian Narrative

Although the definitions of the word do not suggest it has any relationship to spatiality, its doubtful etymology does not prevent the reader from assuming that it has a close relationship with the word 'scene' and, therefore, is a derivative of the Latin word *scaena*. This word, although unchanged in the 1993 and 1997 Additions Series, is given a new definition in the *OED online*, which offers a preview of the draft entries for the forthcoming third edition.

> obscene, a.
> [<Middle French, French *obscène* indecent, offensive (1534; a1592 as *obscœne* (Montaigne)) and its etymon classical Latin *obscēnus*, *obscaenus* inauspicious, ill-omened, filthy, disgusting, indecent, lewd < ob- OB- + a second element of uncertain origin (see note). Cf. slightly earlier OBSCENITY n., OBSCENOUS a.
> Classical Latin *obscēnus*, *obscaenus* has been variously associated, by scholars ancient and modern, with *scaevus* left-sided, inauspicious (see SCÆVITY n.) and with *caenum* mud, filth (see CŒNOSE a.). The derivation from *scaena* SCENE n., one of several suggested by the Latin grammarian Varro, prob. represents a folk etymology.]
> 1. Offensively or grossly indecent, lewd; (*Law*) (of a publication) tending to deprave and corrupt those who are likely to read, see, or hear the contents. [...]
> †**parts obscene** [after classical Latin *parts obscēnae*], the genitals; also in *sing.* (*obs.*).
> 2. Offending against moral principles, repugnant; repulsive, foul, loathsome. Now (also): *spec.* (of a price, sum of money, etc.) ridiculously or offensively high. [...]
> †3. Ill-omened, inauspicious. *Obs. rare*. [...] (*OED Online* Mar. 2004)

The difference is striking. In this new draft, the etymology of 'obscene,' although remaining uncertain, is precisely indicated as having two plausible origins: *ob-scaevus*, meaning 'of / pertaining to the inauspicious'; or *ob-caenum*, meaning 'of / pertaining to filth.' Most notably, the derivation from *scaena* is now included but clearly discounted as a folk etymology. This rules out an etymological origin of the connection between obscenity and space but, at the same time, it stresses the cultural significance of this relationship. Another significant change between editions is the first meaning of the word. In the online draft entry we find that obscene is now defined in the context of "a publication," and that an obscene text can deprave and corrupt those who are likely to read, see or hear the content. The significance of this choice might be gleaned from what is perhaps only a coincidental comment. In 2003 J. M. Coetzee (South African but an Australian resident) published *Elizabeth Costello: Eight Lessons*, a collection of inter-related meta-fictional short stories about an imaginary Australian author. That same year Coetzee won the Nobel Prize. Very significantly, one of *Elizabeth Costello*'s lessons – the reading of which inspired this study – is dedicated to the Problem of Evil and directly confronts the theme of obscenity in literature:

> *Obscene*. That is the word, a word, a word of contested etymology, that she must hold on to as talisman. She chooses to believe that *obscene* means *off-stage*. To save our humanity, certain things that we may want to see (*may want to see because we are human!*) must remain off-stage. (Italics in original. Coetzee 2003, 168)

Coetzee, by making this fictional author embrace the spatial meaning of the word, effectively demonstrates the manner in which obscenity has been fashioned and has reciprocally fashioned our society. As Elizabeth Costello suggests, the word 'obscene' indicates a space beyond the "theatrical scene" of our society, used to ensure that those obscenities that "must remain off-stage" do in fact remain off-scene. The popularization of this meaning by a world famous author in a novel published just prior to his nomination for the Nobel Prize for Literature may have influenced the drafting of the new entry of the *OED Online*. Another clue indicating this possibility is the fact that Coetzee's elderly author explicitly indicates the possibility that the obscene may "deprave and corrupt" (*OED Online*) either the reader or the author himself: "I do not think one can come away unscathed, as a writer, from conjuring up such scenes. I think writing like that can harm one" (Coetzee 2003, 172). Although the influence of Coetzee's work on the redrafting of the *OED Online* is difficult to establish, both texts suggest the existence of a contemporary preoccupation with obscenity and its spatial relevance to post-modern society.

Coetzee did not enter the debate uninformed. One of his critical works, *Giving Offense: Essays on Censorship* (1996), is entirely dedicated to the topic of censorship and, concomitantly, to its off-scene settings. Once we acknowledge this fact, it is easier to understand that Elizabeth Costello's ideas are not Coetzee's own; more specifically, the South African author uses the fictional Australian female author to voice ideas intended to stir a debate, to create self-conscious awareness and to disclose where the problem lies. Indeed, the present study has been inspired by Elizabeth Costello's words and therefore, although incidentally, Coetzee's role has been crucial to the initial framing of obscenity in this study. His definition of obscenity in *Giving Offense* is particularly useful for introducing the socio-cultural implication of obscenity:

> the obscene and the pornographic are not conferential. Scenes of evisceration, for instance, may be obscene but not pornographic. [...] Obscenity has a particular kind of impact on the offended subject: it produces repugnance, shock, or disgust (though, as Feinberg points out, the offending materials can paradoxically be alluring at the same time). (Coetzee 1996, 20)

As Elizabeth Costello points out, *"because we are human,"* we may want to see things that are both repulsive and alluring at the same time (cf. also Pease 2000, 34). For this reason, the relative/subjective nature of obscenity must be examined. It can be argued that obscenity, by appealing to the dignity of the offended, calls into question an entire construct of moral values. The most shocking thing about it is the possible intentionality of the act. The offender voluntarily infringes the law and therefore, in the personal relationship between offender and offended, calls into question the legitimacy of morality. Coetzee notes that "the infringements are real; what is infringed, however, is not our essence but a foundational fiction to which we more or less whole heartedly subscribe" (Coetzee 1996, 14). In short, the fact that we are capable of committing obscene acts indicates that the rules infringed are neither innate nor "our essence." On the contrary, they are a set of rules imposed by the all-encompassing discourse which stage-manages our society. This implies that obscenity and transgression are mere tools of that same discourse that so outspokenly banishes them. It is for this reason that so much critical attention has been dedicated to censorship and, also, why the many studies on censorship deal specifically with obscenity.

The implementation of this discursive construction of obscenity has been thoroughly studied by Michel Foucault, who, in the three volumes of *The History of Sexuality*, tries to establish whether "the workings of power, and in particular those mechanisms that are brought into play in societies such as ours, really belong primarily to the category of repression" (Foucault 1984, 10). His study demonstrates that repression is not always what it seems. For instance, in the case of sexuality, repression was strategically used to induce the dialogization of sex, which then was aptly utilized as an instrument of power over society. Sex was never censored at all; on the contrary, through its supposed banishment, an immense attention was devoted to it: "Rather than a massive censorship, beginning with the verbal proprieties of the Age of Reason, what was involved was a regulated and polymorphous incitement to discourse" (Foucault 1984, 34). Through the flourishing of both text-writing and every-day speech on and around the topic, the general perception of sexuality was reshaped and fashioned according to the need to structuring society: women first became sensual, later hysterics and afterwards fit only for caring jobs; men were entrusted with rationality; and, finally, any kind of deviation from the previous categories was to be repressed and punished. By simply engendering its subjects, the discourse thus managed to seize each individual and firmly locate him/her in his/her assigned role. The ontological importance of deviance should now be clear: deviance is imagined, produced, cornered and suppressed, not only in order to validate the authenticity of the norm but also to structure it.

Foucault's theory envisions discourse not as a simple ideology presiding over a certain period of time. Rather, discourse can be more properly envisioned as the battlefield of the self-perpetrating struggle between power and knowledge. As the French philosopher clearly states, "power and knowledge directly imply one another" because "there is no power relation without the correlative constitution of a field of knowledge, nor any knowledge that does not presuppose and constitute at the same time power relations" (Foucault 1979, 27). These fields of knowledge stretch across society and, by meticulously discerning and differentiating it, they classify it. In so doing they effectively exert power over society as a whole. For this reason the power-technology regulating society "cannot be localized in a particular type of institution or state apparatus," but rather, "this technology is diffuse, [...] it is often made up of bits and pieces [and] it implements different tools and methods" (Foucault 1979, 26). As a result, "its effects of domination are attributed [...] to dispositions, manoeuvres, tactics, techniques [and] functionings" which add up to "a network of relations, constantly in tension, in activity, rather than a privilege one might possess" (Foucault 1979, 26). Power does not reside in a person or institution but in the discourse that defines, validates and invests such entities with authority. The existence of such technology is ultimately justified by the exertion of power. The Discourse[1] becomes an all-encompassing entity that traverses innumerable centres of micro-power carefully disseminated throughout society: a network lacking a centre but held together by its intrinsic tension.

Foucault exemplified the functioning of the regulatory use of power focusing on – as previously mentioned – sexuality, clinics, asylums and prisons. Even though never directly confronting geography as a major theme (cf. Foucault 1980, 65-66), Foucault's work introduces concepts and ideas hinting at the domains of spatiality and topography. The disciplinary system used in each of the institutions analysed by the philosopher is rooted in, or at least related to, specific lo-

---

[1] From now on, 'Discourse' will be used with capitalized D to indicate Foucault's use of the term.

cations: the cell, the prison, the classroom, the asylum. Foucault's Discourse seems, therefore, to be implicitly quartering micro-powers in specific locations. More precisely, the consequence of micro-powers is the designation of functional locations upon the territory – the concept of territory itself being an instrument of the discursive control over space (cf. Foucault 1980, 68). The provocative argument at the base of *Discipline and Punish* finally clarifies the relationship between obscenity, spatiality and Foucault's theory: "the penalty of detention seems to fabricate [...] an enclosed, separated and useful illegality" (Foucault 1979, 278). The ultimate individuation, distinction and seclusion of deviance result in the creation of both a social group identifiable as criminal and of a space belonging to these people. The overcrowded city, the slum, the prison and the cell – in an inverse gradient of importance – are all spaces belonging to this "class" and ideally contributing to its manifestation and reproduction. However, the place of reclusion (an ob-scene space par excellence), which is supposed to reform the delinquent, is also, as Foucault says, a breeding ground for "an enclosed, separated and useful illegality". Useful, because the Discourse justifies the necessity of its regulatory function by showcasing the deviance contained within the cell.

Peter Stallybrass and Allon White grasped the importance of deviance and, in a study predominantly based on Bakhtinian theory, charted transgression in British culture. *The Politics and Poetics of Transgression* (1986) posits that "by tracking the 'grotesque body' and the 'low-Other' [...] we can attain an unusual perspective upon [the] inner dynamics [of bourgeois society]" in Victorian times. What they discovered is that "[w]hat is socially peripheral is often symbolically central" (Babcock, B., "The Reversible World"; qtd. in Stallybrass and White 1986, 20) and therefore "the carnival, the circus, the gipsy, the lumpenproletariat, play a symbolic role [...] out of all proportion to their actual social importance" (Stallybrass and White 1986, 20). The study of the slums, the sewerage and all that became symbolically connected to the "perverse," the "scatological" and the "low" exposes the hidden truth about Victorian society. Fixations such as concealing the legs of tables and the nudity of angels in ancient frescoes, reveal the way the scene, whilst trying to carefully drive the obscene other to the margins of society, in fact harboured it at its heart. With *The Politics and Poetics of Transgression*, Stallybrass and White demonstrated why it is necessary to study the obscene side of a society in order to fully understand it. Deviance, although carefully removed, is not only effectively produced by the Discourse but is also an integrating part of it. Hence the importance of documenting its place in society.

The French sociologist Henri Lefebvre, in his seminal text *The Production of Space* (1974), studied and theorized the process that leads to the creation of what we simply experience as the environment of our daily life. For Lefebvre, space is a complex sociological construct that, although intangible and transparent, determines the everyday understanding of our place in society. One of the fundamental ideas explored in this study is the idea that "any determined and hence demarcated space necessarily embraces some things and excludes others; what it rejects may be relegated to some nostalgia or it may be simply forbidden" (Lefebvre 1991, 99). For Lefebvre, one way of understanding the way space is constructed is to imagine that "walls, enclosures and façades serve to define both a *scene* (where something takes place) and an *obscene* area to which everything that cannot or may not happen on the scene is relegated" (Lefebvre 1991, 36). Hence, the obscene space is a space where the rules regulating the scene do not apply.

Although spawning from different theoretical backgrounds and trying to prove different things, Coetzee's take on obscenity and its off-scene "place" in society, Foucault's theory of disciplinary control, Stallybrass and White's conceptualization of Victorian space, and Lefebvre's notion of space, seem to agree on the fact that "whatever is inadmissible, be it malefic or forbidden, [...] has its own hidden space on the near or far side of a frontier" (Lefebvre 1991, 36).

Obscenity, in spite of its etymology, seems to be consistently related to space and so, for the purpose of this study, the word 'obscene'

1 Introduction: Obscene Settings

is henceforth used to imply the dual meaning immoral/off-scene, while the hyphenated variant 'ob-scene' further stresses its spatial connotation. This study proceeds to use Lefebvre's definition of obscene space, postulating the existence of a scene and an obscene space, to explore the furthest reaches of the British empire. Hence, Australian literature provides the raw material for the in-depth analysis of the socio-spatial construction of the colonial/antipodean space.

In *The Production of Space*, Lefebvre explains that a "façade admits certain acts to the level of what is visible" and "condemns [many other] to obscenity". However, the façade is not solely made of material walls "balconies, window ledges, etc." (Lefebvre 1991, 99) it also becomes a new level of signification that transcends the material referents. In a theorization that is reminiscent of Roland Barthes' analysis of the process of myth creation (Barthes 1957), Lefebvre posits the existence of a monumental space hovering over, and giving meaning to, space as perceived in everyday life:

> The indispensable opposition between inside and outside, as indicated by thresholds, doors and frames, though often underestimated, simply does not suffice when it comes to defining monumental space. Such a space is determined by what may take place there, and consequently by what may not take place there (prescribed/proscribed, scene/obscene). [...]
> Any object – a vase, a chair a garment – may be extracted from everyday practice and suffer displacement which will transform it by transferring it into monumental space: the vase will become holy, the garment ceremonial, the chair the seat of authority. The famous bar which, according to the followers of Saussure, separates signifier from signified and desire from its object, is in fact transportable hither and thither at the whim of society [...] as a means of banishing the obscene. (Lefebvre 1991, 224-226)

The arbitrariness implied in the creation of monumental space resonates right through the human experience of natural environment. Space is imperceptibly constructed in the very same way Foucault suggests power structures are erected around distinctions, rationalizations and distributions of deviance. Moreover, space is implicitly entrenched in the power relations expressed through functional allocations, suggestive connotations and explicit banishments of territories. The construction of space is fundamentally an exercise of power upon the spatial dimension of our world:

> The illusory clarity of *space* is in the last analysis the illusory clarity of *power* that may be glimpsed in the reality that it governs, but which at the same time uses that reality as a veil. Such is the action of political power, which creates fragmentation and then controls it – which creates it indeed in order to control it. But fragmented reality […] depends for sustenance on continual reinforcement. […] This is the form under which state-political power becomes omnipresent: it is everywhere, but its presence varies in intensity; in some places it is diffuse, in others concentrated. (Lefebvre 1991, 320-321)

Hence, although distinctly Marxist, Lefebvre's analysis closely parallels the basic assumptions of Foucault's theory on Discourse. Space, as one of the several fields of knowledge (further subdivided in geography, topography, etc.), is a critical site of power/knowledge relations. It thus becomes a diffuse, transparent and immanent presence governing everyday reality. Hence, a Discourse, in order to maintain and reinforce its control over the lands it governs, continually restructures legal and socio-imaginative status of these spaces.

Australia's case is exemplary and, having clarified the strategic importance of spatial control and the ensuing distinction between scene and obscene space, it is now possible to present the underlying theme of this research. That is, the way the spatial organization of this island-continent has changed over time. In the course of the following chapters, this topic will be chronologically and thematically examined as presented in Australian literature. Emblematically, Australia is a land that has long been fantasized about and subconsciously desired even before Europeans discovered it. As a result, although Aboriginal people had lived there for several thousands of years, Australia became *Terra Nullius* much before the British set foot on its shores to

1 Introduction: Obscene Settings 11

lay claim on it. An antipodean landmass was supposedly required in order to balance the overall equilibrium between seas and continents. As Simon Ryan argues in *The Cartographic Eye*, such a remote and mysterious place was made the make-believe vessel of all human eccentricity; a place of wonders that, in the most heightened "orientalist" fashion, was annexed to the Western Discourse prior to its first sighting (cf. Ryan 1996). In Lefebvre's terms, the antipodes were thus elevated to the status of monumental space and became a regulatory instrument of power over space. In fact, the annexation of Australia to the Western Discourse is not casual. In line with the repression-control strategy, the antipodes became the imaginative obscene space of the European scene, so that control could be reinforced on the scene and the obscene area could later be dealt with and placed under control.

Ryan demonstrates the manner in which Australia was caught in a discursive construction that filled the still imaginary continent with descriptions of an eccentric nature and perverse inhabitants. The othering of the still unknown continent and its inhabitants was caused by Europe's need to dispose of its unacceptable urges and confine them to a remote and secure region. In other words, "out of sight, out of mind." Thus, it is not surprising that, when Australia was actually "discovered," Great Britain immediately began transporting its convicts there. For in Australia, the British now had a real place to which they could export not just their fears and obscene impulses but the actual "refuse" of society itself. This process condemned Australia and its inhabitants to become unwilling protagonists of a story that denied them any agency.

The newly-settled antipodean continent could not forever endure such an infamous reputation. Although it came into being as the land of convicts and savages beyond salvation, once the colony grew in population and importance, social order was imported to Australia and the obscene was once again displaced to another off-scene setting. In keeping with this legacy, the image of the outback was later constructed according to European Societies' innate need to seclude the obscene in an ob-scene scenario. It is thus that the wide empty spaces of the Australian interior were filled with an imagery of absolute freedom and autonomy from the Law. Such a space was fit to contain all the human depravity with which the city, as the bulwark of human civilization, was not supposed to be acquainted. In addition, the discursive construction of this obscene setting "eased" white Australians into a socio-topographic space where their subconscious was allowed to materialize. The outback, with its remoteness and inaccessibility, became the preferred scenario. The Aborigines had retreated there, but more importantly it was the outback's vastness and sparseness of population that made it an ideal setting for obscene urges to be acted out.

Elizabeth Povinelli argues persuasively that Britain's claim on Australia, under the concept of Terra Nullius, was largely based upon a late eighteenth century scheme aimed at reorganizing society through sexual regulation:

> In England during the mid- to late 1700s discussions of class and sexual irregularity and of race and criminality were critically informing government plans to settle Australia as a penal colony. The British social elite's discussions of class sexuality were concentrated on theorizing and institutionalizing capitally productive "marriage relations" among the emerging social classes. (Povinelli 1994, 125)

While England was trying to regulate the unclear sexual relations typical of its local village life (which even included deporting the supposed perverts), in order to establish a basis for the coming into being of the proletariat (an economic force which was increasingly required), the Australian colony was established on the mandates of this same social policy. According to Povinelli, Australia was declared *Terra Nullius* because the Aborigines were portrayed as being "sexually irregular and socially disordered" (Povinelli 1994, 126). Hence, the regulation of their "disorderly" socio-economic structure was deemed absolutely necessary.

1 Introduction: Obscene Settings

Sexual preoccupations lasted for over a century and remained entrenched in the socio-spatial configurations of the land. In a fashion reminiscent of Foucault's analysis of the development and control of sexual Discourse, obscenity, locked in a safeguard, became a material that again was continuously talked about but seemingly never handled in the first person. Sexuality and miscegenation, in particular, soon became a favoured topic of discussion. This is because while supposedly nobody was having sex with Aboriginal women, the "half-caste" was growing steadily in numbers. By the 1920s, it had became a major national preoccupation. Once again, the remote rural areas were singled out as the principal setting for the problem. These ob-scene areas thus came into contrast with the scene of major coastal cities.

This marked socio-topographic distinction – between an urbanized and civilized coast versus an untamed and disorderly interior populated by savages – reminds one of the socio-psychological split that Stallybrass and White observed in Victorian bourgeois society. At that time, everything that had anything to do with the lower parts of the body, with the discarded (defecation) and the censored (sexuality), was ideologically transposed to the "city's low" (Stallybrass and White 1986, 145). Via negative projective identification, the bodily low became associated with the slum, the sewerage, the prostitute and the "dirt down there" – here it is important to note that Australia was also a region "down under". As a result, the bourgeois unconscious was displaced in an ob-scene setting. Stallybrass and White conclude that:

> the city's low becomes a site of obsessive preoccupation, a preoccupation which is in itself intimately conceptualized in terms of discourses of the body. But this means that the obsessional neurosis or hysterical symptom can never be immediately traced back through the psychic domain. To deconstruct the symptomatic language of the bourgeois body, it is necessary to reconstruct the mediating topography of the city which always reflects the relations of class, gender and race. (Stallybrass and White 1986, 145)

Therefore, in order to analyse the dissociative disorder of Victorian society, Stallybrass and White use a wide range of primary sources – helping themselves from literature, sociology and psychoanalysis – which contextualize it in space. To decipher the "symptomatic language" of these texts, it is necessary to outline the map of the displacement of deviance. After doing this, we can then observe the Discourse as a whole (with its scene and obscene spaces) and, hopefully, gain access to the "psychic domain" which originated the "fracture" and its "language." Similarly, this research sets out to map the gradual displacement of Australian obscenity – both in time and space – in the hope of gaining access to a vantage point from which to comprehensively examine its contemporary society. To do so, this study will focus its attention on a selection of literary texts – for the most part novels – representative of Australian literature, from its outset to the present.

The novel is an especially appropriate instrument/subject of analysis because, as John Vernon argues in *The Garden and the Map*, it "arose in the great age of classical physics, when the earth was perceived as a map and therefore was being transformed into one" (Vernon 1973, 40). As a consequence, particularly in "realism and naturalism" (Vernon 1973, 40), and with the novelist as a (now inconceivably) omniscient author of a text, the novel emulates the "classical Newtonian and Cartesian consciousness of the world" (Vernon 1973, 41). From this perspective, the world, being observed from a fixed point in space, is reduced to a bi-dimensional and static image of itself. Vernon, quoting Edward Morgan Forster, goes on to explain that "[t]he novelist look[ing] down from a distance upon his materials" (Vernon 1973, 40), and the "ideal spectator," "sitting up on a hill at the end [of the novel]," viewing all the "cross-correspondences (145)" (Forster, Aspects of the Novel 1927. In Vernon 1973, 40) are the embodiment of this school of thought in literature. Hence, according to Vernon, the plot can be regarded as "the pattern of the world of the novel" (Vernon 1973, 40) and, therefore, as a map of itself.

1 Introduction: Obscene Settings 15

It is important to evaluate the pretence of self-contained objectivity of the novel in relation to its being – either consciously or unconsciously – an instrument of the Discourse in the transformation of space into a consumable commodity (cf. Vernon 1973, 10-11). As Chris Tiffin and Alan Lawson, in *De-Scribing Empire: Post-Colonialism and Textuality*, explain, "[i]mperial relations may have been established initially by guns, guile and disease, but they were maintained in their interpellative phase largely by textuality, both institutionally [...] and informally" (Tiffin and Lawson 1994, 3). Novels, with their mimetic pretence to objectivity, shaped and consolidated the spatial organization produced by the Discourse. However, this is only one level of integration of spatiality into the written medium. Johan Jacobs, in an essay which provides an informative summary of the dynamics and inter-relations between spatial construction and creative writing, formulates an important interpretation of J. Hillis Miller's *Topographies* (1995). As Miller puts it:

> Place names make a site already the product of a virtual writing, a topography, or, since the names are often figures, a "topography"' (3-4). Every narrative, therefore, in the way it constructs an arrangement of specific places, provides 'an exercise in spatial mapping' (10). The novel itself may also be seen in a larger sense as providing 'a figurative mapping' (19). (J Hillis Miller, *Topographies*, 1995; qtd. in Jacobs 2000, 209)

This means that the topography of the novel, as a would-be topography of the physical space it refers to, can be used to gain access to the strategic intention of the Discourse. Therefore, novels can be analysed by searching for the spatial referents that, according to the spatial disposition enforced at the time, contributed to the fashioning of their contemporary reality.

Starting from this assumption, this research uses a range of novels, to present and corroborate the way in which deviance and obscenity, have been gradually displaced in Australia. Different spatial configurations will be addressed in separate chapters respectively dealing with: chapter 2, the configuring of Australia as an obscene space *par excellence*; chapter 3, the shaping of the outback as Australia's principal obscene setting; chapter 4, the reflux of obscenity and subsequent corruption of the city; chapter 5, a contemporary perspective on the resurgent obscenity of the outback. As a character from a novel later analysed says, "Words are maps" (Turner Hospital 1996, 63). It is in this fashion that the present study uses words and texts. Novels in particular, apart from being independent textual/cartographic entities, also establish inter-textual bonds. They indirectly or directly talk to each other and create an even more complex structure mapping our cultural space. Therefore, the first novel considered in this study is Marcus Clarke's *For the Term of His Natural Life* (1874); a colonial novel that actively enforces Australia's strategic configuration as England's obscene Other, in the tangible form of a penal colony. The second text, Peter Carey's *True History of the Kelly Gang* (2000), is a post-colonial novel that clearly responds not only to the early portrayal of Irish people and emancipists as degraded people belonging to marginal and obscene spaces, but also to the misconstructions subsequently generated by the elaboration of myth. Although the literary chronology might at first seem disjointed and syncopated, it must be considered that, in order to second and interpret the dialogue between the texts, fictional chronology had to be privileged over the former. Furthermore, it must be stressed that that the intention of this study was never to present itself as an anthology of obscenity in Australian literature; rather, it is meant to be a study of the socio-topographic construction of obscenity in Australian literature. Although the case of chapter 2, "The Establishment of the Antipodes," with the coupling of Clarke's and Carey's novels is the most striking – 126 years separate them – other cases of deliberate inconsistency in chronological arrangement of the texts can also be found in the subsequent chapters.

Short stories and ballads by Henry Lawson, Banjo Paterson and Barbara Baynton are used in the first section of chapter 3, "Nineteenth Century Idealizations," to introduce the stereotyping of the bush as either an arcadian or as an earthly inferno. In the following sub-section,

1 Introduction: Obscene Settings   17

Lady Joan Lindsay's novel *Picnic at Hanging Rock* (1967) is used to unravel the ambiguity of this space and to explore its construction as a predominantly masculine area. From here, section 3.2, titled "White Man in the Outback," uses Patrick White's *Voss* (1957), David Malouf's *Remembering Babylon* (1993), Catherine Susannah Prichard's *Coonardoo* (1929) and Xavier Herbert's *Capricornia* (1938) to examine the process of spatial construction and the effect of the displacement of deviance and obscenity. *Voss* is particularly apt for this purpose. Not solely it is an exploration narrative that addresses the vital role played by explorers and cartographers in making space available for general fruition (in the form of diaries and Maps) but also because it clearly delineates the ambiguous contrast between the city and the bush. In this novel, the outback – along with the explorer who disappears into it – can be seen as a space both relegated to the realm of treacherous obscenity, and appropriated by the prudish Sydney bourgeoisie. *Remembering Babylon* examines the challenge posed by having to transform the space imaginatively produced by cartographers and politicians (on maps and allotments) into a "civilized space." The serenity of an isolated Queensland settlement is disrupted by the arrival of a white man "gone native." His presence questions the most basic moral constructs embodied in the fences enclosing the ploughed fields. The fences represent the boundary separating the scene from the impenetrable "darkness" of the territory and perceived hostility of the natives. The next step into the evolution of the Australian space is presented with *Coonardoo* where, on a station managed by white people but run with native labour, the problem of miscegenation and the immoral behaviour of white males is addressed for the first time in Australian literature. The outback is again an obscene space threatening to corrupt white heroes or providing refuge to those seeking immoral pleasures. Concluding the section "White Men in the Outback", Xavier Herbert's *Capricornia* is a celebration of the outback. The newly settled territory of Capricornia (a thinly disguised Northern Territory) is not a place to be feared but a land of opportunities. The novel therefore exposes the working of the power structure governing the outback and slowly transforming Capricornia into a redeemed space. Remarkably, the novel attempts to give a voice to the Aborigines, however, this results in a perhaps unconscious exploitation of their role in the novel. Section 3.3, "An Aboriginal Perspective," is dedicated to redressing all the cultural tropes which have so far victimized the natives and their space. Mudrooroo's *Doctor Wooreddy's Prescription for Enduring the Ending of the World* (1987) contests the vilification of the Tasmanian natives as savages from an historical point of view. The novel, proposing itself as an alternative history, unsettles the founding myths that justified colonization and rescues Aboriginal culture from the obscene status with which it has so long struggled. Kim Scott's *Benang* (1999) similarly contextualizes white history, but also actively reframes space by revisiting the sites where the silenced Aboriginal history was made. The last novel examined in this section, and also in this chapter, is Alexis Wright's *Plains of Promise* (1997), a novel that offers a compendium of the institutionalisation of the natives. With each policy, obscenity is discursively created and bureaucratically enforced by the successive institutions governing the life of the Australian natives.

Chapter 4, "The City: A Crumbling Bulwark," is a chiastic match to the previous sections. Five novels are used to contrast the initially idealized image of the city as a site of rationality and civilized purity against contemporary reality. For this reason, the first section (4.1) in this chapter, "The Ubiquitous Closet," is dedicated to Christos Tsiolkas' *Loaded* (1995), which provides an exhaustive portrayal of the dispersal of deviance into the complex structure of Melbourne's social scene. With this novel, Tsiolkas questions not only the positioning of the line dividing scene and obscene spaces, he also intrinsically questions the validity of such definitions. Homosexuality, transvestism and a scathing social critique are the weapons used to strike against a social order that has lost its grip on reality. Section 4.2, "The Vanishing of the Scene," uses Peter Robb's short story "Pig's Blood" (*Pig's Blood and Other Fluids*, 1999) to investigate the otherwise silent retrocession of the scene behind the dazzling façades of Sydney's skyscrapers. Melissa Lucashenko's *Steam Pigs* (1997) draws attention to racial discrimination as induced by the spatial configuration of suburbia. "From the Periphery to the Centre" (4.3) retraces the path followed by a young Murri girl through Queensland's areas of social segregation. In her quest for a position of self-empowerment, the protagonist has to first abandon her disadvantaged community, only to later flee domestic violence triggered by a socially degraded suburban environment. With her arrival in Brisbane and enrolment at university, what initially appears to be a reinstatement of the centre/periphery stereotype, actually is actually a sharp criticism of the government's failure to handle the situation. Section 4.4, "Ostracized From Society," similarly addresses the problem of Aboriginal marginalization. However, the protagonist in Archie Weller's *The Day of the Dog* (1981) fails to disengage himself from the path of self destruction imposed on him by Perth's racist society. In the end, he is literally expelled from society through a symbolic police chase ending in a fatal car accident. However, marginalization does not affect natives alone. The relatively unknown *A Bunch of Ratbags* (1965) by William Dick offers an alternative perspective on Melbourne's cityscape as viewed by an Anglo-Celtic youth growing up in the 1950s. In this novel, under the pressure of social disadvantage and marginalisation, the protagonist is driven to rage and despair. As a consequence, suburbia is turned into an obscene space where the unconscious overflows into the real world and fills this space with anger, violence and psychosomatic illness.

The final chapter "Back to the Outback," returns to the themes of chapter 3 but from a more contemporary perspective. Jeanette Turner Hospital's *Oyster* (1996) and Vivienne Cleven's *Her Sister's Eye* (2002) represent the bush as a space condemned to remain obscene as long as it remains saturated with secrets and guilt from the past. In *Oyster*, the silence clutching Outer Maroo is a self-imposed regimen of mutual protection from the indiscreet gaze of the scene. In this town, ob-scenity is sought in order to enjoy ultimate freedom from the corruption of the scene, the intransigence of the law and from the skeletons of the past. The result is catastrophic. In *Her Sister's Eye*,

Vivienne Cleven, who is of Aboriginal ancestry, counters this perspective by portraying the past as an ob-scene space needing to be freed from the clutch of silenced grief. The price to be paid when failing to do so is to be haunted by the ghosts of the past and to be uprooted from one's own country.

These four chapters of textual analysis provide a framework for understanding obscene spaces in Australia. Numerous texts could not be included in this study. For each chapter there are at least two books that, at one point in time, were temporarily part of the list of texts to be analysed. The most important of these novels were: Hal Porter's *The Tilted Cross* (1961) and Richard Flanagan's *Gould's Book of Fish* (2001) in chapter 2; Kate Greenville's *Secret River* (2005) and Jessica Anderson's *Tirra Lirra by the River* (1978) in chapter 3; Elliot Perlman's *Seven Types of Ambiguity* (2004) and Christos Tsiolkas *The Jesus Man* (1999) in chapter 4; and, Elizabeth Jolley's *The Well* (1986) and Gerald Murnane's *The Plains* in chapter 5. In the end, these novels, in spite of their relevance and value, were excluded either because their contribution would have been marginal or, as in the case of *Secret River*, because at the time of this research they were yet to be published. Nonetheless, as previously mentioned, this research does not have an anthological intent. On the contrary, the texts work independently as single analytical units but also, and most importantly, as a group – almost like a team – united in the purpose of exploring the "obscene spaces in Australian literature."

2 The Establishment of the Antipodes

Robert Hughes' *The Fatal Shore* (1987), with its imposing 600 pages, is one of the most well-known and exhaustive studies of the Australian penal past. In spite of the criticism it drew for its "gorification of convict hardship" (Turcotte 1998, 15), the book provides a vivid and informative picture of the dawn of white settlement in the antipodean continent. In addition to describing the way class segregation served to rule the young colony, Hughes' study also endeavours to illustrate the socio-cultural conditions that willed into being such a highly structured system of control. The frightening portrait it paints of the reality created in the penal colony – an outpost of civilization but also, being a continent-prison, its intrinsic negation – reflects the internal politics of the culture that produced this space. In the very first page of this study the author unveils the deep and dark allegiance binding Australia with its mother country; the image sketched is one of Manichean contrast and, most importantly, of utterly obscene resonance:

> The late eighteenth century abounded in schemes of social goodness thrown off by its burgeoning sense of revolution. But here, the process was to be reversed: not Utopia, but Dystopia; Not Rousseau's Natural Man moving in moral grace amid free social contacts, but man coerced, exiled, deracinated, in chains. [...] [T]he intellectual patrons of Australia, in its first colonial years, were Hobbes and Sade.
>
> In their sanguine moments, the authorities hoped that it would eventually swallow an entire class – the "criminal class" [...]. Australia was settled to defend English property [...] from the marauder within. English lawmakers wished not only to get rid of the "criminal class", but if possible to forget about it. Australia was a cloaca, invisible, its contents filthy and unamendable. (Hughes 2003, 1-2)

The driving forces of the social project ruling the foundation of Australia were displacement and forgetting. The terms used by the author brings to mind the subject of Peter Stallybrass and Allon White's *The Politics and Poetics of Transgression* (1986), where the London sewerage and its connected underworld are said to become the dark mirror of the soul of a society struggling with its moral values. Thus, the bourgeois ruling class projected all its fears and repressed passions upon the lower classes. According to this vision, the convicts were not filthy and unredeemable because of the immorality of their crimes, but because of the role that the dominant Discourse had projected upon them. Above all they were the scapegoats of a system that actively displaced its internal Otherness upon a social class which would be in its turn displaced in "an-other" space. In the early days of the colony, this vast scheme of social purgation, as Hughes argues, created not Thomas More's Utopia – which, as a non-place, is by definition inexistent – but a Dystopia firmly rooted in culture and space. Set at the furthermost point from the British Isles and in tune with the legacy of stories that portrayed the antipodes as a place of oddity and perversity, Australia was born through the convergence of myth, social planning and colonial desire, and was thus deliberately set aside as an obscene space of Western culture.

In *The Dark Side of the Dream* (1991), Bob Hodge and Vijay Mishra expose the strategic importance of the establishment of a penal colony. They argue that Australia was founded with the Althusserian intent of keeping deviance at bay while contemporarily having it close at hand and easily repressible. According to Althusser the repressive state apparatuses – police, military and justice – worked in cooperation with what he calls ideological state apparatuses – religion, media and education – which had the function of justifying the physical coercion imposed by the state (Althusser 1994). In Hodge and Mishra's words:

> The deviants justify the repressive apparatus, aligning the 'normal' majority with the rectitude of the state. The construction of deviance is carried out by a collaboration between [repressive state apparatuses] and [ideological state apparatuses], and then confirmed by systems for the circulation of images. (Hodge and Mishra 1991, 118)

Hodge and Mishra make use of Althusser's theory to demonstrate that Australia was used both to construct and to reform deviance by exemplarily channelling it away. As the two scholars remark, the project for the establishment of the Australian penal colony was conceived at a very particular time. As Michel Foucault explains in *Discipline and Punish* (1979), between 1760 and 1840 the disciplinary system of the European states underwent a profound transformation that changed the old way of spectacularly exerting power on the bodies of the offenders – through public torture and executions (cf. Foucault 1979, 26, 43, 47-46, 56) – to a more humane policy of "reformation" of the offenders associated with a subtler and more pervasive system of "panoptical' control over society (cf. Foucault 1979, 217, 250-251, 264).

However, this change came at a time when the English law was being altered in order to suit the interests of the rapidly increased importance of the new social power, which is the bourgeoisie. As a result, as Hughes argues, between 1660 and 1820, 187 capital statutes became law, "all [...] drafted to protect property, rather than human life" (Hughes 2003, 29), With a rapidly swelling population and a rampant poverty rate inducing a fast and steady process of urban migration, the old system of punishment combined with the new laws protecting property produced an exorbitant amount of convictions mostly resulting in capital punishments: "One could be hanged for burning a house or a hut, a standing rick of corn, or an insignificant pile of straw; for poaching a rabbit, for breaking down 'the head or mound' of a fishpond, or even cutting down an ornamental shrub; or for appearing on a high-road with a sooty face" (Hughes 2003, 29).

If nowadays these facts provide what seems to be certain proof of one of the founding myths of Australia – the unjust transportation of people solely guilty of crimes of poverty – at the time of convict transportation, they were at the heart of the production of the image of deviance. As Foucault explains, the judiciary system was and still is the primary means of producing normality:

> [T]he sentence that condemns or acquits is not simply a judgement of guilt, a legal decision that lays down punishment; it bears within it an assessment of normality and a technical prescription for a possible

normalization. Today the judge – magistrate or juror – certainly does more than 'judge'. (Foucault 1979, 21)

This means that the "criminal class" was initially conceived by the promulgation of the laws defining the crimes against property and later "carved" into society enforcing rules which confined people or, as in this case, an entire social class outside the borders of "normality." As the inflexible English law firmly applied this distinction, capital executions on the gallows served to publicly re-present the moral boundary lines. However, as previously mentioned, the idea of convict transportation to Australia was conceived at a crucial moment in the transformation of the European penal system. It was thus that commuting the capital sentence to transportation became common practice in England:

> When the Royal Mercy intervened as it commonly did, transmuting the death penalty into exile on the other side of the world, the accused and their relatives could bless the intervening power of patronage while leaving the superior operations of Law unquestioned. The Law was a disembodied entity, beyond class interest: the god in the codex. (Hughes 2003, 30)

This provisional system allowed for a relaxation of the system of punishment without simultaneously renouncing the discursive productivity implied by the execution of the sentence. Implicitly, the rhetorical meaning of capital punishment was shifted to the secondary means of punishment. As a result, transportation synecdochically – as the part for the whole – stood for the old spectacular coercion of deviance. Halfway through the process of reforming the system of punishment, convict transportation created a structure – part exemplary punishment and part redemption via confinement – which topographically demarcated and represented the image of bestiality and deviance. As Hughes meaningfully argues, Australia was used as a "cloaca" in order to purge England from its "criminal class" and possibly "forget about it" (Hughes 2003, 1-2). However, far from being forgotten, Otherness was thus psychologically and physically displaced to the other side of the world and conveniently used to mould into shape the English Self.

In this way, detention started to take over the functional role of physical punishment. The figures reported in *The Fatal Shore* confirm this: the percentage of executions per capital convictions slowly declined to almost nothing in the period between 1749 (69.3%) and 1808 (15.7%) (Hughes 2003, 35). However, as a part for the whole, Australia was still meant to epitomize the old ways and for this reason, as Hodge and Mishra contend, the colony partly "maintained the punitive practices that were also intrinsic to the system" (Hodge and Mishra 1991, 119). In the penal colony the body of the convict was still used as the primary medium for immediate coercion. Fetters, floggings and all sorts of cruel physical and psychological tortures were used to subdue those who misbehaved. Thus, although Australia ideally substituted the gallows, while in exile the convict's body was still firmly held in the king's grasp. As a result, the royal mercy offered in England was counter-balanced by a concomitant display of royal power in the colony.

Australia was thus born as a place of Otherness in a mutual relationship to its mother country. Deportation shaped normality by defining deviance and theatrically keeping it at bay. In *The Dark Side of the Dream*, Hodge and Mishram point out that this system was also redeployed in the newly founded colony:

> The split that gave birth to the colony spawned analogous divisions within it, displacing fragments of penality from Botany Bay into such notorious settlements as Norfolk Island, Port Arthur and Moreton Bay. These acted as 'spectacles of punishment' for the colony as the hulks and Botany bay did for England and Ireland. (Hodge and Mishra 1991, 119)

What becomes apparent is the way, at the time of the First Fleet, the socio-topographic construction of Australia was based on the displacement of deviance and the implicit othering of peripheral areas. This situation foreshadows the implementation of the ever more pervasive system of power symbolically embodied in Bentham's panoptic prison: surveillance. In *Discipline and Punish*, Foucault argues that "[o]ur society is not one of spectacle, but of surveillance [...]" (Foucault 1979, 217). This affirmation would initially seem to clash with Hodge and Mishra's argument regarding the spectacle produced by the institutions of secondary punishment in the penal colony. However, when considering this, it is important to consider that Port Arthur, Moreton Bay or Norfolk Island were less and less part of the old power structure, where torturing the offender meant for "the king [to] take revenge for an affront to his very person" (Foucault 1979, 48). Rather, they were posited in a new order where the exposure of deviance justified the need for surveillance.

The amazing revelation in Foucault's study is that "prison, and no doubt punishment in general, is not intended to eliminate offences, but rather to distinguish them, to distribute them, to use them" (Foucault 1979, 272). Australia's history seems to perfectly match this idea: the project of establishing a penal colony at Botany Bay, although reputed economically unviable (cf. Hughes 2003, 64-66), was nevertheless initiated in order to displace the "criminal class." What Foucault's theory proves is that the intent of transportation was "not so much [...] [to] render docile those who are liable to transgress the law, but [...] [to] assimilate the transgression of the laws in a general tactic of subjection" (Foucault 1979, 272). In light of this theory, it becomes clear that the penal system, and along with it the transportation system, do not really try to reform criminals or to prevent their crimes; rather, they use them to justify the existence of the coercive methods used to shape society. Therefore, the confinement of the criminal class to isolated spaces of exemplary punishment was not solely intended as a process of expurgation of English society, but one intended to seize control over it and thoroughly transform it through surveillance. The criminal class, craftily singled out and orderly defined by the penal system, thus became the Other to the normalized Self of English society. Concomitantly, Australia, with its hierarchical structure of punishment, became the litmus test for its mother country's alterity.

2 The Establishment of the Antipodes 27

As Australia became a free-settler colony, it soon tried to wash the convict stain away by initiating a process of "purification" similar to that used by its mother country. The convicts, both the Other and the Subconscious of the young antipodean society, were displaced to the margins. From being a uniformly ob-scene space the continent rapidly evolved to become a diversified setting with Sydney, the centre of political power, standing in contrast to the variously dislocated institutions of secondary punishment or, more generally, to the threatening alterity of the untamed continent. This redemption was made possible not solely by the deployment of the repressive state apparatuses but also, and most importantly, by using the more deviously persuasive influence of ideological state apparatuses. Marcus Clarke's *For the Term of His Natural Life* (1874) is probably the text that had the most significant influence in the shaping of the young nation's identity. Almost as exemplary as Hughes' *The Fatal Shore*, the novel explores all the corners of the Australian system of punishment and gives a detailed account of the moral landscapes traversed by the protagonist. The next section of this chapter will be devoted to analyzing the socio-topographic construction of Australia proposed by Clarke in this novel and the resulting justification and outlining of the obscene spaces of the continent.

2.1 The Carceral Archipelago

The 1874 edition of *For the Term of His Natural Life* is accompanied by a preface in which the author states his reasons for writing a novel prying in the darkest corners of Australia's short history. The significance of this brief piece of writing – both a programmatic declaration and a justification for the possible offence provoked by the themes covered in the novel – is telling of the kind of society this text speaks for. As the author himself explains, convict life was a topic which had long remained unspoken: "Charles Reade has drawn the interior of a house of correction in England, and Victor Hugo has shown how French convict fares after the fulfilment of his sentence. But no writer

– so far as I am aware – has attempted to depict the dismal condition of a felon during his term of transportation" (Clarke 1992, 19). Clarke's claim of being the first author to discuss convictism, raises the question of why fiction had never been addressed this topic before. In a society that had until recently publicly tortured and hanged people, such prudery is hardly explicable. Yet, while bourgeois morality promoted the deportation of convicts, it had a rested interest in keeping its ostracized unconscious concealed from the gaze of literary texts. For this reason, it can be argued that Clarke makes amends to his audience and explains that his reasons are purely philanthropic and aimed at exposing past wrongs so that they may not recur, hence couching this potentially subversive text firmly in a bourgeois moral sensibility. Accordingly, in *Marcus Clarke*, Brian Elliot questions the honesty of this affirmation and affirms that the whole preface "was an afterthought," that "he had no intention of writing a pamphlet against the system" and that "he was merely interested in writing a novel" (Elliott 1958, 145). Elliott supports his argument with several quotations where Clarke's attitude towards convicts is demonstrated to be not in the least sympathetic. Laurie Hergenhan, in "The Contemporary Reception of *His Natural Life*," explains that Clarke, with his preface, might have been seeking a "justification" or "guarantee of respectability" since "in Victorian times a reforming social purpose had become an acceptable reason for probing into the darker areas of life, into suffering and degradation, especially in low life" (Hergenhan 1971, 51).

Whether or not Clarke was supporting the ideals he declared to be heralding, his case demonstrates the way the Dominant Discourse substituted the coercive function of public executions with the less conspicuous machinery of ideological state apparatuses. This means that novels, journals, bureaucratic institutions, etc took the place of lashes, fetters and gallows in the everyday effort of imposing an order to society. Through these new media, the Discourse artfully showcased and dialogised the concealed vindictiveness of the repressive state apparatus and – as Foucault argues in regard to sex in *The History of Sexuality*, vol. 1 (cf. Foucault 1984, 17-35) – effectively amplified the final impact of punishment due to its concealment. Hence, texts like *For the Term of His Natural Life*, even when proclaiming to be written for philanthropic purposes, provided a feedback for the isolation scheme and contributed to the divulgation and establishment of the social organisation induced by the Discourse.

Marcus Clarke's novel is an excellent instrument of analysis for the understanding of the socio-topographic organization of penal Australia. The story follows Richard Devine, who vows never to use his genteel name again in order to protect his mother's secret,[2] and so is suddenly projected in an overturned reality when, unjustly accused of having killed a man, he is transported to Australia under the name of Rufus Dawes. The ensuing story is a tragedy of epic dimensions, where the protagonist traverses all the levels of punishments reserved for recidivist convicts and becomes either the protagonist or closely connected to all of the most relevant events in convict history. For this reason, as Leslie Robson contends, although the novel is often well informed, the reader's perception of the general convict experience is distorted by the narrative choices made by the author to heighten the overall tragic effect:

> Up to 1840, nearly all convicts were assigned and for any breaches of the regulations charged by their masters before magistrates. Punishments varied greatly and only the persistent or serious offenders were re-transported to a place of secondary punishment such as Macquarie Harbour, Port Arthur or Norfolk Island. [...] Thus, although the author seizes upon his material where it suits his purpose to entertain the reader, historically speaking we must conclude that the novel cannot help but be a misleading account of convict colonization. (Robson 1963, 107)

The fact that *For the Term of his Natural Life* is "the best novel produced in nineteenth-century Australia" and that "for most Australians it, and not the history books, has provided the main image of the

---

[2] Sir Richard Devine is an illegitimate child, conceived by his mother from lord Bellasis, and therefore not legally entitled to inherit the Devine's fortune.

convicts" (Hergenhan 1993, 47), may give an idea of the huge impact that the liberties taken by the author must have had on the Australian collective imaginary. The distortion of reality begins with the description of the voyage on the Malabar, where overcrowding is exaggerated (Robson 1963, 108-109) to emphasize the calamity suffered by the protagonist. On the ship, a second misfortune seals Rufus Dawes' fate. He is accused of being the ringleader of a mutiny that he actually thwarted. Thus, as soon as the vessel reaches Van Diemen's Land, he is consigned to the authorities and sent into "the jaws of Macquarie Harbour" (Clarke 1992, 94), one of the most dreaded institutions of secondary punishment. With this expedient, the pure-hearted protagonist is denied the ordinary experience of being assigned to a master – either a free-settler or an official of the colonial government – and is dispatched directly to one of the darkest and most obscene corners of the penal colony.

The exaggeration of Rufus Dawes' ordeal to appear effectively causes the general experience of transportation to appear all the more distinctly reprehensible. Yet, the aristocratic origin of the protagonist and his unquestionable innocence distort the perception of the reader and insinuate false ideas. Dawes/Devine's innocence seems, on one hand, to confirm the idea that convicts were victims of a vindictive system but, on the other hand, it displaces the real socio-political significance of this fact. As Hodge and Mishra observe, Clarke, by making his hero victim of "a series of malign coincidences that no system of justice could be expected to circumvent," shifts the attention of the reader away from the functioning of the institution he claims to be condemning (Hodge and Mishra 1991, 127). In the end, the situation of the protagonist stands in stark contrast to that of the average convict who could not possibly have received such an unfair treatment. The author highlights this distinction by asking the reader to "imagine" how it would feel to be in Rufus' position:

> Is it possible to imagine, even for a moment, what *an innocent man, gifted with ambition, endowed with power to love and to respect*, must have suffered during one week of such punishment? [...] We know

> that were we chained and degraded, fed like dogs, employed like beasts of burden, driven to our daily toils with threats and blows, and *herded with wretches among whom all that savours of decency and manliness is held in an open scorn*, we should die, or perhaps go mad. [...] No human creature could describe to what depth of abasement and self-loathing one week of such life would plunge him. [...] Imagine such torment for six years! (Emphasis mine Clarke 1992, 116)

His being herded with common criminals – which the author unsympathetically describes as little more than beasts – is in fact one of Dawes' main sources of despair. The overall effect is that, while the reader can safely identify with the untainted protagonist, the narrative further debases convicts as social refuses. The clear-cut subdivisions between villains and hero is also accentuated by what becomes a perpetual rivalry between the hero and John Rex:

> In vain had been his first dream of freedom. He had done his best, by good conduct, to win release; but the villainy of Vetch and Rex had deprived him of the fruit of his labour. Instead of gaining credit by his exposure of the plot on board of the Malabar, he was himself deemed guilty, and condemned despite his asseverations of innocence. The knowledge of his "treachery" – for so it was deemed among his associates – while it gained for him no credit with the authorities, produced for him the detestation and ill-will of the *monsters* among whom he found himself. (Emphasis mine Clarke 1992, 116)

The story appears to want to prove that "blood and breeding do matter after all, even in the hell-hole of a penal colony" (Hodge and Mishra 1991, 128). By preventing the mutiny – with which he would have gained immediate freedom – Dawes affirms his ultimate moral superiority: with his disinterested act he saves the lives of his jailers. As a result, the protagonist remains consistently estranged from his peers largely because they are not his equals: Rufus Dawes always remains Sir Richard Devine. He is a representative of the society that has not merely condemned the convicts to exile, but also created their class in the first instance. Accordingly, Dawes/Devine initially sides with the authorities and, reaffirming the moral standards of his social class, he immediately sets himself apart from the monstrous criminal class.

What would initially seem to be a novel engaged in contesting the convict system, at second glance actually appears to emphasize class division and reinforce the socio-topographic distinction between mother country and penal colony. In spite of the fact that Clarke exposes and condemns the mechanisms operating within this separation, the novel still confirms the pertinence of the division itself, in great part by characterizing the landscape according to the stereotyping imposed by the Discourse. Sylvia – a girl, and later, a woman, to whom Dawes becomes platonically attached – summarizes this paradox:

> What if the whole island was but one smouldering volcano of revolt and murder – the whole convict population but one incarnated conspiracy, engendered and bound together by the hideous Freemasonry of crime and suffering! [...] Oh, how strangely must the world have been civilized, that this most lovely corner of it must be set apart as a place of banishment for the monsters that civilization had brought forth and bred! (Clarke 1992, 254)

In this virtuous rationalization, although the system is expressly criticized for producing its own monsters, the hideous nature of the convicts is never itself called into question. This tacit allegation is also rendered implicit by the use of Rufus Dawes as an incorruptible instrument for the probing of ob-scenity. The protagonist's innocence is contrasted with the savagery of the average convict, whose position is consequently aggravated and ultimately deemed irredeemable. As a result, the narrative also reinstates the distinction between scene and ob-scene space. Sylvia's argument confirms that Australia, although "a lovely corner of this world," has been indeed set apart as England's obscene Other. Clarke's weak criticism of the Discourse only concedes that the world must be "strangely civilized" in order to produce this space; on the other hand, by unconditionally condemning the obscenity of this place, it only confirms its prejudice. Laurie Hergenhan,

2 The Establishment of the Antipodes   33

drawing inspiration from Foucault, concisely recapitulates the functioning of the mechanism instigating this subdivision:

> This natural class conflict [...] shows the transformation society enforces through its authority figures of magistrates, jailers and parsons. The transformation aggravates and yet controls the divisiveness, the "war", which is blamed on the lower criminal classes. The creation of wild beasts legitimizes the exercise of total power by jailers who in *His Natural Life* are far removed indeed from the sentencing magistrates. (Hergenhan 1993)

When Clarke, in *For the Term of His Natural Life*, exposes this cultural trope, he does so mainly to justify the creation of his intensely Gothicized settings. As a result, the transformations enforced upon society become unquestionable realities. It does not matter if the Australian space is a by-product of the English judiciary system; rather what is important is that the vicious cycle between transgression and repression creates monsters in both factions and that the protagonist is superior to both. Captain Frere, the merciless officer in charge of the institutions where Dawes is held captive, is not an anti-hero – otherwise the hero would be the villain John Rex – but the other side of the coin of the absolute obscenity of the penal system. Frere and Rex, being the only two possible embodiments of the brutal penal system, are equally distant from Rufus Dawes who represents a piece of England which remains unscathed until the end. Ultimately, it is the isolation of Australia that is responsible for the transformation of each individual into a monster. Being off-scene, "far removed from the magistrates" and from the British public opinion, it provides the perfect setting for an ob-scene scenario.

The plot of the novel coherently represents Rufus Dawes' experience according to a strict socio-topographic organisation of the land: following an increasing level of obscenity and isolation, the titles of the four books composing the novel name each of the circles of the Australian earthly inferno: "At Sea, 1827"; "Macquarie Harbour, 1833"; "Port Arthur, 1838"; and "Norfolk Island, 1846." The gradual displacement of deviance with its coupled means of punishment results in the constitution of a factual carceral archipelago. Foucault envisions this system as one mimetically dispersed through society and based on multilateral surveillance engendering silent definition, judgment and repression of deviance:

> Incarceration with its mechanism of surveillance and punishment functioned [...] according to a principle of relative continuity. [...] A continuity of the punitive criteria and mechanisms, which on the basis of a mere deviation gradually strengthened the rules and increased the punishment. (Foucault 1979, 299)

This continuity and the gradual intensification of punishment are at the very basis of the societal organization described by Clarke. For this reason, when Foucault argues that "the prison transformed the punitive procedure into a penitentiary technique" and that "the carceral archipelago transported this technique from penal institutions to the entire social body" (Foucault 1979, 298), one can deduce that Australia became the first and foremost actualization of this attitude. There, the penal institution truly corresponded to the entirety of the social body. As Gillian Whitlock notices, "England exported to [...] the penitentiaries of Van Diemen's Land and Norfolk Island the structure of a meticulously regulated and disciplined cell" where "each individual had a place, and each place an individual" (Whitlock 1987, 50). The network of power relations linking England, the Australian mainland, Van Diemen's Land, the Islands/Institutions of Maria Island, Sarah Island and Port Arthur, and the remote Norfolk Island formed a wide-reaching archipelago that fulfilled this need of socio-spatial rationalization. *For the Term of His Natural Life* reiterates this socio-cultural configuration and makes the protagonist traverse all of these spaces in order to experience the escalating levels of punishment set aside for each type of deviant subject therein confined. Each book clearly exemplifies the increasing obscenity of the punishment inflicted upon the convicts and the maddening effect it had upon the jailers. In these terms, it is Frere that accompanies Dawes in his journey through the carceral archipelago.

The opening of the second book of the novel faithfully portrays the socio-spatial organization of convict life in Van Diemen's Land:

> Seven classes of criminals were established in 1826, when the new barracks for prisoners at Hobart Town were finished. The first class were allowed to sleep out of barracks, and to work for themselves on Saturday; the second had only the last-named indulgence; the third were only allowed Saturday afternoon; the fourth and fifth were "refractory and disorderly characters – to work in irons;" the sixth were "men of the most degraded and incorrigible character – to be worked in irons, and kept entirely separate from the other prisoners;" while the seventh were the refuse of this refuse – the murderers, bandits, and villains, whom neither chain nor lash could tame. They were regarded as socially dead, and shipped to Hell's Gates, or Maria Island. Hell's Gates was the most dreaded of all these houses of bondage. The discipline at the place was so severe, and the life so terrible, that prisoners would risk all to escape from it. [...] During the ten years of its existence, one hundred and twelve men escaped, out of whom sixty-two only were found–dead. The prisoners killed themselves to avoid living any longer, and if so fortunate as to penetrate the desert of scrub, heath, and swamp, which lay between their prison and the settled districts, preferred death to recapture. Successfully to transport the remnant of this desperate band of doubly-convicted felons to Arthur's new prison, was the mission of Maurice Frere. (Clarke 1992, 101-102)

It is, in fact, with the arrival of Lieutenant Frere – who has been in charge of Maria Island – at Macquarie Harbour that the second book resumes the narration after six years of fictional silence. As the *Ladybird* sails through Hell's Gate with orders to evacuate the settlement and to take the convicts to the new Port Arthur penitentiary, the protagonist is held in solitary punishment on Grummet Rock for having attempted to escape. Major Vickers, the officer in charge of the settlement, prefers solitary confinement to the cruel and spectacular methods used by many of his colleagues:

> Barton, who was here before me, flogged tremendously, but I don't think it did any good. [...] [I] flog the worst, you know; but I don't flog more than a man a week, as a rule, and never more than fifty lashes. They're getting quieter now. Then we iron, and dumb-cells, and maroon them. [...] When a man gets very bad, we clap him into a boat with a week's provisions and pull him over to Grummet. There are cells cut in the rock, you see, and the fellow pulls up his commissariat after him, and lives there by himself for a month or so. It tames them wonderfully. (Clarke 1992, 104)

The use of the small island as the ultimate method of punishment underscores the importance of the "interrelation (or 'articulation') of power, discipline and space" in the penal colony society (Whitlock 1987, 51). Foucault writes that the changing society of the industrial age had "its fundamental reference [...] not [in] the state of nature, but [in] the subordinated cogs of a machine, [...] and not [in] the general will but [in] automatic docility" (Foucault 1979, 169). Major Vickers' punishment embodies this choice: by wanting to tame the convicts he wants to transform them in the reformed "docile bodies" (Foucault 1979, 136) needed by modern society. Vickers' choice also parallels another fundamental mechanism of the disciplinary system that, "in organizing 'cells', 'places' and 'ranks', [...] create[s] complex places that are at once architectural, functional and hierarchical" (Foucault 1979, 148). In the Australian case, the "cells" organized by the Discourse – from islands to continents – are delimited by topographic boundaries. The ob-scenity of what lies beyond the charted territory encloses each functional place.

The coercive role of nature is in fact at the centre of this book. The six years spent by the protagonist as a "Pariah among those beings who were Pariahs to all the world beside" (Clarke 1992, 117), are briefly dismissed with an account of the sufferings endured during this time. What the novel really seems to stress is "The Power of the Wilderness" (Clarke 1992, Ch. 20). Proof of this power is initially given by Gabbet's voluntary return to the penitentiary – Gabbet is one of the convicts with whom Dawes attempted to escape. Later, when Dawes escapes from Grummet Rock he similarly tries to reach a settled area only to discover that "as a cat allows a mouse to escape her for a while, so had he been permitted to trifle with his fate [...]. He never could escape" (Clarke 1992, 129). Australian nature is the ultimate ob-scene space. It is not a space of confinement, rather, it lies outside the moral boundaries of the western world. For this reason the wilderness is given a cruel will of its own, one that plays at cat and mouse with the convicts and that drives them to ultimate folly. As Dawes runs in circles trying to find a way to freedom he discovers the horrific remains of another of his companions:

> Stooping over it [...] he found the body was mangled. One arm was missing, and the skull had been beaten in by some heavy instrument! The first thought – that this heap of rags and bones was a mute witness to the folly of his own undertaking, the corpse of some starved absconder – gave place to a second more horrible suspicion. [...] He was standing on the place where a murder had been committed! A murder! – and what else? Thank God the food he carried was not yet exhausted! (Clarke 1992, 128)

Beyond the moral outposts of Western Civilization, anything is possible, even cannibalism. Ultimately, the bush is a space so ob-scene that all the moral conventions fall apart and leave individuals to behave freely according to their character. This idea is demonstrated when Dawes, left for dead, meets Frere and Vickers' wife and daughter marooned on the coast near Macquarie Harbour. Victims of a mutiny on the Osprey, they have been left with little food and no means of transportation. In this space, as Frere clearly states, "he is as helpless as [Dawes] is" (Clarke 1992, 153), and as a result his equal. Accordingly, Hergenhan argues that Dawes' replacement of Frere as "the leader and saviour of the [...] society of four" demonstrates "that power and authority, which in society are based on arbitrary class distinctions, are replaced in natural surroundings by individual abilities" (Hergenhan 1993, 58). Of course this "social fable" (Hergenhan 1993, 58) can only exist in the cultural void of the bush and, in fact, as soon as the survivors reach civil society, Frere takes credit for Dawes' gallant achievement and swiftly re-establishes the previous artificial power structure.

The two following books plunge the protagonist further down into the circles of the penitentiary inferno. The third book, "Port Arthur 1838," deals with both the debasement of convict life and with the failing character of the officials in charge of the bodies and the souls of the convicts. About them, John Tinkler writes that they are not merely gothic monsters, but "English types transported, intensified and distorted" (Tinkler 1982, 15). The novel implicitly suggests that this transformation is induced by the ob-scenity of Australia, where each character "would be innocuous enough in a suitable English [environment], but [they become] a positive evil when transplanted to Australia" (Tinkler 1982, 15). Tinkler takes Mr Meekin, a "clerical dandy," as an example and proceeds to explain how "all the material horrors of [...] faith – stripped, by force of dissociation from the context, of all poetic feeling and local colouring – were launched at the suffering sinner by [...] ignorant hand" (Clarke 1992, 290). *For the Term of His Natural Life* describes a world were even the spiritual guides are not capable of offering consolation to the convicts. In different ways the two ministers, Mr. Meekin and Mr. North, become corrupted by the iniquity they face. Meekin, by threatening the convicts with "the pains of Hell," "the never-dying worm," "the unquenchable fire," "the bubbling brimstone," and the "bottomless pit" (Clarke 1992, 290), becomes an accomplice of a system that brands the convicts as unredeemable subjects. North, who sides with the convicts, is overwhelmed by the injustice around him and drowns his troubles in alcohol; he thus both becomes corrupt and fails to administer the spiritual and physical salvation he might afford to dispense.

In a crucial episode, the cruelty of the system converges with the moral failure of the chaplains. Mr. North fails twice to save Kirkland, a cultured convict son of a Methodist minister, from the malicious hands of the jailers. As Robson remarks, it is at this occasion that Clarke "introduce[s] obliquely but unmistakably the subject of homosexuality, which offence, asterisked in parliamentary reports, caused such horror to commentators at the time" (Robson 1963, 115). In the morning, after a night spent with the "old hands,"[3] Kirkland implores the reverend to let him out: "Mr. North! Would you see me perish, body and soul, in this place? Mr. North! Oh, you ministers of Christ – wolves in sheep's clothing – you shall be judged for this!" Although North tries to save him by petitioning to Commandant, "my good sir, [...] [y]ou can guess what that unhappy boy has suffered," he is faced with the sadism of the officer who retorts: "Impertinent young beggar! [...] Do him good, curse him!" (Clarke 1992, 290). Clarke's world is one gone astray, one where the system has transformed both convicts and jailers into ferocious beasts. To add to the horror of this incident, Kirkland is later condemned to one hundred lashes for trying to escape the gang where he is called "Miss Nancy." Again, North is not capable of preventing the worst from happening: in the morning he sleeps in with a hang-over while the ex-bank clerk succumbs after fifty lashes. The vivid description of the lashing also becomes the excuse to reaffirm the superiority of the central character: ordered to administer the one hundred lashes to Kirkland, after the first fifty and just before the boy dies, he refuses to continue in his task and, undaunted, he faces the resulting merciless flogging. Avis McDonald explains that with this conduct, "if only by saying 'no' to the convict system that holds his body in bondage," Dawes "exercises the choice that defines and sustains him as a human being" (McDonald 1986, 180). In this situation, to be a human being means to refuse to be transformed into one of the "docile bodies" that the "disciplines" seek to control and contain into prefabricated roles. Ultimately, Dawes refuses to be the beast the system wants him to be.

To further lay bare the horrors of Port Arthur, Clarke also invents what Hughes defines "one of the finest heart-wringers in Victorian Fiction" (Hughes 2003, 602). The suicide of two young inmates of

---

[3] The term 'old hands' does not simply indicate seniority in a class system based on experience and connections within the convict system; it also assumes a pejorative meaning: the old hands are those who have inevitably sunk morality.

Point Puer – the reformatory of Port Arthur – definitively demonstrates the inhumanity of this space:

> "I can do it now," said Tommy. "I feel strong."
> "Will it hurt much, Tommy?" said Billy, who was not so courageous.
> "Not so much as a whipping."
> "I'm afraid! Oh, Tom, it's so deep! Don't leave me, Tom!"
> The bigger boy took his little handkerchief from his neck, and with it bound his own left hand to his companion's right.
> "Now I can't leave you."
> "What was it the lady that kissed us said, Tommy?"
> "Lord, have pity on them two fatherless children!" repeated Tommy.
> "Let's say it together."
> And so the two babies knelt on the brink of the cliff, and, raising the bound hands together, looked up at the sky, and ungrammatically said, "Lord have pity on we two fatherless children!" And then they kissed each other, and "did it". (Clarke 1992, 299)

Although Hughes reminds us that "[n]othing like this ever happened at Point Puer" (Hughes 2003, 602), the author's dramatization of reality surely serves its purpose and labels this space as an entirely obscene one.

Book IV, "Norfolk Island 1846," is named after the last and most remote penitentiary institution visited by the protagonist. Hughes, commenting on Governor Brisbane's definition of the Island as "the ne plus ultra," explains that "[t]here was no point of exile beyond this point; its convicts were at their ultimate distance from reasoned legality and open transaction" (Hughes 2003, 461). Clarke's account of the horrors of Norfolk Island is probably the most accurate in the novel as the island was truly used to induce fear of the system into the Australian convict population. The absence of a judge on the island and its isolation from both Australia and England made of it an ideal obscene space were it was possible to produce a securely remote spectacle of punishment. As Hughes recounts this was rendered necessary because:

> Too many letters had come back from emancipists and from assigned convicts who had found easy masters, praising the conditions of life in New South Wales and Van Diemen's Land, where wages were high and a man could make a new life for himself with his two hands. [The authorities] did not want Australia to lose its reputation. Morriset seemed just the man to [...] put a dose of iron back in the convict soul. The increase of terror [...] must begin from the bottom of the System, which meant Norfolk Island. (Hughes 2003, 459)

For the Term of His Natural Life reflects this intention with Captain Frere's appointment to Norfolk Island (although this happens seventeen years after Morriset's arrival Frere is clearly his alter ego) who is sent with orders to regain control over the unruly convicts. Reverend North, who also happens to be in charge of the island, documents in his diary the changes effected by the brute:

> So great have been the changes which have taken place that I scarcely know how to record them. Captain Frere has realized my worst anticipations. He is brutal, vindictive, and domineering. [...] So long as the island is quiet, he cares not whether the men live or die. "I was sent down here to keep order," said he to me, a few days after his arrival, "and by God, sir, I'll do it!" (Clarke 1992, 371)

The viciousness of the captain and his brutish handling of the convicts make this the most gothic part of the novel. The tortures capable of making the reader cringe from the page establish the absolute obscenity of this space. Thus it is through the pages of the diary of an ever more contrite and indignant Reverend North that this upturned side of the world is revealed to the reading public. In this section Clarke explicitly condemns the behaviour of Frere who, more than a tyrant, resembles an ogre – just as Morriset, due to a disfigured face, had physically resembled one (Hughes 2003, 459). Thus, the author lingers on the description of details of this reign of justice as if to underscore the inhumanity of the commandant:

> The floggings are hideously frequent. On flogging mornings I have seen the ground where the men stood at the triangles saturated with blood, as if a bucket of blood had been spilled on it, covering a space three feet in diameter, and running out in various directions, in little streams two or three feet long. (Clarke 1992, 372)

On this blood-stained island, completely isolated from the justice system that created it, the officers in charge became what Clarke defined as "God's viceregent[s]" (Clarke 1992, 272) on earth. Although the novel obliquely lays responsibility for this degradation on the unparalleled brutishness of Frere, it is clear that this is a space purposely excised from the map of the so-called civilized world in order to allow the Captain to act in undisturbed freedom.

In this environment, North starts to doubt the effectiveness of the system but, when commenting on the change in appearance of Dawes, again betrays the prejudice against the criminal class:

> Seven years ago he was a stalwart, upright, handsome man. He has become a beetle-browed, sullen, slouching ruffian. [...] His face has also grown like other convict faces — how hideously alike they all are! – [...] How habitual sin and misery suffice to brutalize "the human face divine"! (Clarke 1992, 368)

The Reverend describes the change with what seem to be a clashing mixture of sympathetic use of sociology and discriminatory application of physiognomy. The paragraph, when read in its context, conveys the idea that the protagonist has been changed by the many wrongs he has suffered. However, North, who is ignorant of the ill-fated destiny of this noble character, regards him as an average convict thus producing the unsympathetic image of a subhuman creature. The system is proved to have certainly succeeded in its intent: it has first herded and later created its criminals. Yet, after doing so, there is one last feat to be accomplished, namely subjugating the souls of such beasts. Hergenhan, quoting Foucault, states that "[i]n *His Natural Life*, punishment is seen in this way, as conquering souls, not simply subjugating bodies, as the "key of heart" in the sense of locking them up or raping them" (Hergenhan 1993, 49) It is in fact Captain Frere's intention to mould the prisoners in subdued docility by using their bodies as a means of access to their hearts. Having a particular dislike for Dawes – whom he has wronged by denying him recognition of the saving of the marooned party at Macquarie Harbour – he sets to brutishly bend his will through incessant bodily and mental torture. In order to break his spirit he flogs him, puts him in solitary confinement, flogs him again and makes him work at the pepper mill:

> This was a punishment more dreaded by the convicts than any other. The pungent dust filled their eyes and lungs, causing them the most excruciating torments. For a man with a raw back the work was one continued agony. In four days Rufus Dawes, emaciated, blistered, blinded, broke down.
> "For God's sake, Captain Frere, kill me at once!" he said. (Clarke 1992, 387)

Thus, in this space of confinement the convicts definitively lose all hope and come to consider death a way to escape this situation. Dawes, after further physical and moral coercion, eventually consents to participate to a form of group lottery-suicide:

> The scheme of escape hit upon by the convict intellect was simply this. Three men being together, lots were drawn to determine whom should be murdered. The drawer of the longest straw was the "lucky" man. He was killed. The drawer of the next longest straw was the murderer. He was hanged. The unlucky one was the witness. He had, of course, an excellent chance of being hung also, but his doom was not so certain, and he therefore looked upon himself as unfortunate. (Clarke 1992, 396)

However shocking and incredible this scheme may seem, it has an historical basis. The horrors of Norfolk Island were so unbearable that prisoners resorted to an analogous scheme of "escape." Yet, and once again, the novel distorts historical facts by making the plan entirely suicidal. Hughes indicates that convicts proceeded to these murder/suicides in order to be shipped to Sydney to be tried by a judge, and there, possibly hanged or maybe spared their lives. (Hughes 2003, 468-470). Without diminishing the tragic nature of such an act, it is important to notice how Clarke overstated the desperateness of the plan by denying the convicts even that final hope represented by the judge in Sydney.

Clarke denies any way out of this bottomless pit. Those who are cast so far away from the "scene" become unfit to return to society, whether it be England, the free colonies on the Australian mainland, or even one of the less peripheral penal institutions. For this reason, Dawes is led to a tragic death at the end of the novel. Although purehearted, he has become irredeemable and, in order to favour Australia's progress, he must be forgotten. It is here worth noticing that *His Natural Life* (1870) – which is the lesser known serialized version of the novel – ends in a radically different way. When the novel was edited for publication in its unabridged form (1874) the last book of the novel was excised. When also considering this section, the novel more exhaustively portrays the segregating system set up in the new continent: there, the aristocratic protagonist manages to escape to Victoria and, under the name of Tom Crosbie, experiences the life of a free settler. However, as Hodge and Mishra argue, "Australia had more need of a purified Dawes locked safely in the past than a reformed Dawes living on into the present" (Hodge and Mishra 1991, 130). As a result, the end of *For the Term of his Natural Life* was changed in order to neutralize the peril represented by the surviving convict. Dawes is sacrificed with what appears to be his last act of self-denial. When North confesses to him his intention to flee with Frere's wife – who is also the amnesic girl he saved 15 years earlier – the protagonist heroically sets to save the lady's soul. Thus, when Dawes substitutes himself for North and manages to embark on the ship supposed to take the reverend and Sylvia to Sydney, with one last gallant act, he saves the lady's honour and altruistically effaces himself from the face of the earth: as the vessel yields to the indomitable power of a hurricane Sylvia recognizes him as her saviour and they die locked in an embrace.

Although in the novel Clarke argues that men are made beasts by the penal system, his genteel protagonist is destined to prove that the "reassuring lesson from the ghastly past [is] that the present is now much better" (Hodge and Mishra 1991, 130). By locking the obscenity of the system into the past, the author favours the construction of a sanitized socio-topographic image of Australia. This need and intention is also explicitly addressed in a section of the suppressed book. A dialogue between a gold digger and the disguised protagonist reveals the danger posed by the haunting presence of the ex-convict:

> 'Of course, a man can be a convict innocently [...]. But that is misfortune. He could never come back to society again, you know. He may be proved innocent and all that, but one could not look upon him as the same. The memory of the frightful scenes through which he had passed would taint him.' [...] 'You are right, young man' Crosbie [a.k.a. Dawes] said, 'the society of the good and pure would justly refuse to be contaminated by the presence of such a man. He is a leper, from whom all healthy beings shrink with disgust. For him remains no love of sister, wife, or child. He is alone in the world – a being apart and accursed [...]. (Clarke 1970, 754)

The contamination of purity is the principal danger. For this reason, Dawes must not only be set apart accursed and ostracized, he must also die. Only through this ultimate displacement is the scene of that time's reading public secured from the resurgence of the not too remote obscenity of its setting. In Clarke's *For the Term of His Natural Life*, the Australian space is thus contemporarily othered, purified and identified through the strategic production of an obscene space which is subsequently effaced. Deviance was thus tactically used to configure the norm exported and implanted at the antipodes.

2.2 True History: Squatters, Selectors and Bushrangers

The excised ending of *For the Term of his Natural Life* symbolized the need to contain and swiftly censor the carceral space from nineteenth century Australia. However, when ignoring Tom Crosbie / Richard Devine's story, the account of the socio-topographic construction of Australia is left incomplete. The foundation and growth of free colonies needs to be taken in consideration as well. Due to its elaborate portrayal of one of Australia's founding myths, Peter Carey's *True History of the Kelly Gang* (2000) is an ideal text to engage with the study of the free settler colonial space. Ned Kelly, nowadays one of Australia's legendary figures, was squarely typified by the mid-century Australian Bourgeoisie as Irish, catholic, currency[4] and lastly a criminal. Although romanticised and far from being the "true" story of the Kelly Gang, Carey's novel has the merit of conjuring the social unrest feeding the legend of the bushranger and of placing it in an environment delightfully portrayed. Thus the setting of the novel becomes the stage of an intense power struggle between social forces which embody the same stereotypical categories found in Clarke's penal settlements. The bourgeoisie rules over a subdued and strictly controlled underclass – mostly Irish – secluded at the fringes of the colonial space.

Almost all the reviews or critical essays written about the novel stress the historic distortion performed by the text – Susan Martin quotes one international reviewer falling for the manuscript material on which the novel is supposedly based (Martin 2004, 231). In the "Melbourne Public Library" there is no such thing as manuscript "V.L.10453" (Carey 2000, 2), composed of thirteen parcels and being the truthful story of the Kelly gang as written by Ned himself. Indeed, as Andreas Gaile reminds the reader, Melbourne does not even have a

---

[4] 'Currency' is an Australian term to define the offspring of either a convict or an emancipist: born free but tainted by their parents' culpability (Hughes, Robert (2003). *The Fatal Shore: A History of the Transportation of Convicts to Australia, 1787-1868*. London, England: Vintage.

Public Library any more: it did in "Kelly-time but Carey's present-day reader will find in its place only the State Library of Victoria" (Gaile 2001, 39). Thus, although the veracity of the novel is inherently discredited to the eyes of the attentive reader, the title of the novel assumes a new and particular significance. For Laurie Clancy "the dropping of the definite article and the claim to generic completeness" is the way in which Carey "mock[s] the notion that there can be a definitive truth" (Clancy 2004, 54). In fact, in an interview with Nathaniel O'Reilly, Carey remarks that the words 'true' and 'history' together should immediately catch the attention of a literary audience because "each word calls the other in question" and "everyone is going to know what the game is" (O'Reilly 2002, 164); the game of course being the writing of fiction, not biography. *True History of the Kelly Gang* is therefore principally a piece of creative writing where Ned's letters to his inexistent daughter function as a literary device that Carey uses to "save the past and make it available to our present-day imagination" (Gaile 2001, 39). If the initial intent was to copy the style of the Jerilderie Letter,[5] the use of a more confessional tone – Kelly is talking to his unseen child – allows for the creation of a more personal narrative (cf. O'Reilly 2002, 164) which explores the everyday life of the protagonist of the fictional autobiography and resurrects the everyday life of the settlers. Therefore, it is the images of young Ned running barefoot around the countryside, of the houses where the Kellies live, of the refuges of the Kelly Gang and of the society revolving around these sites that most effectively make this 'history' come 'true.'

The reality so vibrantly portrayed in the pages of the novel is one that closely reflects the social order described by Marcus Clarke in *For the Term of His Natural Life*. Although Rufus Dawes is symboli-

---

[5] The Jerilderie Letter is the only surviving document written by Ned Kelly; he tried to get it published during the seizing of Jerilderie but only failed to do so when the printer's wife turned it in to the authorities. In this letter, Kelly stated his case and explicitly challenged the discursive construction of his character and state of affairs.

cally killed in order to purge Australia from the convict stain, the protagonist/narrator of *True History of the Kelly Gang* draws an unequivocal parallel between the old penal system and the present convict free Victoria by declaring that "the colony [is] ruled like Beechworth Gaol" (Carey 2000, 350). Ned's father's demise is probably the best example of the legacy evidenced by the narration. Once unjustly accused and imprisoned for having stolen a heifer that his son has slain for food, he succumbs to the pressure exerted upon him:

> You may think it strange that a man can survive transportation and the horrors of Van Diemen's Land and then be destroyed in a country lockup but we cannot credit the torture our parents suffered in Van Diemen's Land – Port Macquarie – Toongabbie – Norfolk Island – Emu Plains. Avenel lockup were the final straw for your grandfather […]. (Carey 2000, 36-37)

Van Diemen's Land, Norfolk Island, the Avenel lockup and Beechworth Gaol are all power-related locations pertaining to the Dominant Discourse that originally fashioned the Australian space in accordance to the need of British society. Ned's father is therefore crushed by the realization that not even as a selector in "country Victoria" can he be a free man. His life is still ruled by the same powers that uprooted him and tormented him. In the end he is subdued into "automatic docility" (Foucault 1979, 169). As Gaile argues, Carey describes a "highly hierarchical and class-ridden society […] [that] is united in the haunting memories of convictism" (Gaile 2001, 37). Thus, a social class that can be controlled outside the penal system has been artfully produced by the Discourse. This new class, serving a specific social function in the Australian colony, is also assigned a precise spatial collocation. The paupers of the British Islands – either free settlers or ex convicts – are confined at the margins of the colony working at barely profitable leases of crown land: "The Duffy Land Act of 1862 […] gave a man or a widow the right to select a block between 50 and 640 acres for £1 per acre […]. [M]y father were against it he said the great Charles Gavan Duffy was a well intentioned idiot leading poor men into debt and lifelong labour" (Carey 2000, 19).

Thus, the narration repeatedly reiterates the injustice of this scheme. Hence, the incredible prowess of young Kelly is measured in trees he can fell in a day – 5 per day (Carey 2000, 63) – and his blind loyalty to his mother – which is also almost incestuous – is continuously underscored by his preoccupation about her meeting the requirements of the lease of the land:

> I told him the Land Act was a b----r of a thing they would take our land away if we did not comply. [...] My ma can't run that selection by herself the government will take our land off her. (Carey 2000, 77, 104)

> I suggested to young Jem he come outside. As we left the veranda I picked up 2 axes and once behind the cowbails advised my brother that we must do the labour which the boundary rider had no taste for. It were this or we would surely lose our land. (Carey 2000, 77, 104)

Clearing the land, fencing it and improving it are the works demanded of the working class. As Ned's father clearly states and as Ned's anxiety demonstrates, the selectors are used as pawns in the programmatic territorial expansion of the colony and thus transformed into near-slaves by the unreasonable and despotic demands of the colonial power.

Laurie Kelly, in the "The Selective History of the Kelly Gang" argues that "Carey's use of history is not only subjective and highly selective but it is also highly partisan" (Clancy 2004, 58). This exaggeration, unquestionably true in the case of the construction of an implausibly flawless and heroic Ned Kelly, essentially underscores the societal repartition of the time. In this configuration, the Australian-based but British connected bourgeoisie is in stark contrast to the entirely disconnected and British rejected Australian working class. Andreas Gaile identifies this issue and appropriately frames into its spatial setting:

> Kelly Country is a place where the old oppositions between "convict" and "jailer" have only been replaced by new – and no less harsh – ones such as "rich" vs. "poor"; "insatiable squatters" vs. "poor selectors," "authorities" vs. "common people" – and very importantly "English" vs. "Irish." Carey leaves little doubt about the culprits for these social inequities: the British. (Gaile 2001, 37)

Without a doubt, Ned's fictional autobiography proves that the Kelly Outbreak[6] is the exemplary materialization of a "historic moment of UNFAIRNESS" (Carey 2000, 342). The "Kelly Country" is therefore the exemplary stage of a struggle that encompasses a much wider space. As in the case of the variously dislocated penal settlements, the Australian "class-ridden" and "hierarchical" society also imposes a spatial configuration which, once again, confines its Other to the margins in an (almost) ob-scene scenario. On the theme of otherness, Susan Martin explains that Ned's whiteness is so "tenuous" and "uncertain" that in a police gazette of the time he is described "as having the appearance of a half-caste" (Martin 2004, 32). For Martin, this is the cue to clarify how, in the late nineteenth century, the Irish were regarded as an inferior race and thus, clearly identified as Others in society (Martin 2004, 32). Concomitantly, Carolyn Bliss identifies a series of cultural masterplots that "spawned and revivified" times of the "Kelly Outrage". Most interesting among them are "the story of oppressed Irish convicts, emancipists, and currency lads cheated, harassed, robbed and generally abused by the Anglo power structure" and "the related story of small selectors hounded by prosperous squattocracy" (Bliss 2005, 290). The masterplots individuated by Bliss condense the most crucial strategies of the Discourse in the socio-topographic construction and appropriation of the Australian land. The "Anglo power structure," by discriminating the Irish emancipists/currency, pushes this segment of society to the fringes of the

---

[6] 'Kelly Outbreak' is just another term used by the contemporary press to sensationalize and demonize the challenge posed by a small gang of outlaws.

empire and invests it with the back-breaking role of "opening" the country and broadening the frontier. The oppressed selectors are later, in Bliss' words, hounded by the squattocracy who, favoured by tailor-made laws, take over their cleared selections at bargain prices.

Exploited in order to colonize the margin, the prejudice against the working class creates an interstitial zone between the social order imposed by England and executed via Sydney and Melbourne, and the unexplored space lying beyond the last fence erected by the settler. This space, similar to the areas of the penal colonies, is ob-scene because it provides the authorities the isolation and freedom necessary to securely abuse the law. In this advantageously isolated setting the "traps," as Ned calls the representatives of the repressive state apparatuses, misuse their power and, with the cooperation of these apparatuses, work to the persistent and cautionary repression of the subaltern. Clancy gives a detailed summary of the prevarications suffered by the Kellies and coherently organizes them in order to demonstrate the cruel – but also overstated – intentionality of these acts:

> The police trick [Ned] into jail and when they can't capture him indiscriminately arrest his family, friends and acquaintances. There is a long list of brutal and predatory police in the novel – Sergeant O'Neil, Sergeant Whelan, Constable Alexander Fitzpatrick, Constable Hall, Constable Flood, Constable Farrel. Magistrates hand out heavy sentences without questioning the police evidence. Judge Barry is portrayed as a power-crazed sadist [...]. Newspapers refuse to print Ned's statements [...]. Squatters steal the selectors' land and animals and levy fines for their recovery of the latter. (Clancy 2004, 56-57)

Being at the mercy of this rapacious system, the Irish selectors – and the Kellies in particular – are given only one last choice: bushranging, which was in its actual practice a self-serving and ineffective opposition. At fourteen, Ned is apprenticed to Harry Power, the bushranger/suitor of Ned's mother. Although this turns to be the experience that will give the protagonist his enviable knowledge of the country, the opinion he forms of the activity is completely negative.

After participating to a number of luckless highway robberies he returns home and, to his mother's utmost disappointment, reveals that "bushranging aint as profitable as you'd expect" (Carey 2000, 102). Harry's robberies, although principally targeted against the squattocracy, are nothing more than a crude survival technique which has nothing to do with insurgence or a Robin-Hood like redistribution of property. On the contrary, the mighty bushranger is often ridiculed either for the meagre booties (once it is only marbles for young Ned (Carey 2000, 82)]) or because of the facility with which he is fooled by his hostages, as when he is tricked into believing that the wealthy Miss Phoebe Martin Boyd is a poor school teacher (Carey 2000, 92). Essentially, what is demonstrated is that the breaching of the law imposes a taxing decision: either being captured and put in jail – a place of obscene confinement – or living on the run in a space that is altogether outside of society. Harry Power, although a comic character, is therefore respected for his unparalleled knowledge of the bush: "[Harry] could not feed himself or even clean his teeth but he had more bootholes than a family of foxes he had secret caves and mia mias and hollow trees throughout the North East of the colony of Victoria [...]" (Carey 2000, 84).

The land beyond the last fenced paddock is the ob-scene realm of the outlaw, a space that, as demonstrated by Harry's solemn declaration, the British law does not reach: he has "been haunted by every trap from Wangaratta to Benalla and Beechworth besides and none of them can find their way around the Wombat Ranges" (Carey 2000, 83), The police are at a loss in this space because the bush is not only a territory beyond the British sphere of influence, but also because it is an area that is largely construed as dangerously Other by the Dominant Discourse. Uncharted, uncultivated, homeland of the surviving Aborigines and most importantly refuge to the outcasts of society, the bush is imaginatively appropriated as the ob-scene setting of Australian obscenity.

Accordingly, the Discourse, in the attempt to brand the adult Ned as the quintessence of the undesirable criminal class, portrays him as a degenerate man. A news article recounting the events of Stringybark Creek includes a picture "of a demonic kind of man" (Carey 2000, 296):

> The author of this so called LIKENESS were not content to show my natural imperfections he must join my brows across my nose and twist my lips to render me the Devil the Horror of the Ages. [...]
> The title headline said MURDER OF POLICE AT STRINGYBARK CREEK. I don't know who wrote it but it made us Irish Madmen. I had mutilated Sergeant Kennedy he claimed I had cut off his ear with my knife before murdering him. Moreover I had forced my 3 mates to discharge their pistols in to the bodies of the police so all would be guilty of the crime the same as me. (Carey 2000, 296-297)

This passage clearly demonstrates the way in which the ideological state apparatuses cooperatively work with the repressive state apparatuses in the shaping of society. In this instance the engraving presented by the media transforms Ned in the prototypical image of the criminal as exemplified by the phrenological studies of the time. In this fashion and through the biased account of the events leading to the death of the police officers, the Discourse clearly defines both the character of the outlaws and the space in which they move. The bush is utterly obscene and, in fact, according to Carey's version of the facts, the intent of the police is also in tune with the lack of restrictions granted to this space: they undertake their scout with the unlawful intent of murdering the gang, a fact proved by the straps the police had purposely made for carrying the bodies (Carey 2000, 267,275).

Trying to escape the rigid categorization imposed by the Discourse, the protagonist writes his own "true history." As Gail argues, by reporting and contradicting articles from *The Jerilderie Gazette* and *The Morning Chronicle*, Ned tries to "correct public misconceptions about his history" and "by appropriating the power of Discourse, writes his own damned history and inserts his narrative into the grand narrative of history" (Gaile 2001, 38). It is, however, not so simple to find a point through which to speak freely; on the contrary, as demonstrated by the seizure of his narrative by the schoolteacher Thomas Curnow and the heavy editing made by his and other hands, it must be doubted whether Ned's voice really manages to surface in the narration (cf. Bliss 2005, 293). Significantly, Graham Huggan states that "the voice through which [the narrative] claims to speak is never Kelly's own" (Huggan 2002). Thus, as appropriately argued in Gaile's paper, "Gayatri Spivak's cognition that the subaltern cannot speak is exemplified in Kelly's futile attempts to break through the barrier of colonial snobs" (Gaile 2001, 38). Therefore, Carey's narrative, with its numerous and contradictory points of view, does not try to present a historically correct "true history of the Kelly Gang," rather, it "draws attention to the pitfalls inherent in the process of constructing any kind of history" (Gaile 2001, 38).

Gaile believes that Ned Kelly's story belongs to myth (Gaile 2001, 38) and Clancy echoes him by demonstrating the way this myth started: "The announcement of his death sentence prompted a petition for clemency which attracted no fewer than 32.000 signatures – just over 10 percent of Victoria's population of 300.000" (Clancy 2004, 53).

Ten percent of the Victorian population had the courage of speaking up and asked for "justice" to be suspended. With this petition 32.000 people – which perhaps is only a fraction of the real portion of those controlled and marginalised by the Discourse – asked to be included into society because the execution of Ned Kelly as the ultimate bushranger also symbolized their difference and predestined them to the same destitution suffered by the Kellies/Irish/Emancipists/Currency. Bliss notes that Carey's text principally suggests two ideas: that "there is no such thing as uninflected historical accuracy" and that "Ned is ambushed by all sides by masterplots." What must be borne in mind is that the surviving masterplot, which is also the one reiterated by the novel, is the one of "Kelly as a much put upon victim who rose against his oppressor and fought for the rights of little people and against the misuses of authority everywhere" (Clancy 2004, 54). Ned Kelly's story was thus raised to myth and he became the sort of symbol inspiring national unity. However, at this point it becomes clear how *True History of the Kelly Gang* shows the way all the other metanarratives contending for Ned's voice are somehow silenced in myth: "To Mary, he must be a knight errant, to Curnow a dastardly villain, to some of the reporters a savage beast who must be brought to bay, to many of his compatriots a kind of hounded Robin Hood (Bliss 2005, 293).

The most surprising thing is that, out of all these voices, the ones that end up being silenced are the ones that most closely represent the repressive apparatus of the Dominant Discourse. One starts to wonder if it is the Discourse itself that first stigmatized and later sanctified Ned Kelly. Martin, amending Huggan's argument, gives an answer to this question by explaining that Kelly is not only "predestined to become the pathological host for malevolent ancestral forces" (Huggan 2002, 148), he is also "a punisher of the white establishment [...], but recuperable to one strand of that establishment" (Martin 2004, 35). Hence, Martin suggests that the "victimological narrative with Ned Kelly as white male hero of an acceptable alterity" (Martin 2004, 35) is used to integrate the Irish into the Australian national identity, and, at the same time, to strategically appropriate the space of the bushranger. The obscene space beyond the last cleared field is thus reappropriated by discourse via the dismemberment of the outlaw and his voice. He is othered, prosecuted, executed and violently appropriated (as Huggan and Martin evidence, Kelly's story, his armour, and even his skull are seized by various bodies of the Dominant Discourse) only to be later reshaped and re-embodied into an acceptable figure of cultural normalcy.

With this "twist of the masterplot," the Dominant Discourse gains a foothold into the bush. It does not yet guarantee a complete appropriation but rather it could be said that the process of incorporation of the outback is activated through the use of this "dead white male hero" (Martin 2004, 23). Ned Kelly, as the personification of the bushranger and simultaneously a "typical" Irish, currency, settler, is used as yet another pawn by the Discourse dynamically shaping the socio-topographic organization of the Australian landscape. It is thus that the obscene, being progressively displaced, recedes towards the heart of the country and is confined into the remotest areas of the outback.

3 The Outback

3.1 Nineteenth Century Idealizations

The question of how the bush came to be so important to Australian literature and culture becomes enmeshed in a continuum of lived experiences, their infinite recounting in a series of "yarns" and the consolidation of an informal oral tradition celebrating a way of life that would become central to the national ethos. Thus, much before Australia "came of age" by offering its blood to England during the Great War, the Australian national character was being forged by the controversial relationship of the European settlers with their new country. The harsh living conditions of the interior, the vastness of the island-continent and the sparseness of the cities scattered along the coast, created an environment that continuously challenged the white Australians' capacity to adapt. Within one century from the arrival of the First Fleet, the result of the continuous oral elaboration of the themes central to the lives of the settlers came together in a literary production that would from then onwards represent the foremost representation of the young nation's identity. The productions of Henry Lawson, A. B. Paterson (also known as the Banjo) and Barbara Baynton represent the crux and the most accomplished example of this literary feat: the immortalization of a highly representative and emotively charged way of life and its establishment as a founding myth of Australian culture – emblematically Paterson's "Waltzin' Matilda" was soon to be adopted by the Australian troops as an unofficial national anthem during the Great War. This crucial part of Australian literary history is also fundamental in the formation and fixation of certain obscene spaces in the Australian tradition and therefore this period cannot be excluded from this study. However, this being the introduction to the more extensive and more relevant literature of the twentieth century, this section will be restrained to an introductory part adherent to the overall theme of the study. Only few selected works by Andrew Barton Paterson, Henry Lawson and Barbara Baynton will therefore be analysed to demonstrate the importance of their contribution in the construction of the founding Australian myths.

According to Edouard Glissant, epics are instrumental in the socio-cultural formation of the conscience of a people. *The Old Testament, The Iliad, The Odyssey, The Song of Roland, The Song of the Nibelungs*, the Finnish *Kalevala* and numerous other western texts from ancient times are all examples of the crystallisation of the conscience of a people in a text that frames and guarantees its rightness and solidity by making it holy and exclusive to their culture (cf. Glissant 1996, 35). The stories recounted by the great Australian authors in the late nineteenth century do not solidify into a single and clear-cut epic, but they are grounded in and they elaborate on a myth reflected in the infinite fragments of the dismal but always extraordinary lives of the settlers. The great Australian epic is based on the lives of the jolly swag man, the solitary drover, the ever travelling prospector, the in-fatigable miner and the patiently waiting wives raising the children on isolated selections of land. The national ethos was thus born and centred around the "legendary" survival of common individuals; it is a story celebrating the way strength and endurance prevailed against adverse situations and, in the communal or similar struggle, bound people together.

3.1.1 Lawson, Paterson and Baynton

In 1896, with *While the Billy Boils*, Henry Lawson immortalised these small adventures and thus transfigured them in tales of epic importance. Interestingly, the public of this fiction were the city dwellers that, right from the start, were the vast majority of the Australian population. The ambiguous relationship of the white Australian population to their land is best described in Henry Lawson's "His Country – After All" (first published in *While the Billy Boils*), where an Australian expatriate complains about his mother country until, while on his way to Christchurch in New Zealand, he encounters some gum trees planted by the road. At that moment he is overcome by a sudden and irresistible sense of nostalgia:

> "So you're a native to Australia?" said the bagman to the greybeard, as the coach went on again.
> "Well, I suppose I am. Anyway, I was born there. That's the main thing I've got against the darned country." [...]
> "The worst and hardest years of my life were spent in Australia. [...] I worked harder and got less in my own country in five years then I ever did in any other in fifteen. [...] What's Australia? A big, thirsty, hungry wilderness, with one or two cities for the convenience of foreign speculators, and a few collections of humpies called towns."
> [...]
> "What trees are those?" asked the stranger. [...] "They look as if they have been planted there. There ain't been a forest here surely."
> "Oh, they are trees the Government imported," said the bagman, whose knowledge on the subject was limited. "Our own bush won't grow in this soil." [...]
> Here the stranger sniffed once by accident, and then several times with interest. It was warm morning after rain. He fixed his eyes on those trees.
> They didn't look like Australian Gums; they tapered to the tops, the branches were pretty regular, and the boughs hung in shipshape fashion. There was not the heat to twist the branches and turn the leaves.
> "Why!" Dang me if they ain't (sniff) Australian gums!" (Lawson 1927 v.1, 66-71)

This is an important moment of recognition, where nostalgia is not simply conjured by the scent and sighting of gum saplings; also implied is a positive projective identification of the protagonist with the trees. The nostalgia is for what the gums represent, the toughness and stamina of Australians; people that, just like the gum trees, grow toughened by the adverse conditions they live in. The sun, the heat, the droughts do not only shape the Eucalypts in their typical ragged shapes, they also harden the Australians in body and in spirit. Thus, the stranger changes his mind and decides to "hop" to Australia before returning to San Francisco. At the end of his trip, while conversing with an English-man, he even ventures to defend his old country:

> "Well for my part," said a tourist in the coach, presently, in a condescending tone, "I can't see much in Australia. The bally colonies are ..."
> "Oh, that be damned!" snarled the Australian-born – they had finished the second flask of whisky. "What do you Britishers know about Australia? *She*'s as good as England, anyway." (Emphasis mine. Lawson 1927 v.1, 73)

Suddenly the native land becomes feminized and, as a true mother country, it seems nurturing and attractive. The text suggests that the relationship of the typical Australian to his land is one of love and hate and that, in the end, it is the hardship endured that, after all, definitively binds the people to the land. It is in fact to have a yarn with an old mate that the protagonist of this story decides to return to Sydney. The best reward for the honest hard-working Australians is the chance to share their stories – yarns – in a jovial conversation. This is a fashion that the literature of the end of the nineteenth century condenses, celebrates and returns to the people in a dignified form. For this reason, Lawson, Paterson and Baynton are not simply spokepersons of a tradition, but also heroes of a culture. In their work, while maintaining the spirit of the oral folklore intact, they managed to metamorphose the simple yarn into praiseworthy prose and verse.

The bush, with its odd characters and their entertaining stories, consequently became an iconic image of Australianness. Banjo Paterson's "Clancy of the Overflow" (*Bulletin*, December 1889) gives one of the finest examples of the nostalgic relationship that the city dwellers established with the remote interior of the continent. In this poem the narrator/protagonist, mostly with the power of his imagination, visits Clancy in his wanderings. The incorporeal nature of this call is first implied in the sending of a letter:

3 The Outback 61

> I had written him a letter which I had, for want of better
> Knowledge, sent to where I met him down the Lachlan, years ago,
> He was shearing when I knew him, so I sent the letter to him,
> Just "on spec", addressed as follows: "Clancy, of The Overflow".
> (Paterson 1902, 20)

With this opening passage the poet affirms his authority on bush matters by clarifying that he has been there "years ago," but he also proclaims his estrangement from it by clarifying that he writes "for want of better knowledge." The context of this poem, immediately framed within the boundaries of nostalgic imagination, is thus set in the ambiguous space lying between the actual city and its socio-culturally produced counterpart, the bush. The idyllic vision evoked by Paterson is nothing but the projection of the city's fantasies being glorified and eternalized by poetry:

> In my wild erratic fancy, visions come to me of Clancy
> Gone a-droving "down the Cooper" where the western drovers go;
> As the stock are slowly stringing, Clancy rides behind them singing,
> For the drover's life has pleasures that the townsfolk never know.
>
> And the bush hath friends to meet him, and their kindly voices greet him
> In the murmur of the breezes and the river on its bars,
> And he sees the vision splendid of the sunlit plains extended,
> And at night the wondrous glory of the everlasting stars.
> (Paterson 1902, 21)

As the following passage clarifies, the "pleasures that the townsfolk never know" are predominantly generated by the city's longing for a nurturing nature. The description given of the bush is thus a romanticised version of reality conceived in reminiscence from within the enclosures of an office:

> I am sitting in my dingy little office, where a stingy
> Ray of sunlight struggles feebly down between the houses tall,
> And the foetid air and gritty of the dusty, dirty city

Through the open window floating, spreads its foulness over all.
(Paterson 1902, 21)

For need of compensation, the bush becomes a glorified Arcadia. Raymond Williams, in his seminal study *The Country and the City* (1973), gives an historical account of the transformation in the connotation of these areas in English literature:

> On the country has gathered the idea of a natural way of life: of peace, innocence, and simple virtue. On the city has gathered the idea of an achieved centre: of learning, communication, light. Powerful hostile associations have also developed: on the city as a place of noise, worldliness and ambition; on the country as a place of backwardness, ignorance, limitation. A contrast between country and city races back to classical times. (Williams 1973, 1)

According to Williams, what appears to be the key for the construction of an ideal Arcadian space is the longing for a state of past grace that can be connected to that place. The country is thus often seen as a location of peace and beauty because it upholds all the values that are felt to be lost through the process of modernization. "Arcadia" is therefore the projection of nostalgia for a state of lost grace and it is substantially a Utopia, a no-place.

Arcadia, in Australia, is beyond doubt a utopian space because of the lack of an extensive history and a sense of belonging to the land. Raymond Williams explains that in the English tradition Arcadia is always lost in time, something that has been but that is no more. Australia, at the end of the nineteenth century, could not afford this retrospective gaze and was therefore forced to a direct confrontation with reality. Banjo Paterson's flattering depiction of the outback is thus contested by a more realistic portrayal given by Henry Lawson. Well renowned is the so called Bush Controversy where Lawson and Paterson – with the addition of a few others along the way – attack each other's points of view with verses published in the *Bulletin* between 1892 and 1894. Even though the controversy was a set up – the contributors had agreed to "have some fun" pretending to have a bitter argument around their differing perspectives while hopefully getting paid for the resulting publications – it still retains an extreme importance in the construction and solidification of the myth that in time would create a real Australian Arcadia.

In "Borderland" (*Bulletin*, July 1892), Henry Lawson very poignantly describes the bush as a sun-baked thirsty land:

> Miles and miles of thirsty gutters – strings of muddy waterholes
> In the place of "shining rivers" (walled by cliffs and forest boles).
> "Range!" of ridges, gullies, ridges, barren! where the madden'd flies –
> Fiercer than the plagues of Egypt – swarm about your blighted eyes!
> Bush! where there is no horizon! where the buried bushman sees
> Nothing. Nothing! but the maddening sameness of the stunted trees!
> Lonely hut where drought's eternal – suffocating atmosphere –
> Where the God forgotten hatter dreams of city-life and beer.
> (Lawson 1896, 138-139)

It was not long before an answer was published in the *Bulletin*. On the 23rd of July 1892, with "In Defence of the Bush," Banjo Paterson insisted that the hardship of the bush is nothing compared to the dull ways of city living.

> But you found the bush was dismal and a land of no delight –
> Did you chance to hear a chorus in the shearers' huts at night?
> Did they "rise up William Riley" by the camp-fire's cheery blaze?
> Did they rise him as we rose him in the good old droving days?
> And the women of the homesteads and the men you chanced to meet –
> Were their faces sour and saddened like the "faces in the street"?
> And the "shy selector children" – were they better now or worse
> Than the little city urchins who would greet you with a curse?
> Is not such a life much better than the squalid street and square
> Where the fallen women flaunt it in the fierce electric glare,
> Where the seamstress plies her needle till her eyes are sore and red
> In a filthy, dirty attic toiling on for daily bread?
> Did you hear no sweeter voices in the music of the bush

Than the roar of trams and buses, and the war-whoop of "the push"?
(Paterson 1902, 157-158)

In Paterson's depiction of the bush it is the contact with nature, even in spite of its poverty and destitution, that leads people to a joyful way of life. The two points of view clash, yet, they are two sides of the same coin. The authors confronted the same topic from two diametrically opposed perspectives. The glorification of the bush, in whichever form, passes through the controversial need to have a counterpart for the socio-cultural role invested by the city. As Raymond Williams clarifies, the urban centre of illumination and culture also becomes a hostile environment from which people seek shelter, even if only in their fantasy, by fleeing to the backward but amiable way of country life. The city needs the country and the country needs the city. They are the extreme of an antithetical couple basing its existence on the presence of its opposite. Australia, with Lawson's and Paterson's bush controversy, was striving for this same equilibrium.

Emblematic is also the fact that the two authors, as Richard Hall argues in *Banjo Paterson, His Poetry and Prose* (Hall 1993, 218), had agreed to write against each other not out of spite but to get more of their work published and earn in proportion. Later, in "Banjo Paterson Tells His Own Story" (*Sydney Morning Herald*, 4 Feb-4 Mar 1939), Paterson clearly stated this intention:

> We were both looking for the same reef, if you get what I mean; but I had done my prospecting on horseback with my meals cooked for me, while Lawson has done his prospecting on foot and had had to cook for himself. Nobody realised this better than Lawson; and one day he suggested that we should write against each other, he putting the bush from his point of view, and I putting it from mine.
> "We ought to do pretty well out of it," he said, "we ought to be able to get in three or four sets of verses before they stop us."
> This suited me all right, for we were working on space, and the pay was very small – in fact, I remember getting exactly thirteen and sixpence for writing "Clancy of the Overflow" – so we slam-banged away at each other for weeks and weeks; not until they stopped us, but

until we ran out of material. I think that Lawson put his case better than I did, but I had the better case, so that honours (or dishonours) were fairly equal. (In, Hall 1993, 219)

After all, the "Bush Controversy" is no controversy at all. The antithetical representations of the land serve the same purpose; "We were both looking for the same reef" explains Paterson, meaning they were not only working on the same subject but on different grounds; on the contrary, they were both contributing to the construction of the same tradition glorifying the bush as the keystone of Australian identity. The synergistic effort of this feat is testified by the postscript of "In Answer to "Banjo", and Otherwise" by Henry Lawson (*Bulletin*, August 1892). The last stanza of this poem clarifies the nature of that tension that the two poets were probing:

> You'll admit that "up-the-country," more especially in drought,
> Isn't quite the Eldorado that the poets rave about,
> Yet at times we long to gallop where the reckless bushman rides
> In the wake of startled brumbies that are flying for their hides;
> And to feel the saddle tremble once again between our knees
> And to hear the stockwhips rattle just like rifles in the trees!
> And to feel the bridle-leather tugging strongly in the hand
> And to feel once more a little like a "native of the land."
> And the ring of bitter feeling in the jingling of our rhymes
> Isn't suited to the country nor the spirit of the times,
> Let us go together droving and returning, if we live,
> Try to understand each other while we liquor up the "div."
> (Lawson 1896, 157)

What is offered in these verses is not a simple truce; on the contrary, it is the affirmation of the sharing of a fascination for the way of life that, be it rough or merry, embodies the true spirit of the nation. Lawson's stress on the need to feel like a "native of the land" and on the unsuitability of the quarrel for the enhancement of the country, draws attention to the true uniting value celebrated by both authors: the work of common people. By inviting Banjo to go droving, Lawson does not simply affirm his love for the land, he also reinstates the importance of work (droving in this case) as the principal way of belonging to the land and making it one's own.

The picture presented here clearly illustrates how the founding myth of Anglo-Celtic Australia is closely connected to the protestant value of work and the idea that in the fallen world it is God's people's job to make the earth flourish again. As Foucault explains, work becomes a Christian duty:

> The poor man who, without consenting to "torment" the land, waits until God comes to his aid, since he has promised to feed the birds of the sky, would be disobeying the law of Scripture: "Thou shalt not tempt the Lord Thy God." Does not reluctance to work mean "trying beyond God," as Calvin says? It is seeking to constrain the miracle, whereas the miracle is granted daily to man as the gratuitous reward of his labour. (Foucault 1967, 56)

Australia, with its often-poor soils, long droughts and fierce sun, posed the ultimate challenge to the industriousness of God's people. As it will become clear later in this section and in the following ones (see 3.2.4 and 3.3.3), the respect of this God-given law is at the base of the definition of the outback as an obscene space. The land is moralised distinguishing between productive and unproductive people. It is thus that the work of drovers, shearers, squatters and women dispersed throughout the bush, can be envisioned as a concerted effort ideally aimed at reclaiming the land from its post-fallen-world state and at creating a new Garden of Eden. The ideology feeding this drive is clearly illustrated in the hymn *Onwards Christian Soldiers* by Reverend Sabine Baring-Gould (1824-1934):

> Onward Christian soldiers marching as to war
> With the cross of Jesus going on before.
> Christ, the royal master leads against the foe
> Forward into battle, see His banners go,

Onward, Christian soldiers, marching as to war,
With the cross of Jesus going on before.

Like a mighty army moves the church of God;
Brothers, we are treading where the saints have trod.
We are not divided, all one body we,
One in hope and doctrine, one in charity.
(Bradley 1990, 333)

The passage here quoted depicts Christian people as an army united in a holy mission, the spreading of the doctrine and the salvation of all human souls. As Baring-Gould suggests, this goal is achieved through righteousness and unity; however, it is exactly this unity that turns all those who do not stand in the close ranks of the "Christian army" into "foes." The natives, by keeping the land unproductive, offend God's benevolence. As a consequence, they are enemies of the Christian people and to seize the land from them becomes almost holy duty. In the end, this way of thinking led to the establishment of an Australian ideal: that in this vast new continent everyone has "a fair go". Which literally means to have the opportunity of improving oneself through hard work. For this reason, the two poets, despite their difference in opinion, should go droving together and "liquor up the div."

In accordance with this vision, Henry Lawson does not consider the outback an Eldorado; rather, his poetry and prose celebrate the effort made in transforming the rough land into a homely environment. The honest portrayal of places and circumstances makes his work extremely relevant to the introduction of the theme of obscenity in the outback. Where Paterson's idyllic celebration hides all the negative aspects of the Australian interior, Lawson's depiction finds its strength in the overcoming of the innumerable threats posed by the bush. Henry Lawson's short story "The Drover's Wife" (1896) and the almost unambiguously corresponding "The Chosen Vessel" (1902) by Barbara Baynton are here particularly useful in disclosing the brutal aspects of the bush. The two opposing views, already subject to numerous studies, become exceptionally relevant when compared to one another; in doing so it is possible to discern the creeping obscenity threatening the life of the drover's wife. Both stories focus on the isolation endured by the female characters but Lawson's narration, being once again functional to the celebration of the conquering of the bush, introduces a heroic and strenuously enduring female protagonist which, with her work, protects her children from the numerous perils of the bush. The small house almost feels like a fortress when weighed against the nineteen miles in radius of emptiness around it; no sign of civilization, only the treacherous natural elements. It is thus that this unnamed woman is left alone (unaided by male characters) to raise her children and protect them from the external world and, more specifically, against a snake. Sue Rowley, in "Inside the Deserted Hut: Representation of Motherhood in Bush Mythology," points out how the simplicity of the plot hides a rough and clear-cut schematization of space:

> We learn simply that the Drover's Wife gives the children some supper, and she has a sewing basket by her side. But the focus of the night's vigil and of her memories is on her actions to protect the family against dangers that threaten their lives and livelihood. To think of these she puts down her sewing. [...] The dangers against which she struggles are associated with the world beyond the hut. [...] [T]he disasters are not seen to be consequences of the social order: bushfire, flood, pleuro-pneumonia, crows. The hut is besieged by intruders; swagman, mad bull, and the snake itself. The differentiation of space is integral to the heroism of the woman. She does not extend her domain into the bush beyond the yard, and nor is she successful in her struggle against fire, flood and or pleuro-pneumonia. But she repels intruders, protects her family and maintains the integrity of her own sphere. (Rowley 1989, 82)

Rowley very poignantly distinguishes between two spheres of influence: the homestead and the bush. The bush is exclusively a masculine domain and for this reason each of the woman's heroic attempts at contrasting nature beyond the yard – which is her assigned domain

– is doomed to fail. While sitting in the hut by the fire, she recalls how during the flood she fought to save the dam across the creek "[b]ut she could not save it. There are things a bushwoman cannot do" (Lawson 1927, 19). And so it is for every attempt to challenge men's space; she is overcome by the flood, saved by men from the bushfire and fails to seek help in time when riding with a dead baby to the closest station. She is literally confined to the house where her first and unique role is that of mother. For this reason she has to protect her small domain from the external world. The bush is male in gender and its intruders threaten her virtue and role as a mother: the mad bull, the swagman and the snake all represent a threat against her assigned matriarchal role.

Lawson's short story is not simply a celebration of motherhood; rather, according to Rowley, it is driven by a precise agenda:

> Lawson explicitly intervened in the debates about birthrate. He supported the pro-natalist position, and his demands for high white fertility are articulated in terms of national and race survival. He too attributes the decline in birthrate to selfishness, particularly on the part of women. [...]
> Lawson is contributing to the shaping of a nationalist discourse in which feminists have "never a thought for their country's sake".
> (Rowley 1989, 88,89)

When at the turn of the century the nation started to be concerned about the decline in birthrate, Lawson responded with stories such as this one, where the woman is glorified as an accomplished mother of many children. In Lawson's story, the drover's wife is the incarnation of this stereotype and her struggle is indicative of the role that has been assigned to her: she has to defend her children at any cost.

The swagman is only mentioned very briefly but, when considered from this new perspective, his visit is particularly significant because, as soon as the intruder ascertains that he is the only male in the homestead, he first orders food and, secondly, he claims his right to sleep with the woman:

Only last week a gallows-faced swagman – having satisfied himself that there were no men on the place – threw his swag down on the veranda, and demanded tucker. She gave him something to eat; then he expressed his intention of staying for the night. It was sundown then. She got a batten from the sofa, loosened the dog, and confronted the stranger, holding the batten in one hand and the dog's collar with the other. "Now you go!" she said. He looked at her and at the dog, said "All right, mum," in a cringing tone, and left. She was a determined-looking woman, and Alligator's yellow eyes glared unpleasantly – besides, the dog's chewing-up apparatus greatly resembled that of the reptile he was named after. (Lawson 1927 v.2, 21-22)

Isolation in a male dominated environment is the most perilous threat posed to women; nevertheless, Lawson depicts an optimistic picture where the strong-willed bushwoman courageously defeats her opponent and avoids being raped. In spite of this, it is a snake that keeps her waking all night. At any time the creature, which is hiding under the house, could penetrate the living area through the cracks in the floorboards and kill her children in their sleep. It is difficult to fail to recognize the symbolism of this image, the snake – incarnation of evil but also of the original sin – is the definitive embodiment of the masculine land around the house. Once again, the woman courageously defends her citadel armed of stick and dog, and, when the snake finally enters the kitchen from one of the cracks, she crushes its spine with several blows and throws the dead body into the fire.

The role model proposed by Lawson in "The Drover's Wife" subtly constrains the woman to a domestic role by chaining her to her function as a mother. If from a male perspective this is a heroic role, Barbara Baynton's short story discloses a different reality. The woman in the bush is not simply isolated from any assistance, but also prisoner of the patriarchal logic that burdens her with children and abandons her to care for them. Sue Rowley offers an insightful analysis of this situation:

In the bush mythology, settling the land is achieved by men by clearing it and by women bearing children to inherit it. The division of labour between men and women is articulated in terms of a spatial metaphor. The notion of men and women occupying their "separate spheres" is an expression of the complementary relationship between them. However the insistence on spatial segregation and differentiation in the construction of gender sets the terms within which the representation of motherhood is shaped. Whilst mothers are placed under virtual "house arrest", the positioning of the implicitly masculine observer renders the domestic interior only partially legible. In consequence the point of view of the mother is excluded and the meanings she might ascribe to her domestic and mothering practices are negated. (Rowley 1989, 95)

Therefore, in the "The Drover's Wife," the attempt to describe the feminine space in the bush is yet another way of silencing the woman's real voice. Deprived of agency and subjectivity, she is rendered a devote and efficient servant of the patriarchal cause. Bearing this in mind, Lawson's portrayal of the settlers living conditions almost appears to be a fabrication. With his biased story he obscures the most terrifying aspects of the bushwoman's life. It is here that Barbara Baynton intervenes to set the record straight: "The Chosen Vessel," first published in 1902 as part of the collection *Bush Studies*, offers an alternative view of almost the same story. The protagonist of this story is the wife of a shearer who, just like the drover's wife, is often left alone in the house to mind her baby. In this case, however, the heroine is a simple town-girl and her reactions to the menaces around her are not as heroic; on the contrary, this is a story of absolute terror. Elizabeth Webby, in the introduction to the Angus and Robertson edition of *Bush Studies*, appropriately distinguishes the different attitudes of Lawson and Baynton by juxtaposing the titles of their first collection of short stories:

It is instructive to compare the title of Henry Lawson's first major collection of short stories, *While the Billy Boils* (1896), with Baynton's. Lawson's, evoking a group of mates gathered around a campfire, foregrounds the relationship between narrator and listener. Nearly all his stories are told by someone to someone else. Baynton's *Bush Studies*, however, points to her more dramatic, and seemingly more objective, narrative mode. (Elizabeth Webby, introduction to: Baynton 1993, 4)

If Paterson and Lawson concentrate on the almost solely masculine practice of "having a yarn with one's mates" Baynton finds a different, less biased, point of view for herself and hence her distinct literary production.

Remarkably, the protagonist of "The Chosen Vessel" is a simple town-girl who is afraid of her own milk-cow and its calf. When she confronts it, as well as the creature she fears her husband: "it was he who forced her to run and meet the advancing cow, brandishing a stick and uttering threatening words till the enemy turned and ran" (Baynton 1993, 132). The husband is immediately portrayed as yet another enemy and, with a sharp comment, the woman realizes that "in many things he was worse than the cow" (Baynton 1993, 132). Just like in "The Drover's Wife," the mother's range of action is extremely limited, but in this case the reason of this imprisonment is immediately clarified with a simile: in the absence of her husband the young wife ties up the calf by the creek so that the cow will stay with it and does not roam on the plains. By doing so she replicates her condition because "she had plenty of time to go after [the cow], but then there was baby." Just like the cow, the wife is kept prisoner by her baby. Due to this encumbrance, the emptiness around the house – 15 miles separates her from the shearing shed where her husband works – becomes even more terrifying. With her baby, in case of danger, she cannot run away. To enhance her sense of isolation, her husband scorns her when she discloses her concern about her own security in his absence:

> More than once she thought of taking her baby and going to her husband. But in the past, when she had dared to speak of the dangers to which her loneliness exposed her, he had taunted and sneered at her.

She need not flatter herself, he had coarsely told her, that anybody would want to run away with her. (Baynton 1993, 134)

In this passage Barbara Baynton's criticism of male attitudes is particularly harsh. Motherhood is not a constraining experience per se, it is the social order imposed through chauvinist male attitudes that entraps women to the domestic hearth.

Again, the story evolves paralleles Lawson's "The Drover's Wife". During the day a swagman visits the homestead, the young mother tries to fool him by telling him that her husband is sick in bed and the malicious visitor, after having had some food, cannily proves the absence of the husband: "had asked for tobacco [...] and if there were a man inside, there ought to have been tobacco" (Baynton 1993, 133). From the moment the visitor leaves, the woman is trapped in the house. Just like the drover's wife, she will wake and listen, she will notice the shadow of the man outside as he probes the cracks in the wall and she will fear that he might discover the loose slab with the wedge under it. Starting from this moment the story becomes almost gothic, with the suspense created by the short sentences describing the panic in the woman's thoughts:

> What woke her? The wonder was that she had slept – she had not meant to. [...] Something had set her heart beating wildly; [...] and she prayed, "Little baby, little baby, don't wake!" [...]
> She suddenly recalled that one of the slabs [...] had once fallen out. What if he should discover that? The uncertainty increased her terror. [...]
> Then she saw him find it; and heard the sound of the knife as bit by bit he began to cut out the wooden support. (Baynton 1993, 135-136)

Her alertness to every sound and movement around the house creates a tension that discloses the existence of a reality entirely unmentioned in Lawson's story: outside the hut the uncanny reigns unchallenged. The claustrophobic feeling created by the narration clearly distinguishes between inside and outside: the hut is a tiny familiar refuge from a world extending so vast and unknown around it that it continuously threatens to swallow the small fortress. In this dark atmosphere and after comparing Lawson's and Baynton's story, the parallelism between snake and swagman becomes outstanding as they both could represent the incarnation of all evil.

The swagman and the world around the hut thus become the incarnation of obscenity. The invisibility of the enemy makes him dangerously omnipresent. The swagman is figuratively everywhere, as he belongs to the dark emptiness which surrounds the house. This vision comes into direct conflict with Lawson's and Paterson's celebration of the bush as either an arcadian or rough place populated by good-natured people. The uniquely positive image of the bush is finally challenged in the dichotomy that will ultimately characterize Australian literature. City and bush are persistently juxtaposed, but the connotation of these two locations shifts according to the different perspectives. John Kinsella, in an article titled "The Shifting City and the Shifting Bush," elaborates on the difficulty of defining these spaces:

> The openness of the farmlands, the prospect hemmed in by hills and forest, was threatened by our seeing and potentially reporting to an outside world, maybe taking the message of their violence – shooting animals, racism, bush-bashing and so on – to the media. [...] There's a private world, in which many crimes of violence toward animals and land are hidden. [...]
> [O]ne might level the same accusation at those who live in the cities. [...] the city is a place where you are never alone – outside the privacy of your living place, others will see you. But anonymity comes with numbers. [...] The city creates anonymity through proximity. The outback represents the ability to get lost. [I]t becomes a place of fear, a place that will, dentata-like, consume you. (Kinsella 2002, 25)

Kinsella's analysis presents all of the perspectives encountered in the previously quoted texts; Paterson's resentment of the city is accounted for by the anonymity of individuals lost in crowds but, more poignantly, Barbara Baynton's horrific depiction of the bush is justified by the enticing emptiness of the outback. From this perspective, the swagman represents the fallen man who has been corrupted by the emptiness of the space he has entered and that, in the anonymity there offered, has infringed the primary moral rule of the protestant ethic: he has become an unproductive vagrant.

Lawson, in his short story, recognizes the problem – because the swagman does not fit in his vision of laborious people relentlessly working at the construction of a nation – but minimizes the origin and the importance of the threat posed by this character. Baynton expressly centres the story on the swagman who clearly covers the only active role in the story: he deliberately chooses the defenceless drover's wife as "the vessel" of his immoral crime. The woman, at every level, is just an object in a patriarchal configuration of reality. In this case the "chosen vessel" is not selected for a holy cause; the woman, hearing a horseman go by, dashes out in the open and cries for help to the stranger:

> She called to him in Christ's name, in her babe's name, still flying like the wind with the speed that deadly peril gives. But the distance grew greater and greater between them, and when she reached the creek her prayers turned to wild shrieks, for there crouched the man she feared, with outstretched arms that caught her as she fell. (Baynton 1993, 136)

Highly symbolic is the fact that the swagman becomes one with nature and, just as she falls, he is there to take her almost as if in a welcoming embrace. Of course, she is mercilessly raped and killed.

The second part of the story focuses on Peter Hennessey's rebellious attempt at voting for a candidate not supported by the priest. That night, burdened by superstition and an inner sense of guilt, Peter fails to save the unnamed woman from her faith: when he hears her call for help – "For Christ's sake! Christ's sake! Christ's sake!" – he mistakes what he sees for an apparition of the Virgin Mary and the baby Jesus. Once again the woman has been possessed and reduced to an instrument – objectified – of the patriarchal world order. Thus, she also becomes Peter's chosen vessel as, with her sacrifice, she prevents him from voting against the priest's candidate who is essentially the incarnation of that same patriarchal order. Kay Iseman (a.k.a. Kay Shaffer), in her paper "Barbara Baynton: Woman as 'The Chosen Vessel,' " extensively analyses this theme from a feminist perspective and concludes:

> If one reads through the contradictions, woman is not guilty at all – she is wholly absent. She takes no part in the actions of the story except to represent male desire as either Virgin or whore. Her 'lack', disguised as maternal power, enables 'him' (husband, son, horseman, Priest) to attain or maintain an identity. She has been named, captured, controlled, appropriated, violated, raped and murdered, and then reverenced through the signifying practices of the text. And these contradictory practices through which the 'woman' is disseminated in the text are made possible by her very absence from the symbolic order except by reference to her phallic repossession by Man. Baynton's text, in its deliberate irony, calls attention to these facts while it calls into question the idealization of the bushman as the embodiment of Australian personality. (Schaffer 1983, 36)

As Shaffer points out, Barbara Baynton draws attention to what has been silenced about the bush, or better, to the bush's capacity to silence and abscond and therefore of becoming an ideal ob-scene scenario. This theme will become a fundamental element of the literature of the twentieth century. As it will be presented in section 3.2 of this chapter, Patrick White's *Voss* (1957), David Malouf's *Remembering Babylon* (1993), Catherine Susannah Prichard's *Coonardoo* (1929) and Xavier Herbert's *Capricornia* (1938) explore this ambiguous cultural space where the Australian bushman is often portrayed as either a troubled person or an individual striving not to stray from the righteous path. Thus, Lawson and Paterson's image is slowly abandoned and the bush is construed as a corrupting force. This shift in attitude towards the interior is accounted for in the next section (3.1.2) where Joan Lindsay's *Picnic at Hanging Rock* (1967) is used to testify the formalization of the bush as an uncanny corrupting force in literature.

3.1.2 Picnic at Hanging Rock

Lady Lindsay's novel, *Picnic at Hanging Rock* (1967), even if written sixty-six year after Queen Victoria's death, is particularly relevant as it perfectly embodies the anxieties of the Victorian age and, most importantly, presents an alternative perception of the outback. Set in 1900, the novel presents itself as the true account of events which occurred during a Saint Valentine's Day picnic of that same year. The facts recounted in the novel are actually quite simple: during a picnic at Hanging Rock three young girls, pupils of a nearby college, and a teacher disappear leaving no trace. After eight days, one of them is found in relatively good conditions but oblivious to anything that happened on the rock. The simplicity of the events – the disappearance is dealt with in just eight of the 200 pages– is counterbalanced by the tension caused by the mystery slowly clutching the community and subsequently bringing the college and its mistress to a downfall. Cleverly, Lady Lindsay centres her drama on a pre-existent Australian anxiety; her characters and her story are the distillation of the perennial struggle between nurture and nature. The underlying theme is the one so expressively described by Lawson in "His Country – After All," where the inhospitable mother country remains a mother after all. Kay Schaffer, in an essay titled "Women and the Bush: Australian National Identity and Representations of the Feminine," concisely elucidates this idea:

> We all are the effects of discourse. Meaning does not exist anywhere except where it is lived and made. The pre-eminent meaning encoded in the nationalist myth of the land-as-women is that of harsh, cruel, threatening, fickle, castrating mother. She is dangerous, non-nurturing and not to be trusted. This is "no place for a woman!" But it is also a familiar place of Woman within the Australian tradition. (Schaffer 1989, 11)

Australia as a nurturing/castrating mother can be viewed as the unifying thread between the texts so far analysed in this chapter.

However, so far the threat had been posed to men who, as in the case of the swagman, are left to battle the uncanny forces of the land and to defend themselves from the consuming forces of nature/mother. *Picnic at Hanging Rock* follows this same theme by shifting the focus from the paladins of civilization – the pioneers taming the indomitable land – to the maidens that, in the enclosure of the "bastions" of the college, embody the ultimate achievement of nurture in the battle against nature. Bearing this in mind, the significance of the disappearance of three of the most accomplished and senior girls of the college should become more apparent. Almost as if in a ritual sacrifice, the outback devours the characters that are its symbolic opposite: Mrs McCraw, the mathematic teacher, representing rationality; Marion Quade, another rationally inclined character, and Miranda who, as her name suggests, stands for beauty and grace. These characters embody the moral order imposed to the land (cf. Crittenden 1976, 172). In this vision, with its very well marked spatial contours, women are tokens used in the solidification of a social space supposedly constructed for the benefit of the ladies themselves, but truly shaped to suit the needs of a patriarchal social order. Women, as portrayed in the novel, are ultimately prisoners of this scheme. Victorian maidens, constrained by clothing and manners, are actually just the other side of the coin to Lawson's and Baynton's heroines. Each one in a different role, they are all pawns – some as flawless role models and others as the nation's begetters – in the construction of Australia's social landscape.

In the archetypical representation of the conflict between nature and civilization proposed by Lindsay, Hanging Rock symbolizes all the negative aspects attributed to the bush. The rock is a space completely "other," diametrically opposite to the orderliness of Mrs Appleyard's College. The headmistress' initial remarks and recommendation to her students are highly significant; first she concedes that they "may remove their gloves once the drag has passed through Woodend" (Lindsay 1975, 8) and later she warns them about the dangers posed by the place: "venomous snakes and poisonous ants of various species" (Lindsay 1975, 8). The concession of removing the gloves becomes highly symbolic; the venturing into the wilderness allows for a small relaxation of the rigid rules controlling the girls' lives. It is not however proper to remove the gloves before passing through Woodend or to remove the hats while on the drag: "can't we take our hats off too [...]? [...] Certainly not. Because we are not on an excursion, there is no necessity to look like a wagon load of gypsies" (Lindsay 1975, 11). Nevertheless, at the picnic ground, some of the girls take their hats off and, finally, the senior girls venturing on the rock remove their shoes and stockings. Yet, the removal of the incongruous female apparel is not in this case dictated by necessity; Irma Leopold appropriately remarks that "whoever invented female fashions for nineteen hundred should be made walk through bracken fern in three layers of petticoats" (Lindsay 1975, 29). The ladies fashion is made to constrain movement and to create objects of male adoration. The girls, unlike the more rational and practical Miss McCraw who is seen venturing in the scrub in her "pantalons," are not concerned with making their excursion easier but, as Irma wishes, with enjoying freedom for a bit longer: "If only we could stay out all night and watch the moon rise [...] we don't often have a chance to enjoy ourselves out of school" (Lindsay 1975, 30). The removal of shoes and stockings is a symbolic step out of the realm of civilization and a material step into the natural world. Exhausted, the girls fall asleep on the ground, unconcerned, as the nature surrounding them follows its course – beetles cross Miranda's ankle and a thorned lizard lies in the hollow of Marion's ankle. After this prolonged contact with nature, by walking barefoot and sleeping on the ground, the girls wake up as though enchanted and they simply walk away. This time, the ever caring Miranda fails to hear Edith's insistent calls – she had not removed her shoes – and slips out of view with the others.

> 'Miranda' Edith said again, I feel perfectly awful! 'When are we going home?' Miranda was looking at her so strangely, almost as if she wasn't seeing her. When Edith repeated the question more loudly she simply turned her back and began walking away up the rise, the other two following a little behind. Well, hardly walking – sliding over the

stones on their bare feet as if they were on a drawing-room carpet, Edith thought, instead of those nasty stones. [...] 'Come back, all of you! Don't go up there – come back!' [...] To her horror all three girls were fast moving out of sight behind the monolith. 'Miranda! Come back!' she took a few uneasy steps towards the rise and saw the last of a white sleeve parting the bushes ahead. (Lindsay 1975, 33-34)

The girls seem to be almost drawn by an invisible force – they slide over stones – and they are literally swallowed by nature that, with the final bush closing onto a white sleeve, definitively closes around them and confines them into an off-scene space.

This space draws most of its luring power from its inscrutability. The reader and the other protagonists of the novel are left to imagine what lies beyond the last bush. It thus not only becomes off-scene – what lies beyond the bush is never mentioned in the published version – but also obscene. Immediately after the disappearance of the girls the newspapers start speculating about the College Mystery and, a very clear idea of what fears are projected upon this space, is given by a police detective in an interview with Mrs Appleyard:

MISSING: PRESUMED DEAD [...] The word DEAD leaped obscenely from the printed page. Yes, it was possible, but highly unlikely, said the Senior Detective with whom she was closeted for two hours in a stuffy room, that the girls had been abducted, lured away, robbed – or worse. 'And what,' asked the headmistress, tight-lipped and clammy with fear and the insufferable heat of the room, 'could be worse, may I ask, than that?' It appeared that they might yet be found in a Sydney brothel: such things happened now and then in Sydney when girls of respectable background disappeared without a trace. Not often in Melbourne. Mrs Appleyard could only shudder. 'They were exceptionally intelligent and well-behaved girls who would never have allowed any familiarity from strangers.'

'As far as that goes,' said the detective blandly, 'most young girls would object to being raped by a drunken seaman, if that's what you have in mind' (Lindsay 1975, 111)

Kidnapping, murder, rape; anything could have happened. In fact, the mystery is so intriguing because the actual events are never revealed and, for this reason, it had such a mesmerizing effect over the Australian imaginary. I will therefore deliberately ignore the posthumously published eighteenth chapter (Lindsay and Rousseau 1987) which, by solving the mystery, dissolves the otherwise unresolved tension and deprives the novel of most of its captivating symbolism. The mystery of Hanging Rock is particularly meaningful, as in spite of all the possible conjectures, the focus remains on the un-responding otherness of nature. Fantasy, by projecting its worst fears upon the unknown, transforms nature, in this case Hanging Rock, into an obscene space – where murder or worse are consumed.

In her essay, Kay Shaffer reveals the cultural legacy imprinted by the novel into everyday Australian reality; as an example, she quotes the headings and part of the text likening the disappearance of two boys in Western Australia to the mystery of Hanging Rock (Schaffer 1989, 10). Joan Lindsay's novel – also through the filmic adaptation by Peter Weir – left a mark on the Australian consciousness by addressing a theme that is at the heart of the Australian definition of space. She represented the disquieting effect that, after two hundred years of colonial history, nature continues to have on white Australians and, the ensuing struggle between civilization and the so-perceived indomitable and capricious forces of nature. Lady Lindsay's description of this relationship is impeccable; when Marion Quade reflects on the age of the rock, she exposes their relative irrelevance in the face of the millenary age of the land:

> 'Those peaks ... they must be a million years old.'
> 'A million. Oh, how horrible!" Edith exclaimed. 'Miranda! Did you here that?' At fourteen, millions of years can be almost indecent. [...]
> 'Whether Edith likes it or not,' Marion pointed out, 'that fat little body of hers is made up of millions and millions of cells.' Edith put her hands over her ears, 'Stop it, Marion! I don't want to hear about such things.'

'And what's more, you little goose, you have already lived millions and millions of seconds.'
Edith had gone white in the face. 'Stop it! You are making me feel giddy.' (Lindsay 1975, 28)

Edith's reaction is typical in its kind; the vastness and the often ragged look of the land are overwhelming, they make people feel perilously insignificant. Later, Marion compares the people on the plain – which by now are searching for them – to ants. Curiously, Miranda and the other senior girls dismiss the thought with a laugh, while Edith is terrified by the thought. The youngest and worldliest of the girls, like many before her, fails to establish a connection with the land and feels rejected. The place, as she often repeats, is awful to her.

Prior to the publication of the eighteenth chapter, there had been several attempts to solve the mystery in analytical ways – masterly in the attempt was Yvonne Rousseau's book *The Murders at Hanging Rock* (Rousseau) which counts seven contradicting hypotheses. Then again, it is more important to unlock the veiled symbolism of the novel. In "The mythology of Pan and *Picnic at Hanging Rock*" (1982) Donald Barrett's interpretation correlates the numerous symbols with the ancient myth of Pan. His sharp analysis of the text provides a very convincing picture linking the Greek Deity to the Australian text. The capriciousness of nature, the watches stopping at noon, the sexual tension and the recurring themes of torpor, sleep and nightmares can all be explained in light of the influence of the capricious faun hunting the wilderness. However, the author himself questions whether this may have really been a direct influence on the author or just a culturally mediated one: "To counteract the temptation of reading into the novel only the things one wants to see, I sent a résumé of the foregoing views to Lady Lindsay for comment" (Barrett 1982, 308). The Authoress, in her reply, disclaims any Classical influence but admits that, when Peter Weir proposed to use Pan pipes for the soundtrack of the film she "felt that was good" (Barrett 1982, 308). Nevertheless, as Donald Barrett claims, his analysis should not be entirely discredited.

His observations are important "not only for the sake of balance but because they are highly significant in themselves" (Barrett 1982, 308).

It can be argued that the feeling of otherness in nature is achieved through the conscious or unconscious use of a series of very well established symbols. Barrett points out Pan, which explains the alterity and capriciousness of the virgin land; there are however other ways – not entirely discordant – to interpret the story. Exceptionally illuminating for the purpose of this research is Anne Crittenden's study "*Picnic at Hanging Rock*: A Myth and its Symbols" where the attention is shifted to a more contemporary Christian symbolism. The very initial remark that "Appleyard College" recalls the loss of the Garden of Eden and the entrance of a condition ruled by deprivation, work and ultimately death, draws the attention to a socio-topographic configuration of the environment depicted in the novel: "Appleyard college is not a Garden of Eden itself, that is clear: it is a school, which signifies the deliberately 'knowing', rational side of our civilization, and the effort, basic to education, to train the young generation in the values of society at large" (Crittenden 1976, 167). The school is a space of confinement, a training ground for people who are yet to be broken into the values of moral society. The rock is of course the antithetic opposite of the college. According to Donald Barrett, Hanging Rock is Pan's realm while for Anne Crittenden, who contrasts the material values of the college to the higher spiritual values embodied in Miranda, it is a stepping ground to heaven (Crittenden 1976, 170). The iconic significance of the mountain, best represented in Dante's *The Divine Comedy*, seems initially to clash with the contrasting of civilization and nature. However, Anne Crittenden's analysis also evidences the significance of the date of the Picnic, on Saint Valentine's Day:

> 14th of February has always been kept as Saint Valentine's feast day by the Christian Church, and in the later middle ages there arose a custom of sending love-notes on that-day. This custom originally had nothing to do with Saint Valentine, but was a watered down fertility ritual whose roots went back into magical-religious rites to celebrate

spring. Love notes on this day is thus a custom descended from barbaric rites connected to the gods of nature. (Crittenden 1976, 168)

When the college girls dance barefoot on the rocks they could be seen as performing a fertility ritual in adoration of the Mother Earth embodied in the rock. Hanging Rock is thus an ambiguous space. If it appears menacing and haunting to Mrs Appleyard – after the vanishing of the girls she repeatedly dreams of it – or dreadful to Edith, it is enticing to the other girls. Miranda is of course the central and leading figure among the missing girls and it is under her guidance that the group gets lost in what seems to be a fracture of time. From the start her character is described as being absolutely perfect; she is capable of giving love to everybody and she tolerates anything – even the annoying Edith. As Mademoiselle De Poitiers realizes, this iconic beauty – both bodily and spiritually – is already an immortal archetype: Miranda is a Botticelli's angel from the Uffizi museum in Florence. It is thus that this remarkable girl, by walking towards the summit of the rock, strives for that immortal reunion with the eternal. As Crittenden explains: "In order to ascend to the cloud in which God resides – we think of the frightening red cloud Edith sees – a person must surrender himself utterly to a state of unknowing, and approach the divine mystery in the blindness of self-destruction" (Crittenden 1976, 172).

Miranda is therefore destined to step out of the material world and, by renouncing her earthly life, to step into the realm of the divine. The other girls seem otherwise to be either rejected or punished by the rock itself. One week later, Michael Fitzhubert's disturbance of the scene spares Irma the fate of the others. Exactly a week after the girls walked off in a trance, Michael appears on the scene calling for his loved one. Michael, after a single glance, has mystically fallen in love with Miranda. It is this idealized love for the girl – comparable to Dante's love for Beatrice – that enables the young Englishman to be the only male figure to feel an empathy with the rock similar to the one the girls experienced. However, his love is of a lesser kind to that of Miranda and he is spared her fate. Similarly, Irma, who had fallen in love with Michael, is recalled to the real world by the youth's passionate calls. It could be said that Irma is spared her destiny because of her love for Michael, which pleases the Earth Mother embodied in the rock. In contrast, for Anne Crittenden, Greta McCraw and Marion are punished for their renunciation of the earthly values of love and fertility and for their sterile interest in analytical reason.

The picture emerging from this analysis is not dissimilar to that proposed by Donald Barrett; nature is still depicted as a capricious entity that punishes or spares its victims. Be it Pan or a revered Mother Nature, the essence is the same: the rock stands in contrast to Appleyard College and civilization by representing a perilous space of perdition. Finally, what is more daunting about this space is the unresponding silence that surrounds the mystery. The unresolved case remains a haunting presence in the unconscious of those who witness it. At the end of the novel, the girls of the college reunited in the gymnasium have a vision of the rock and of the corpses rotting in a filthy cave. They also violently attack Irma, who is there for a last goodbye, and try to extort a truth that she herself does not know. It is the impenetrability of the mystery that makes it obscene.

In the end, no matter the reason why, the fact is that the girls have been devoured by nature. As Anne Crittenden points out, this human sacrifice happens on a Saturday (Crittenden 1976, 168) (which does not correspond to the real 14th of February 1900, which was a Wednesday), the day of Saturn, in Greek mythology the God of Time, a deity that devoured his own children. Having established that this is an exemplary punishment, what remains to be determined is its cultural significance. The clues so far collected demonstrate not only that nature, by swallowing the ladies whole, is reinstated as an antagonist to civilization but, at the same time and in a covert way, it also becomes a patriarchal agent reinforcing the demarcation of women's boundaries. As in the late nineteenth-century short stories by Lawson and Baynton, space is constructed around the patriarchal society at large in the 1900s. The exemplary lesson taught by the novel seems to be that Miranda, too spiritual to be interested in marriage, Marion, a bookworm, and Miss McCraw, a spinster, are all punished for their failure to fit in a society that transformed them in male commodities. By infringing this dictum, the girls metaphorically overstepped the boundaries of patriarchal society purposely surrounded by a revengeful obscene world. In this sociologically constructed space women are figuratively and physically confined within a space arranged around their functions of wives and mothers. Edith, who is so ludicrously obtuse, makes a role model citizen in this social order. As a proof, upon reaching the borders of moral society, she responds by feeling rejected and she runs back in a panic. Irma, worldlier than her companions, is spared death because she accepts the rules imposed on her: she will marry, have children and, most importantly, bring her millionaire dowry to her husband.

In every reading the rock remains an obscene site, ob-scene because of its inaccessibility and mystery but also obscene because of the fears projected onto it. Anne Crittenden very clearly outlines the symbolic importance of Hanging Rock: "On the level of individual psychology, Hanging Rock stands for the Unconscious, in its two drives, sexuality – the source of life – and the death instinct – the perversity and hatred inside any person that can lead him to destroy himself or others" (Crittenden 1976, 173).

Beyond the moral boundaries of society, the unconscious reigns unbounded. Women are strictly not allowed in this space, however men can venture in it and, if they are lucky, may return un-scalded to civilization. Thus, the next section of this chapter will be dedicated to the study of this space and to the men who, at their own risk, explored it, first settled there and eventually transformed it into an homely environment. It is the breaking of a frontier in order to widen the boundaries of civilization and to reinstate the social, but also sociotopographic, order of western society. The other, the unconscious and the obscene that lie beyond that frontier are thus slowly pushed backward.

3.2 White Men in the Outback

After having determined that the bush – being a treacherous obscene setting – is presented as a predominantly masculine environment, the novels by Patrick White, David Malouf, Xavier Herbert and Catherine Susannah Prichard – where all the protagonists are white, male, and possibly heroes – can be used to illustrate the compartmentalization of this space and the ensuing transformation of the Australian socio-topographic landscape. As previously mentioned, *Voss* (1957), with its journey into the heart of the country, *Remembering Babylon* (1993), with Gemmy's symbolic intrusion into the civilized space, *Coornadoo* (1929), with its troubling theme of miscegenation, and *Capricornia* (1938), with the unflattering description of the formation of a new state in the far North, all provide an excellent study subject regarding the exploration and settlement of the outback. Each of these texts covers a different period in time and a distinct cultural phase contributing to the appropriation of the bush. Hence, even though written at very different times, the novels fall effortlessly together and create an illuminating account of the evolution of the ever-ambiguous relationship between City and Bush.

3.2.1 Voss

Voss, due to its fascinating exploration of the Australian interior, is the first text to be considered. The plot, although apparently simple, is imbued in a dense symbolism which is open to innumerable interpretations. What becomes immediately evident is that the novel is inspired by the expedition of the German explorer Ludwig Leichardt, and that the text could therefore be read as a fictional reconstruction of real events. Even from this point of view the multi-layering imposed by Patrick White's skilful hand evades an easy interpretation. As John Beston notes in "Will Voss Endure? Fifty Years Later," the novel also "incorporates elements of the journey of Eyre (the spearing of Palfreyman) and of Bourke and Wills (the poorly organized aspect of the expedition and the unknown fate of the explorers) and it is more evocative for suggesting all these three explorers" (Beston 2003, 50). It is not simply an historical figure that is embodied in Voss, it is the archetype of the explorer and therefore of everything that this character represents. Roslyn Haynes, in her seminal text *Seeking the Centre*, argues that "to a greater extent than anywhere else on the globe [...] the nineteenth century explorers shaped the Australian desert for posterity, investing it with the character and significance it continued to bear for over a century." Explorers, whose main intent was to depict themselves as heroes, are thus held responsible for "unwittingly [...] generating the gothic fairy tales with which the nation [now] periodically frightens itself" (Haynes 1998, 58). It is thus that, as Kay Shaffer also points out in relation to *Picnic at Hanging Rock*, the "images of treachery in and by the desert lie dormant in the collective memory ready to erupt at every conforming incident" (Haynes 1998, 58-59). "Geography is never innocent" reads the title of the chapter dealing with explorers in Hayne's study; invoking Foucault she explains that "the quest for truth [...] was intimately related to the 'will to power'" and therefore that "[t]he knowledge conveyed by [the explorers] was thus a form of power presented in the guise of scientific disinterest" (Haynes 1998, 59-60).

Patrick White, by condensing in Voss all the most celebrated Australian explorers, implicitly tackles the problem of the socio-topographic construction of Australia. Emblematically, when asked if he has studied the map of the continent, the German explorer declares "The map? [...] I will first make it!" (White 1994, 23). As Haynes proves in her study, the explorers, with their journeys and their recording in their diaries, shaped and in a way literally created the cultural map of Australia. The novel is therefore not simply the account of an expedition but the account of the making of a continent. Before venturing in the desert with Voss and studying the dynamics of this process, it is interesting to note Patrick White's standpoint in relation to the novel and his country. *Voss* was written after White's return to Australia and after his realization that, in order to conquer the sense of desolation communicated by the cultural scene of the country, he had to "discover the extraordinary behind the ordinary, the mystery and the poetry which alone could make bearable the lives of [Australian] people" (White 1990, 23). This famous quote from *The Prodigal Son* (first published in 1958) refers to *The Tree of Man* in particular, however, it is this drive that induced White to explore the desert interior of the continent and, symbolically, the cultural desert that surrounded him:

> In all directions stretched the Great Australian Emptiness, in which the mind is the least of possessions, in which the rich man is the important man, in which the schoolmaster and the journalist rule what intellectual roost there is, in which beautiful youths and girls stare at life through blinkered blue eyes, in which human teeth fall like autumn leaves, the buttocks of cars grow hourly glassier, food means cake and steak, muscles prevail, and the march of material ugliness does not raise a quiver from the average nerves. (White 1990, 22)

Voss, in a way, is a twofold exploration. It simultaneously engages the past and the present and, almost proposing itself as a new journal of exploration (which as previously noted is not an innocent scientific tool), it re-charts the cultural map of Australia. Accordingly, in 1973, Patrick White was awarded the Nobel Prize "for an epic and psychological narrative art which has introduced a new continent into literature" (Nobel-Prize-Foundation 1973). The continent was not simply introduced in the panorama of international literature but, in a way, it was turned inside out and re-presented by focusing on, as previously mentioned, the extraordinary in the ordinary. It is thus that such a simple tale of exploration – an expedition is prepared, it takes place and fails, and the consequences are dealt with – acquires epic proportions. White, as he declares in *The Prodigal Son*, wanted to attempt to give *Voss* "the textures of music, the sensuousness of paint" (White 1990, 23). It is through the attention to minor details and to the insight provided in the characters' psychologies that the author "paints" a new portrait of the country. John Beston observes that the fact that White "was not much interested in the geographical aspects of the exploration of the Australian Interior is clear from the very vagueness of the geographical details in [the novel]" (Beston 2003, 51). Sydney, Newcastle, Rhine Towers "idyllic rather than realistic" and Jildra "surrounded by a sea of grass" (Beston 2003, 51), are the only "certain" points of reference in the entire journey. From then onwards the expedition traverses an almost indistinguishable landscape that Beston defines "the country of the mind" (Beston 2003, 51). This is the extraordinary feat accomplished by White: *Voss* is deeply Australian because it does not merely describe the dry interior of the continent but, by juxtaposition, it investigates the subtleties of the meaning of being Australian. The society, its history and its suffocating shallowness (that of the fifties) are depicted in an epic form. Taking consciousness of a criticism made by Guy Innes after the publication of *The Aunt's Story* (1948), the author admits that the journalist was right: after coming back to Australia "the colours [came] flooding back onto [his] palette" (White 1990, 23). The colours returned in the form of Australian characters, almost icons, such as Voss, Laura, the Bonners and the other protagonists of the novel. Australia, almost stripped naked in the process, is fascinatingly represented through the exploration of its desert. The continent is thus charted twice, first, in the past by Voss in the act of exploration, and a second time, in the present by White in the act of writing.

The 1850s socio-spatial configuration of Australia is quite accurately depicted in the novel; the shallowness of Sydney's mercantile society is represented in the bigotry of the Bonners and their friends. Laura and Voss immediately distinguish themselves as outcasts. Foreigners in a dull and uncomprehending society, their link is largely forged on the basis of this mutual condition. Veronica Brady, in an essay on censorship, points out the clear-cut distinction between the patrons of the expedition, who fear "the 'other half'" of life, everything that is not orderly and manageable, which is beyond rational control" (Brady 1974, 48) and the man who is about to engage in the actual exploration of this space:

It is White's contention in *Voss* that Australian society, represented by the Bonners and their friends also fear this 'other half' of life, the desert, the irrational country where man loses control. Voss mocks these fears of theirs. "A pity that you huddle" he says "your country is of great subtlety." (Brady 1974, 48)

Voss sets off to explore a space that has already been culturally appropriated as a location of otherness. However, by doing so, the explorer distinguishes himself not by refuting the socio-topographic configuration of the continent but, on the contrary, by daring to venture into a culturally banished – or censored, as Veronica Brady suggests – area. In the end, all the cultural allegations stigmatizing the desert as a place of treacherous otherness are confirmed in Voss' trip: his party never returns, the desert conveniently swallows them. Several years later Judd, the ex-convict, reappears half demented and gives a confused account of the expedition:

"Ah," smiled the aged, gummy man. "Voss." […]
"Voss left his mark on the country," he said.
"How?" asked Miss Trevelyan, cautiously.
"Well, the trees, of course. He was cutting his initials in the trees. He was a queer beggar, Voss. The blacks talk about him to this day. He is still there – that is the honest opinion of many of them – he is there in the country and always will be."
"How?" repeated Miss Trevelyan. Her voice was that of a man. She dared anyone.
Judd was feeling his way with his hands.
"Well, you see, if you live and suffer long enough in a place, you do not leave it altogether. Your spirit is still there."
"Like a God, in fact,' said Colonel Hebden, but laughed to show his scepticism.
Judd looked up out of the distance.
"Voss? No, he was never God, though he liked to think that he was. Sometimes, when he forgot, he was a man." (White 1994, 443)

This conclusive interpretation of the facts merges several of the most important themes of the novel: Laura's bond to her mystical husband, the problem of Voss' nature – good or evil – and his resulting influence in the socio-topographic construction of the land. The novel portrays Voss in fine but ambiguous detail. The subtleties and contradictions of his personality emerge throughout the novel and during his trip, adding to the life-like credibility of the character. Judd's description is extremely appropriate. Voss is an exceptionally strong willed man, however, just a man. Colonel Hebden does not accept this ambivalent version of the facts. In his quest for "truth" (one related to the "will to power") he needs a schematic interpretation of facts. In his words, "history is not acceptable until is sifted for the truth" (White 1994, 413). This man at the service of truth defines himself a "tentative explorer [...] or less than that, even – one who follows in the tracks of another not so much to find him alive in the end, as to satisfy curiosity" (White 1994, 407). The Colonel's goal is not to discover or to explore, it is to distinguish and determine who Voss really was. Inspired by the mystery surrounding the expedition and by Laura Trevelyan's declaration that "Voss could have been the Devil, [...] if at the same time he had not resembled a most unfortunate human being" (White 1994, 414), he leads two expeditions that literally try to prove Voss' monstrosity.

Insisting on the explorer's moral defeat, either pre-existent or caused by the voyage into the desert, Hebden, who is a paladin of the Bonners' society, reinforces the spatial subdivision which confines the unconscious into the heart of the country. Veronica Brady, in her essay on censorship, brilliantly elucidates the situation:

> Many of the appeals for censorship, for authority to save us from what we fear because we cannot control ourselves, suggest fears like the Bonners, of the irrational, the Dionysian forces long repressed but now erupting in our society. Moreover, their sense of morality seems disturbingly immature, resting, it seems, on legislation rather than on inner choice. In fact what Kierkegaard said of the bourgeois of his day may well apply to them. "Their ethics are short summary of police ordinances. For them, the most important thing is to be a member of the state ... They have never felt a homesickness for something unknown and far away." Because of this, because all they know is the horizon

of the present, their standards are conditioned by history. (Brady 1974, 48)

Voss and Laura are the two visionary characters that feel that "homesickness for something unknown and far away." As Miss Trevelyan says in an early discussion with Lieutenant Radclyffe, Australia "is his by right of vision." He thus trespasses all the set cultural boundaries and explores, as suggested by Brady, the territory of the censored and of the repressed (White 1994, 29). Colonel Hebden, on the contrary, is a representative of the "police order" and for this reason his mission is to reinstate those boundaries and to contain Voss' figure in the schematization of the bourgeois ethics he defends. Thus, Hebden's "truth" suggests that Voss is either an evil man or a man subdued by the evil in the land. Patrick White stylishly presents the everlasting struggle between this narrow minded logic and the extraordinary complexity that it tries to conceal. As Laura Trevelyan conclusively says: "All truths are particoloured. Except the greatest truth of all" (White 1994, 444). The explorer aims at finding this type of truth: a whole encompassing and everlasting one, that of God and the infinite.

Voss is portrayed as an immensely egocentric character driven by an indomitable determination. His visionary quest for something beyond rationality means he is very often misunderstood by Australian materialist society. From the beginning Laura is the only person that seems to understand Voss, and very early on she defends Voss from the malignant comments rumoured in the Bonners' household:

> 'He does not intend to make a fortune out of this country, like other men. He is not all money talk.'
> 'Other men are human,' said her uncle, 'and this is the country of the future. Who will not snap at an opportunity when he sees one? And get rich. (White 1994, 28)

"The march of material ugliness [that] does not raise a quiver from the average nerves" (White 1990, 23) constitutes the norm of the

1850s as well as that of the 1950s. Voss is a visionary who has higher aims and it is this cultural difference that makes him appear like an alien to everybody else. Mrs Bonner maternally expresses her concern about this character and, noticing his non-robust build, remarks that "he is already lost," and that "his eyes cannot find their way" (White 1994, 27-28). It is however the inspired gaze already looking into the distance that this society fails to understand; that of the explorer who is already travelling through the desert where he has been summoned. As it becomes clearer throughout the preparation of the journey, the voyage is mostly a spiritual one. The German, when recruiting Le Mesurier, honestly explains that by "crossing the desert from one end to the other end" he has "every intention to know it with [his] heart" (White 1994, 33). This approach, directly in contrast with the "huddling" attitude of the Sydney society, suggests the possibility of reconciliation with the otherness externalized upon the heart of the country. As Laura suggests, Voss is the only person who is not afraid of the desert:

> 'But he is not afraid,' said Laura.
> 'Who is afraid?' Said Tom Radclyff.
> 'Everyone is still afraid, or most of us, of this country, and will not say it. We are not yet possessed of understanding.' (White 1994, 29)

However, Voss' lack of concern about the dangers awaiting him in the heart of the country does not prove his autonomy from the discourse stigmatizing the desert as a place of pure Otherness:

> Have you walked upon the bottom of the sea, Mr Pringle?' said the German.
> 'Eh?' said Mr Pringle. 'No.'
> His eyes, however, had swum unaccustomed depths.
> 'I have not,' said Voss. 'Except in dreams, of course. That is why I am fascinated by the prospect before me. Even if the future of great areas of sand is a purely metaphysical one.' (White 1994, 62)

The journey is after all a purely metaphysical exploration in the country of the mind and of the white men's unconscious. Laura Trevelyan perceptively comments that the "expedition [...] is pure will" (White 1994, 69). This is the first indication of the true nature of the mission and of its ill-fated outcome; Voss sagely considers that he "will be under the restrain of several human beings, [animals] and practical impediments [his] patrons consider necessary" (White 1994, 69). In fact, the clumsily organized expedition results highly unsuited to traverse the desert and, as its catastrophic fate is slowly accomplished, all the unnecessary gear and supplies are gradually lost. This comes in stark contrast with the lifestyle of the Aboriginal tribes who, equipped with nothing other than their knowledge of the land, contentedly roam and are provided for by the region that slowly kills the members of the expedition. It is the failure to understand the continent that kills the explorers. By starting the journey prejudiced against the country ahead of them they fail to see what their Aboriginal guides and the native tribes see: food, water and what can ultimately be a homely environment. Even Dougald, the old Aboriginal guide accompanying the mission, when sent back alone to deliver a letter to Miss Trevelyan, perfectly readapts to that other world that the whitemen cannot see:

> Sometimes the old man would jump down at the butt of certain trees, and dig until he reached roots, and brake them open, and suck out the water. [...] The old man killed and ate goannas. He ate a small, dun-coloured rat. [...] When the horse lay down and died, one afternoon in the bed of a dried creek, the black was not unduly concerned. If anything his responsibilities were less. (White 1994, 218)

Talking to Laura, Voss perceptively expresses the wish to traverse the desert "barefoot and alone." Mrs Trevelyan however, senses the real meaning of this intent and earnestly warns him: "You are not going to allow your will to destroy you" (White 1994, 69). Exemplified here is the symbolic nature of the desert. Voss wants to undertake his metaphysical journey alone because he intends to travel through the western collective unconscious. This perilous voyage belongs to an exclusively western cultural space that inevitably threatens to destroy its participants. For this reason the novel has been so often compared to Joseph Conrad's *Heart of Darkness*. The voyage into the desert parallels the one up the river Congo where Marlow rescues (or fails to rescue) a man that, as it is stated in Kurtz's final ravenous words, has succumbed to "the horror." Mark Williams, in a comparative study of the works of Joseph Conrad, Graham Greene, Wilson Harris and Patrick White, argues that Voss' "is another version of the Conradian journey into the heart of darkness" with yet a major difference, since White does not merely stage a "smash and grab into the primitive" and "Voss remains in the country itself" (Williams 1985, 38). In *Voss*, the exploration is not a simple voyeuristic journey into the regions of the unconscious projected upon an off-scene setting. The novel, with its multiple perspectives, critically questions the legitimacy of this reading:

> The colonial social world is one in which the fixity, hierarchy and air of permanence of the Victorian class structure can appear only as travesties. White is prepared in Voss to question this structure in terms of the 'realities' it excludes, in terms, for instance, of the ways the aboriginals construe their world. [...] The Blacks in *Voss* have their own contradictory and complex inner lives as the Blacks in *Heart of Darkness* or *Journey Without Maps* do not. In White's novel the indigenous people, so long convenient representatives of primitiveness, savagery or otherness, begin to live outside the categories which the mind of the Western explorer imposes on them. Voss, who seeks to impose the map of his spiritual arrogance on the black continent, discovers the writing of the Blacks already there. (Williams 1985, 39)

Mark William's argument clearly illustrates the cultural clash represented in the novel. What is at stake here is the imposition of a cultural map upon the continent. For Voss and the Bonners, even though their views are conflicting, Australia is a blank space waiting to be written on. This is what makes the explorer's demise possible. As Laura's concern first indicated Voss is not subdued by the country itself but by the vision his will projects upon the desert. Williams contends that Voss "is in a sense swallowed by the primitive world he had hoped to subdue by virtue of the superiority of his will" (Williams 1985, 39).

Yet, this is only true in the Western frame of mind which leads the explorer to travel not simply through space but also through his unconscious. David Tacey in *Patrick White: Fiction and the Unconscious*, by analysing the novel through Jungian theory, demonstrates the symbolic relevance of this travel. Voss is a man who seeks to obliterate himself in the embrace of his Mother Goddess, Australia (Tacey 1988, 69).

> Voss identifies with the destructive matriarchal force within his psyche, and it is this which gives him his god-like or demonic character. It is absurd to idealize him in terms of the Nietzschean Übermensch because he is the helpless victim of the archetypal possession, an ego which has become morbidly assimilated to the deep unconscious. In his youth Voss had a penchant for dangerous sports and a passion for near-death experiences, which 'through some perversity, inspired him with fresh life'. We are even told, that prior to his obsession for the deserts of Australia, he had a certain fascination for an insect-devouring species of flower. (Tacey 1988, 69)

Here, Tacey definitely humanises Voss: neither a Übermensch nor a God, the German explorer is simply a man who is victim of his own vision. With this reading of the novel, the Australian desert is identified as a mother figure luring the protagonist to its demise. The archetypal image of the mother country as a feminine dentate-like castrating figure (cf. Kinsella 2002, 25) recalls the revered Mother Nature that swallows the pupils of Appleyard College in *Picnic at Hanging Rock*. The difference between the two novels is that Voss' incursion in the region of the unconscious is promoted and blessed by the civilized world, while Miranda's and her companion's escapade is in stark violation of the rules of decency. The outback is reinstated as an exclusively masculine space; only men are allowed to explore the regions of the unconscious while women remain confined in the enclosure of the western world. Accordingly, Laura, who undertakes a similar journey to that of her spiritual husband, does not move from the Bonners' house in Sydney. In her sickbed – diagnosed with "brain fever" (White 1994, 353) – she telepathically follows the final and ruinous stages of the expedition in the desert and she is "released from the destructive grip of the unconscious" (Tacey 1988, 86) only when Voss' head is finally severed.

Laura's words at the very end of the novel further substantiate this spatial distinction:

> I am uncomfortably aware of the very little I have seen and experienced of things in general, and of our country in particular,' Miss Trevelyan had just confessed, 'but the little I have seen is less, I like to feel, than what I know. Knowledge was never a matter of geography. Quite the reverse, it overflows all maps that exist. Perhaps true knowledge only comes of death by torture in the country of the mind. (White 1994, 446)

Miss Trevelyan is deeply aware of the significance of the sociotopographic boundaries restricting her scope of action and, even if she accepts to live within the area she has been assigned, she is conscious of the possibility of evading such boundaries in "the country of the mind" – hence her sickness and the transcendental voyage through the desert/unconscious. David Tacey dismisses Laura's psychological journey as one returning to the security of the Civil society representing the ego: "*Voss* ends on this divisive note: explorers disintegrate and huddlers, with the addition of Miss Trevelyan, continue to huddle. The novel leaves off with an intra-psychic war between ego and unconscious, and a disastrous rift between social and interior worlds" (Tacey 1988, 87).

However, Laura cannot be simply dismissed as a "huddler" because, by adopting the illegitimate child of her deceased maid and by becoming a teacher, she actively resists the rules that compel her to marry, to have children and to be thus secured in the safety of a domestic space. Laura successfully manages to carve out a niche for herself in the huddler society surrounding her. This does not however change the fact that Laura's character is held under strict control by the patriarchal discourse that imposes on her the role, as her name suggests, of the Petrarchan muse (cf. Morley 1972, 73) illuminating the path of the courageous visionary man. As Patricia Morley argues in *The Mystery of Unity*, *Voss* can also be read as a modern version of Dante's *Divine Comedy* (cf. Morley 1972, 118); Laura's role can thus be compared to that of another muse, Beatrice, that leads Dante in his journey through heaven. Being cast in this subsidiary role she is reintegrated in society as an agent contributing to the fulfilment of yet another masculine project. In the end, it does not matter whether Miss Trevelyan is Beatrice or, as David Tacey argues, a "Dark Inspiratrice" (Tacey 1988, 69) because, just as Dante's muse leads her man towards an ecstatic vision, "Circe, the Sirens, the Lorelei, and all those ancient beauties whose task it was to captivate men" draw their preys "to ecstatic death" (Tacey 1988, 73). The presence of Laura in the outback, even if only in a ghostly form, is thus justified by either her Otherness or her otherworldliness. What is most important, however, is the fact that in both cases women are thus objectified as the medium through which men reach their desired state of fulfilment.

Ecstasy, annulment of the self and an almost mystical drive towards the infinite are a clear-cut sub-theme of the novel. Voss, as early as at the time of the recruitment of his team, discloses this vision:

> In this disturbing country, so far as I have become acquainted with it already, it is possible more easily to discard the inessential and to attempt the infinite. You will be burnt up most likely, you will have the flesh torn from your bones, you will be tortured in many horrible and primitive ways, but you will realize that genius of which you sometimes suspect you are possessed. (White 1994, 35)

These "horrible and primitive tortures" evoke the frightful "horror" that Marlow discovers at the heart of Congo. Similarly, in *Voss* the heart of the country is a place of darkness, however, the reason compelling the German explorer to traverse this utterly Other space is different: his goal is to reach some sort of illumination. During the journey it is not simply the body that will be mortified: abandoning the comforts of civilization will humble human pride and, in a possible interpretation of the novel, deliver the human soul. As Veronica Brady says, it is "no wonder that the Bonners are glad to see the last of such man, for he threatens them, challenging the complacencies by which they live" (Brady 1974, 86). It is here important to stress the fact that the gratifications of the bourgeois world are not exclusively material ones. Voss' expedition challenges an entire moral system. Whether Voss' expedition is an allegorical journey towards God or a psychological one into the depths of the unconscious, the regions he ventures into are strictly prohibited to the Sydney mercantile society. Jeffrey Robinson, in *The Aboriginal Enigma: Heart of Darkness, Voss and Palace of the Peacock*, gives a beautiful insight into the relationship between these novels and the social boundaries that they traverse:

> At the end of *Heart of Darkness* [...] as it becomes evident that chaos or darkness has no specific geographical location; it is a condition rather than a peculiarity of the place Marlowe has visited. Its opposite, order, has no specific geographical location either but is the result of some system of cultural norms which constitute "restraint". [...] "Restraint" is obviously an aspect of the comfortable domestic world of Marlowe's listeners where there is a constable around the corner and of the ordered world of seamen on board their ship. Marlow looks ironically at the smug domestic kind of order. Yet those who, like Kurtz and the steersman, go beyond this cultural restraint risk horror. What, in *Heart of Darkness*, is horror becomes, in both *Voss* and *Palace of the Peacock*, a condition of existential freedom in which there is both danger and creative potential. (Robinson 1985, 150)

In *Voss*, those who gladly embrace the cultural restrains of western society and enjoy its "comfortable domesticity" are the "huddlers." The vast majority of people, just like the Bonners, content themselves with living their lives within the cultural boundaries imposed upon them. Voss, conscious of the risk he is taking, breaches these boundaries and brakes into a space of "free creativity" (Robinson 1985, 151).

In *The Prodigal Son*, Patrick White explicitly suggests that the cultural desert he has found in Australia has set him free from what he "considered desirable and necessary" (White 1990, 24) and enabled him to see that "even the boredom and frustration presented avenues for endless exploration" (White 1990, 24). In the end, Voss, just like his author, is set free by his travel through the desert. As Laura Trevelyan says: "When man is truly humbled, when he has learnt that he is not God, then he is nearest to becoming so. In the end, he may ascend" (White 1994, 387). For Voss liberation is the gradual despoliation of his egocentric will. This transformation can be best accounted for by reconsidering Voss' role as an explorer in the light of Simon Ryan's study *The Cartographic Eye*:

> The attitude of the explorers in the journals towards the outside is Cartesian. Space, fixed and Newtonian, may be mathematically proscribed and described by the central observer. [...] Michel de Certeau describing the Cartesian system's positioning of the observer, describes exactly the explorer's point of view: 'His elevation transforms him into a voyeur. It puts him at a distance. [...] It allows one to read the [world], to be a solar eye, looking down like a god.' (Ryan 1996, 6)

Voss' megalomania perfectly fits this description. As many characters claim, the German starts by thinking of himself as a God and presumes to be able to conquer the country solely by the power of his will. It is this attitude that prevents him from entering into contact with the country he is supposed to be exploring. Effectively, as he is actually traversing a "country of the mind," he continuously fails to meet his duties concerning the material organization and leading of the mission. It is thus that during the trip the company slowly loses the cattle, the sheep, the provisions, the compass and, finally, expedition members, either in the form of casualties or mutineers. Judd, whose will has already been subdued by the cat-o'-nine, proves significantly more apt at leading the way through the actual desert – and in fact he takes command of the mutineer's party – yet, Voss' destination is not spatial but rather a cultural one. At the end of the journey, when Voss, as Laura says, "is truly humbled," he finally accepts his humanity and the coming sacrifice. This truly horrific part of the novel, where Frank Le Mesurier cuts his own throat, Harry Robarts' body is desecrated and the horses and mules are slain during a corroboree, ends in Voss' ritual killing. Only at this stage the explorer possibly descends from his visionary heights and finally confronts reality. By dying in the desert, as Judd testifies, Voss is capable of "leaving his mark" and to permanently "remain in the country." Even though the country overcame the explorer, and not vice versa, the outcome is positive. This is the only way in which the explorer could truly become part of land. The significance of the fact that the blacks still talk about him is that he has not only penetrated the corporeal space fenced off by Western culture, he has also breached the cultural barrier created by Otherness and entered the cultural space existing on the other side. In the end he becomes a ghost of the land. Similarly, Patrick White, in the years that passed between the publication of *The Aunt's Story* (1948) and *The Tree of Men* (1955), has been won over by the subtle charm of his homeland and been made capable of penetrating its cultural desert – made of tedious bourgeois shallowness and working-class carelessness – with his writing.

It is however important to notice that Voss' figure is ultimately reappropriated by the huddler society that financed his expedition in the desert. Firstly through the expeditions of Colonel Hebden, which only find a button under a tree (*Voss* 406), and second, through the casting of Voss' figure in bronze, the Sydney Bourgeoisie rescues its prize. Voss did not return with a map of Australia but his "courageous" and "disastrous" journey is readily used to reinstate the socio-topographic arrangement of western society. The interior is a dangerously obscene space which threatens to consume the men who venture into it. God or

Devil, Voss becomes another landmark in the construction of the Australian space.

3.2.2 Remembering Babylon

The process revealed in *Voss* (1957) is one of discursive annexation principally through cartographic means. As demonstrated, the explorer is used as pawn intended to map and, most importantly, to signify – in western cultural terms – a space that would otherwise feel persistently blank. David Malouf's novel *Remembering Babylon* (1993) explores the construction of the Australian cultural space from an entirely different perspective. In his narrative it is not the explorer that confronts the otherness of the land but the humble settler who, with the work of his plough, is involved in a struggle that, without his knowing, goes much beyond the need of supplying for his family. Set in a small isolated community of coastal Queensland, Malouf's novel explores the feebleness of the moral barriers between nurture and nature as experienced by 15 families living at the margin of civilization. The farmers, caught in an overwhelming national effort that uses them as simple pawns, are scattered upon the Australian land with the implied objective of opening the country. If on one side the explorer, with his cartographic seizure of the land disclosed new spaces to the people, it was then up to the farmer to transform the "newly discovered" land into inhabitable and civilized spaces. Perceived by the individual as a remarkable opportunity to make a living, the taking of a lease of crown land placed the settler in the frontline of an imperial battle: that of the definitive socio-topographic appropriation and reconfiguration of the land. The author of the novel sets out to rescue from oblivion the human aspect of this experience and, therefore, to recover the many voices that did not surface into history yet were at the centre of the actual process of boundary production set by the Discourse.

David Malouf, in an interview with Nikos Papastergiadis, discloses what lies at the heart of the enormous and troubling feat faced by innumerable people that were involved in this process:

> When those early European settlers came to confront the Australian landscape, it wasn't the hostility of extreme drought and rain that was most frightening to them, rather it was the sense that the landscape reflected nothing back to their own humanity. They would look at it and it would remain something quite separate. It had not been shaped by them and so they could not see their humanity in it. That in itself is a very frightening thing, to be faced with an entirely unmade landscape when the very notion we have of landscape is of something made. [...] Whereas, if you live in a little village in England or in Ireland or in Scotland, where you know the name of every field, where every part of the landscape has events and a story related to it, where you know every steeple on the horizon, where the churchyard has all of your forebears in it going back a thousand years, then you can comfortably tell yourself that you absolutely belong in that landscape and there is no metaphysical problem. (Papastergiadis 1994, 84 - 85)

The explorer willingly ventures into this unmarked space and accordingly celebrates himself as the courageous individual who, almost biblically, first names the things and places he encounters. However, as Malouf points out, the bulk of the process of re-signification of this space is left to the settlers who, even if un-glorified ordinary people, are confronted by the immensely troubling metaphysical problem of relating themselves to the utter Otherness of the land. To the advantage of the Discourse, these people, who were utterly unprepared to face such a situation, reacted in the most obvious way. They started to reshape the land into a more familiar form. They cleared the land, ploughed the soil, planted their crops and, as a result, created a homely environment that reproduced the distinction between civilization and wilderness signified by the boundary posts at the edge of the fields:

> To the North, beginning with the last fenced paddock, lay swamp country, bird-haunted marshes; then, where the great spine of the Dividing Range rose in ridges and shoals of mist, rainforest broken by sluggish streams. The land to the South was also unknown. Settlements here proceeded in frog leaps from one coastal place to the next.

> Between lay tracts of country no white man had ever entered. It was disturbing, that: to have unknown country behind you as well as in front.
> [...] Out here the very ground was strange. It had never been ploughed. [...] And all around, before and behind, worse than weather and the deepest night, natives, tribes of wondering myalls who, in their traipsing this way and that all over the map, were forever encroaching on boundaries that could be insisted on by daylight – a good shotgun saw to that – but in the dark hours, when you no longer stood there as a living marker with all the glow of the white man's authority about you, reverted to being a creek-bed or ridge of granite like any other, and gave no indication that six hundred miles away, in the Lands Office in Brisbane, this bit of country had a name set against it on a numbered document, and a line the was empowered with all the authority of the Law. (Malouf 1993, 8-9)

This passage concisely recapitulates not merely the disquieting and frightful environment confronted by the settlers, but also their position in relation to the imperial project of conquest of the continent. They really were "living markers" of the expanding boundaries of the so-called civilized areas: last of a long chain of power, they were entrusted the menial work necessary to seize the space lying beyond the grasp of the central socio-topographic planning. While the explorer furnished the central authority with the imaginative means to rationalize space (maps), it was up to the settlers to validate the arbitrary subdivisions operated with concrete "improvements" to the land. From the outset, Malouf's narration, with its explicit reference to the native tribes "traipsing this way and that all over the map," clearly remarks on the ambiguous nature of these boundaries. The nightly permeability of the frontier embodies the haziness of the moral values on which the small settlement is based. The lack of a clear-cut socio-topographic subdivision between civilization and savagery questions not only their right to be there, but also the stability of the accepted distinction between good and evil. It is the troubling experience of being confronted with this indefinite space that transforms the protagonists of this novel, even in their wrongdoings, into heroic figures:

> These people really are pioneers, not just of another country, but pioneers of the human state. These people are not adventurers; they have gone there because they were poor and uneducated – because they had no power at home. But they are the people who have to go out and confront that metaphysical question. I am interested in their struggle.
> (Papastergiadis 1994, 87)

This celebration is however a honest depiction of a painful process endured by people that did their best with very limited means. The pioneers are not heroes in the epic sense of the term and they are not the embodiment of all noble qualities; on the contrary, they are full-rounded characters easily lost in the intricacies of the moral maze in which they are abandoned. As a consequence, fear, rage, violence and brutality are honestly portrayed as an integrating part of their lives.

The moral order embraced by the settlers is definitively unbalanced by Gemmy Fairley's arrival in the community. By stepping out of the outback and into the settled area, Gemmy disrupts the accepted conception of the equilibrium between civilized and uncivilized people and areas. Coming out of the "the world over there, [...] abode of everything savage and fearsome, [...] and all that belonged to Absolute Dark" (Malouf 1993, 3), the settlers "see him as a reflection of what they fear" (Papastergiadis 1994, 88). The Conradian resonance of the "Absolute Dark" – capitalised in the original text – emphasises the author's intention to probe the Manichean distinction between good and evil imposed upon the land and the psyche of the settlers.

Malouf, in his interview with Nikos Papastergiadis, openly discloses his intentions in constructing the narrative of this novel:

> If you have a little society as this is, it's a little settlement of 15 families – all in the same place, all facing the same dangers, trying to make the land produce food – then they are drawn together into something that looks like a community. But all communities are extremely fragile. I wanted to introduce in such a community a kind of catalyst.
> (Papastergiadis 1994, 89)

As demonstrated by this affirmation and as previously noted by Sathyabhama Daly in "David Malouf's *Remembering Babylon* and the Wild Man of the European Cultural Consciousness" (Daly 2000, 13), the sense of community developed by the settlers is obtained via a process that Hayden White calls self-definition by negation. The essence of the idea is that

> in times of socio-cultural stress, when the need for positive self-definition asserts itself but no compelling criterion of self-identification appears, it is always possible to say something like: "I may not know the precise content of my own felt humanity, but I am most certainly not like that," and simply point to something in the landscape that is manifestly different from oneself. (White 1972, 13)

In *Remembering Babylon*, the settlers are brought together by their common fear of the Other and "are only able to define themselves by distancing themselves from the aborigines and by projecting onto them all that is antithetical to their beliefs about civilization" (Daly 2000, 13). Malouf, who has been accused of "turning his text into a retreat from the real political and material violences of colonialism" (McCredden 1999), by introducing Gemmy actually confronts the very heart of the political foundation of colonialism. Gemmi undermines the distinction between "us" and the "Other" from its foundation. As the collective voice of the village asks: "Could you lose it? Not just language, but *it. It*" (Malouf 1993, 40).

The moment in which Gemmy steps out of the "Absolute Dark" and, after having crossed the imaginative border delimiting the western civilized space, falls at Lachlan and his cousin's feet, poignantly reveals the significance of this trespassing:

> A black! That was the boy's first thought. We're being raided by blacks. [...] But it wasn't a raid, there was just one of them; and the thing [...] was not even, maybe, human. [...] The creature, almost upon them now and with Flash at its heels, came to a halt, gave a kind of squawk, and leaping up unto the top rail of the fence, hung there, its

arms outflung as if preparing for flight. Then the ragged mouth gapped.

'Do not shoot,' it shouted. 'I am B-b-british object!'

It was a white man, though there was no way you could have known from his look. He had the mangy, half-starved look of a black, and when, with a cry, he lost his grip on the rail and came tumbling at their feet, the smell of one too, like a dead swamp water; and must have been as astonished as they were by the words that had jumped out of his mouth because he could find no more of them. (Malouf 1993, 3)

The crossing is frozen in time: Gemmy balances on the fence that separates the two worlds he has known, the kids have enough time to consider the "object" they are faced with and sense everything it brings with him (the look, the odour, the feel of a black), there is a moment of recognition, a few words are spoken and, finally, the ragged man collapses to the ground. Not really black but certainly not white, Gemmy, by returning to the "civilised world," is lowered to a sub-human rank. As his lexical confusion indicates he is not a British subject any more, he has become an "object" of the British colonial Discourse. He is the materialization of the most haunting western fear – a white man gone native.

Gemmy is not gladly welcomed in the little farmer community. His presence is disturbing because it disrupts the supposed moral order topographically marked by the fence and the implied distinction between "us" and the "Others." This definitively invalidates the firmness of such division. Gemmy's return from the void beyond the fence, a space which had been entrusted the settler's worst fears and most repressed lures, reintroduces – or better, it causes to surface – the socio-topographically secluded unconscious of the settlers. What had seemed to be a serene and pleasant village is suddenly clutched by acrimony and resentment that unforeseeably wells from the very heart of the community. This contamination becomes evident on one particular occasion: after a group of natives visits Gemmy by a shed he is repairing, the majority of the settlers are taken by a frenzy and one, in a most explicit act, expresses his outrage by vandalizing Gemmy's shed:

> The new planks in its wall, the new nails heads showing plainly in the weathered grey of the rest. And there, smeared across them, was a stain, a gathering of greenflies that heaped and bubbled, and the air that came to his nostrils rich with its stink. Someone had plastered the place with shit.
> [...] Some man had done this. Someone he knew. Someone whose eyes he had looked into, and recently; maybe at the very moment he was planning the thing. [...] He saw the hand with its load of filth moving across the wall and understood now the what it was setting there was a word. (Malouf 1993, 115-116)

The vandal could not have gone lower. Symbolically, the use of faeces is offensive because it is invested with all the emotive charge connected to ob-scenity and therefore all that lies beyond the last fence. This demonstrates that, as argued by Stallybrass and White in their study of Victorian society and its obsession with the "low," i.e. the slums, the sewerage, the lower parts of the body and their implication with defecation (Stallybrass and White 1986, 125-148), the subconscious cannot be successfully ostracized. Obscenity might be effectively concealed and seemingly placed off scene, however, being born in the bosom of civilization and being a complementary part of it, it cannot be definitively expelled. The fictitious boundaries between probity and incivility clearly account for the permeability of these two areas and for the relative freedom of the interstitial and more isolated areas. Thus, the outback, exactly because it is an obscene setting, becomes the setting not merely of an alleged Aboriginal immorality (the one needed to justify colonization) but also a site where white men could disobey their own rules.

As Jock McIvor's indignation suggests (the McIvor family "adopted" Gemmy), the most disturbing thing is that what is considered to be so below humanity is actually in the midst of the community. Well hidden but ever present. From that moment, Jock will feel haunted by this abomination. The awareness of living in the presence of a creeping obscenity will take away his confidence in society's moral order and its boundary setting. Concomitantly, the rest of the community starts questioning Jock's standing:

> McIvor's hesitation between the 'one side' and the 'other' shows that he, like Fairley before him, is the victim of binary judgements as soon as he finds himself in the position of the *object* of discourse. The irony, from McIvor's perspective, of his relationship with Fairley, is that it demonstrates to him, first, that colonial identity is *produced*, not *threatened*, by the engagement with cultural difference, and, secondly, that his rejection by his neighbours suggests that 'otherness' is a mobile concept capable of reconfiguration according to immediate local and pragmatic needs. (Spinks 1995, 171)

Lee Spink's analysis explains how *Remembering Babylon* can be regarded a highly confrontational text. Although the crudeness of the colonial enterprise is confined to the margins of the text – at the end of the novel, Lachlan, searching for a reconciliation with his past, discovers that Gemmy has been killed in the "dispersal" of a native tribe – the novel focuses its attention on the power of the discursive construction of the colonial space. Carolyn Bliss, paying attention to this characteristic of the novel, focuses her attention on the myths driving the plot of this novel:

> The novel's very title already invokes one failed myth, for like all "new" civilizations, white Australia might have been Jerusalem, but instead became a Babylon, a trajectory which should be but usually is not remembered by its inhabitants.
>   It is certainly forgotten by the group of white settlers [who] see themselves as bearers of light to another dark continent, builders of barricades between civilization and the land on which they have imposed it [...] (Bliss 2000, 730)

According to Bliss, Malouf uses mythologies – as intended by Roland Barthes[7] (cf. Barthes 1957) – not in order to validate old ones or to create new ones, but to unmask their devious way of working and to create a consciousness that would reveal the dangers of subscribing to the realities evoked by myth. The danger of myth-making, with its capacity of creating the illusion that the signifier gives a foundation to the signified, is that, as in the case of the settlers, it blinds people and subdues them in obedience to the discursive construction of reality. Hence, the myth of a new promised land drove herds of people who failed to see that "the continent had already been completely humanized by the people who lived there" (Malouf 2000, 85). *Remembering Babylon* stands as a silent but symbolic critique to this process but, even more daringly and with extreme caution, the author attempts to not simply unmask the past wrongdoings, but also to cause them to resurface from the unconscious of the Australian people and heal the wounds that they left:

> A good many of my novels deal with verifiable moments in Australian history, not with known events but with that underside of events which is where most of us experience them, and in many cases go on experiencing them as pain or loss. I would want to call this an interior history, and what interests me is that in the ordinary way of things, so much of this, in Australia, goes unexpressed: unwritten about but also unspoken. [...]
> But until such things are spoken about, and, most of all, have been taken inside and lived through in the imagination, re-experienced as meaning rather than muddle, individual lives, and the larger life of the community, cannot recover and be healed. [...] It's a matter, as always, of the writer's dealing with what touches him personally – these things cannot be taken up coldly or out of duty – but by doing

---

[7] For Roland Barthes (1957) mythologies are part of a system of signification that evades the simple relationship between referent, signifier and signified. A myth rises to a metonymic level of signification where the indeterminacy of the semiotic triangle crystallizes in the unity of a symbol and where this artificial referent is given a new and broader meaning; one surging to whole-encompassing cultural importance.

so, he also provides a kind of healing for the world he comes out of, whose sorrows and losses he shares with the rest. (Malouf 2000, 704)

This passage, originally intended for the literature dealing with World War I trauma, is evidently more vastly applicable. Speaking about the myths of the past allows one to rediscover the functional myths that in time the Discourse substituted with new ones, while never explicitly refuting the old ones. Accordingly, the Jerusalem/Babylon myths – describing Australia as a foreign land of either blissful arrival or exile – lay dormant under the new Australian myths which Patrick White poignantly described in *The Prodigal Son* (cf. Section 3.2.1). In the land of opportunities, youth culture became the new formulation of the atavic myth on which Australia had been founded. Malouf's use of myth intentionally draws attention to myth-making and the role it had in the construction of the Australian nation. The brutality of the frontier period is very effectively portrayed by the tension generated by Gemmy's arrival. The psychological and physical violence that Gemmy endures (culminating in his near drowning at the hands of a group of exasperated settlers) symbolically evokes the much larger extent of violence used to uphold the idea of Australia being a promised land. The unspoken truth about the dispossession of the Aborigines and the violence used against them silently becomes an inherent theme in the novel. Lyn McCredden, focusing on this idea, reveals that this is a two-sided story: "I would argue that the necessarily imperfect imprinting of the Aboriginal world [...] onto the body of Gemmy speaks eloquently and provocatively to white audiences of the violent dispossession perpetrated upon Aboriginal cultures, as well as by and upon the white, working class colonisers" (McCredden 1999, 11).

Thus, the novel speaks not simply of the violence used against the Australian natives, it also deals with the implications that this violence had on its perpetrators. *Remembering Babylon*, as the title suggests, explicitly aims to rediscover the trauma caused by the colonial experience. McCredden reminds us that the "white colonial perpetrators [...] were also dispossessed labouring emigrants with their own set of narratives about victimization" (McCredden 1999, 11), and that moving to Australia was their last chance to escape their own dispossessed status. However, in order to create their own "promised land," they had to endure the bewildering metaphysical experience of dislocation, to re-imagine the land according to their own expectations and – by also becoming the perpetrator of unspeakable crimes – to materially reshape it. Babylon is the realm that they entered in the new colony and Malouf, with his narrative, re-evokes the trauma that has been concealed by the later accomplished myth of the Promised Land. To remember Babylon does not mean to merely acknowledge the existence of a gruesome colonial past and to blatantly say "sorry" to the Aborigines; rather, it means to re-explore that past and to expose the wounds left in the nation's unconscious. As the author wishes, the disclosure of this failed myth will hopefully initiate a process of healing, culminating in the acceptance of the ob-scene past which keeps haunting Australia's conscience. To re-admit this past into the present and onto the scene would also definitely undermine the deceptive myths of Promised/Exile Land.

According to Caroline Bliss, the novel introduces a third myth. She argues that Gemmy might embody "the future Australian, truly at home in and honouring a land whose ancient signs he can recognize, honouring also its first peoples and their ability to read those signs" (Bliss 2000, 703). This myth, easily dismissible as a simple form of wishful thinking, acquires a more significant importance when weighed against the actual events of the novel. Gemmy's hybridity is strongly opposed by both the settlers, for whom he "brings to the fore [...] the fear of the descent into the barbaric and godless state of the wilderness" (Daly 2000), and by the colonial government in Brisbane. Mr Frazer, the pastor of the community, had seen in Gemmy "a forerunner [...] no longer a white man, or a European, [...] but a true child of the place" (Malouf 1993, 132) and had envisioned a sort of sustainable development in which he proposed to make use of the entirely ignored native resources. Quite obviously the Governor of Queensland regards this idea an amusing curiosity and dismisses it without a second thought. The blinding power of the Discourse reduces the available options to the ones proposed by the founding myth of the Promised Land: the world split between us and Others, nature and civilization. Malouf's novel offers no easy way out to this state of affairs; on the contrary, it is clear that the harsh refusal of Gemmy's hybridity is an unambiguous warning to the readers. It is not through another myth (that of hybridity) that Australia can maturely look at its past and resolutely work for a better future. Carolyn Bliss explains: "Were Gemmy's myth to be enacted in the novel's plot, [. . .] then this myth too would [. . .] lull readers into belief that the gaping wound of black-and-white division in postcolonial Australia not only could be healed, but in some sense had been" (Bliss 2000, 730).

Gemmy does not fit this position. Having resisted all sorts of appropriations, he returns to his adoptive Aboriginal tribe. Moreover, before running away, he symbolically tries to recover his stolen identity. He breaks into the school and steals from the teacher what he thinks are the pages containing his story. Gemmy intuitively understands the importance of that document. His identity and his position in society were forged by the laborious work of interpretation led by the Pastor and the teacher. The story surfacing from his broken English had not simply been altered by inaccurate interpretation but, as in the case of Voss' enterprise, it had also been appropriated by the Discourse. Through that process his alterity had been framed and established.

For similar reasons Janet McIvor's outstanding achievement is also locked in "sterility". When, as a young girl, thousands of bees swarm on her attracted by her menstrual blood, she learns to surrender to nature and become one with it. However, in later in her life, she disconnects herself from society and becomes a nun. The meaning of this choice is that she does not yet represent the wished-for "new Australian". Her accomplishment, being based on an ecstatic experience, is an entirely personal one and cannot be shared. The closure of the novel is gloomy yet realistic. The moral borders drawn upon the land by the Dominant Discourse are definitively reinstated. All over again,

3 The Outback   115

with the coming of World War I, Australia rehearses the process of Othering but this time at the expenses of the Australians of German origin, who, once again, become mythical objects of the Discourse:

> A fortitude Valley pastry cook, Walter Goetz by name, a naturalized German, had had his windows broken the week after Paschendaele by a gang of patriotic football fans. When he complained he was himself arrested, charged with disturbing the peace, and found guilty. He and his Australian wife and four children were to be deported and their assets confiscated. (Malouf 1993, 188-189)

The swift and most unreasonable repudiation of this man – a fellow Australian one day and a hideous German the next – is justified only by the strategic shift in the positioning of the line dividing and identifying the "us" and the "Other." Janet's closing prayer definitively reflects and summarises this state of affairs: by remembering Gemmy "as she saw him, [...] up there on the stripped and shiny rail, never to fall, [...] overbalancing now, drawn by the power, all unconscious to them, of their gaze," (Malouf 1993, 199) she acknowledges the contemporary relevance of that event. She thus prays that none of this will be forgotten: "Let none be left in the dark or out of mind, on this night, now, in this corner of the world or any other, at this hour, in the middle of this war [...]" (Malouf 1993, 200). What must be remembered is the power of the gaze that caused Gemmy to fall on one side of the fence. In the eyes of a nun who has been recently accused of treason because of her correspondence with a German apiculture, the combined flimsiness, arbitrariness and violence of cultural and moral border setting becomes ever more apparent. It is this consciousness that she prays will not be forgotten and it is this knowledge that Malouf offers to his readers. Not an easy way out of Australia's dilemmas, just a reminder of their origin.

3.2.3 Coonardoo

Voss (1957) and *Remembering Babylon* (1993) respectively presented two different phases in the socio-topographic construction of Australia: the cartographic opening and the newcomers' settling of the country. At that time obscenity was purposefully created but always displaced in an ultimately obscene setting, one in which the explorer could venture or out of which the native could come out. The next stage, here presented through *Coonardoo* (1929), is one in which the land has now been unequivocally settled, the natives have been integrated – although in a marginal position – in the society of the time, but the outback remains a treacherous and obscene setting. Katherine Susannah Prichard's *Coonardoo*, in spite of its inestimable value as a pioneering literary work attempting to document the life of the underprivileged classes, falls in the scope of this research by unconsciously responding to the interpellation of the Discourse and proposing an illuminating yet distorted image of life in rural Australia. Based on the author's personal experience of outback life – in 1926 she was guest at Turee Creek, a cattle station in the North of Western Australia – the novel sets out to probe the moral boundaries of western civilization and to expose realities unknown to city dwellers. However, despite Prichard's commitment to truthful sociological representation and even considering the scandal and outrage provoked by the 1928 serialization of the novel in *The Bulletin*, the plot still responds to and reinstates the prejudices of the time (cf. Lever 2000, 59). For this reason, in spite of the different perspectives of the two texts, *Remembering Babylon* can be used to introduce an analysis of *Coonardoo*. As Janet McIvor's prayer suggests, Australia's socio-topographic structure is still intimately related to the pioneering stage of settlement. As a consequence, spaces and cultures are polarized in terms of moral opposites. As JanMohamed argues, this is a "power- and interest-related" model common to all colonial societies that, by stating "the putative superiority of the European Culture and the supposed inferiority of the native, provides the central feature of the colonialist cognitive framework and colonialist literary representation"(JanMohamed 1985, 63). Malouf's novel consciously investigates the effect of this discourse on its individual recipients. He explores the moral struggle endured by those who conform to the stark yet interchangeable opposition between: "white and black, good and evil, superiority and inferiority, civilization and savagery, intelligence and emotion, rationality and sensuality, self and Other, subject and object" (JanMohamed 1985, 63). Thus, while the colonized slowly succumbs and internalizes these categorizations (with all the devastating consequences described by Frantz Fanon in *Black Skin, White Masks*), the colonizer undergoes an inversely reciprocal transformation that will ultimately distort his/her perception of reality. Accordingly, in spite of Prichard's effort in seeing through the maze of prejudices blindfolding the society of the 1920's, her text is not immune from the dichotomial stereotypization of whites and Aborigines. As JanMohamed conveniently explains, "[t]he power relations underlying this model set in motion such strong currents that even a writer who may indeed be highly critical of imperial exploitation is drawn into its vortex" (JanMohamed 1985, 63). By considering this notion it is possible to analyse *Coonardoo* from a more neutral perspective, one that, rather than trying to prove or disprove the complicity of the author with the Discourse, attempts to reveal the influence exerted by the Discourse on the text under discussion. After all, as Sandra Burchill states in the title of a paper on Prichard, "She Did What She Could" (Burchill 1993).

Leigh Dale, in her essay "Coonardoo and Truth," provides a concise yet clear view of the cultural standing of the novel:

> Although radical for its time – as evidenced by readers' hostile responses to the *Bulletin* serialization and the difficulty which Prichard experienced in finding an Australian Publisher for her prize winning novel – *Coonardoo* reiterates conservative stereotypes of Aboriginal people as 'dark, passionate and childlike', people who are fundamentally passive in their response to the invasion of their country, and

who are now happy to work on 'good' stations such as Wytaliba for food, clothing, and the occasional gift. (Dale 1994, 134)

Coonardoo, by addressing themes like women's sexuality, miscegenation and love between a white man and a black woman, unquestionably transgressed the accepted idea of a moral novel. Nowadays, the novel's probing of certain boundaries (miscegenation and male-female power relations) and the simultaneous reinstatement of others (racial connotation of the Aborigines), provides a perfect tool for the assessment of the socio-topographic construction of the society of the 1920's. Provocatively, the author gave an Aboriginal woman, Coonardoo, the central role in the novel. If in 1928 this alone would have been a confrontational act – empowering a female Aborigine to an active role in a novel – nowadays an attentive reader would see things quite differently. The supposed protagonist is rapidly transformed into a disempowered "object" dominated by white male characters who speak and make decisions for her. Considering this, the fact that the novel actually begins and ends with Coonardoo's singing in Wytaliba should also become suspect. On both occasions she sings for Hugh, initially her playmate and later her boss, friend, one-time-lover and husband. In spite of the title, the real protagonist of the novel is Hugh Watt, the white boss of an outback station where Coonardoo is all but an instrument in the construction of his patriarchal role. The cultural trope of the native women embodying nature/land is here completely and doubly reinstated. Coonardoo is there to be possessed and, as Coonardoo herself considers, she is the well in the shadow: "Was she not the well in the shadow? Had she not some sort of affinity with that ancestral female spirit which was responsible for fertility, generation, the growth of everything? (Prichard 1956, 225).

Clearly she represents the key to the fertility of the land and, most prominently, the pretext of both the novel and the colonial enterprise itself. Thus, the significance of her voice containing the novel is made explicit: filled – almost impregnated – with the tropes of the Dominant

Discourse, Coonardoo (both as a text and as a character) is reduced to being a "chosen vessel" of the colonial enterprise.

The first remark that can be made of Prichard's novel is the complete absence of any reference to the frontier period and to the way Aborigines came to live on the stations. As Leigh Dale's comment suggests (Dale 1994, 134) it is as though the Aborigines were passive to the taking over of their land and their virtual enslavement. Anne Brewester, in an article on Doris Pilkington's *Following the Rabbit Proof Fence*, also notes that *Coonardoo* does not mention "the elaborate and pervasive governmental management of "the Aboriginal problem which came to a head in the 1930's with the formulation of the notorious assimilationist policies" (Brewster 2002, 155). In this sense Ion Idriess' account of his visit to the Kimberley on a Police Patrol during the 1930's is more accurate. Even though in a very conservative way, *Over the Range: Sunshine and Shadow in the Kimberley* (1937) depicts the coercive methods used to subdue the natives of the North West. The text accounts for everything: indiscriminate use of rifles, violent dispersals, Aboriginal people walking for hundreds of miles chained by the neck to be tried for cattle killing and, of course, station life. Mary Anne Jebb, in her extensive study of the settlement of the Kimberley, notes that Ion Idriess, although "he avoided writing anything which suggested immorality, exploitation or avoidable conflict between settlers and Indigenous people," wrote books that "are useful social documents for developing a picture of a fringe community" (Jebb 2002, 19). Adam Shoemaker, in *Black Words, White Pages*, also insists on the relevance of this author who, on the basis of the huge sales of his novels, largely outnumbering those of Herbert's and Prichard's, had an outstanding influence on the perception of Aboriginal people (Shoemaker 1988, 54). Mary Anne Jebb's study subverts the sweetened version of truth given by Idriess. The cattle killing trials were farces used to disperse tribes, bind the native women to the stations and disrupt the native independent culture (Jebb 2002, 41). Prichard, by not spending a single word on this subject, passively accepts and endorses a version of truth similar to that established in *Over the Range*: that the Whiteman was involved in a civilizing mission of the continent and its people.

Mrs Bessie Watt and her son Hugh are thus depicted as benefactors of the Australian natives and their gentle rule over Wytaliba is never questioned throughout the novel. The only doubts cast upon the legitimacy of the settlers' right to possess the land are based on moral concepts strictly related to the socio-topographic configuration of the land. Sam Geary's right to own the land is undermined by his immoral behaviour. By living in concubinage with several Aboriginal women, he renounces his role of praiseworthy redeemer of a childish race, while also confirming the idea of the outback as an obscene space capable of corrupting the white men's integrity. Prichard, in spite of her communist ideals and her commitment to the labourers' cause, chooses to take sides with the Watts who, in their endeavour to control the land, are more amicable and respectful to the Aborigines. Geary, from the outset of the novel, tries to take over Wytaliba. His interest lies not exclusively in the property, but also in the natives who live there and that would become his with the passing over of the property. In particular, Geary is trying to get hold of Coonardoo. Until the very end, Hugh's strenuous efforts prevent this from occurring. This is of course more than a simple financial struggle. Hugh, driven by a profound distaste induced by his schooling, fights a moral battle against his contender in affair: "'No stud gins for mine – no matter what happens' he swore to himself, disturbed and irritated" (Prichard 1956, 51). As Sue Thomas remarks in her essay on the topic, "[t]he dark evil force Hugh perceives in the northwest is white male lust for black women, a lust epitomized in Sam Geary" (Thomas 1987, 240).

Noteworthy is the fact that the novel begins precisely at the moment when Hugh leaves the station to go to boarding school. Education and morality inherently belong to the city centre while, as Sue Thomas suggests, the outback is the location of dark evil forces. For this reason Mrs Bessie sends her son to Perth and for this same reason, on the day of his return, Coonardoo knows that he will come back a changed man. More specifically, he will return with a fiancée. The most important lesson imparted by the central moral authority is that, because of his moral superiority, he cannot love a black woman. The problem posed by this dictum is best exposed by Mrs Bessie's advice to her son regarding the choice of a wife: "I'd rather you took a gin than a white woman like that for the keeps. [...] It's a man's country ... and you are a man, Hugie, not a boy any longer [...]. I don't want you to go mucking around with gins. But I'd rather a gin than a Jessica" (Prichard 1956, 64).

The truth is that Hugh is left with little choice: he cannot marry a lady because she would not be suited for the "job" and he cannot take a gin because it would dishonour him. His mother's second piece of advice is that "sex hunger's like any other. Satisfy it and you don't think about it" (Prichard 1956, 65). It is thus that, as a sort of insurance policy, he marries Mollie, a very down-to-earth maid who is initially more than happy to join him on the farm. However, after giving birth to five girls, she bails out and moves to the city. Her comment as well will be: "Oh, it's a man's country, [...] A woman can go mad and clear out for all anybody cares" (Prichard 1956, 134). This is exactly where Prichard reiterates one of the major cultural tropes regarding the bush. It is man's country, it is inimical to women and as Clare Corbould notes, it is only masculine women that survive there:

> In order to make sense of women whose behaviour did not concur with the dominant prescriptions of womanhood – that women are weaker and less resilient then men – Prichard masculinised them.
>
> Prichard's characterization reinscribes the dominant gendered stereotypes of the 1920's, by continuing to equate masculinity with endurance and ability, and femininity with weakness. (Corbould 1999, 417, 419)

Accordingly, the only women that "survive" the bush are equated to men. Both Mrs Bessie and Phillis, Hugh's first-born daughter, are excellent horsewomen and perfectly capable of doing the job of any man. Phillis, when joining her father on the station, emblematically declares that she "hates female's life," that she is "as strong as a bullock" and that she had "ought to be his eldest son" (Prichard 1956, 162). However, this characterization does not to apply to Coonardoo. In spite of the masculine qualities that Hugh admires in her, she remains feminine and, most importantly, extremely attractive to Hugh.

It is, in fact, in Coonardoo that Prichard embodies all the major characteristics of the outback: it is both a man's country and an alluring feminine environment. Sam Geary, who is depicted as an exploitative white pioneer, is more frank about his moral behaviour and openly challenges Hugh:

> "You're one of those god-damned young heroes. No 'black velvet' for you, I suppose?"
> "I'm goin' to marry white and stick white," Hugh said, obstinate lines settling on either side of this mouth.
> Geary laughed.
> "Oh, you are, are you?" he Jeered. "[...] Well, I'll bet you a new saddle you take a gin before a twelvemonth's out – if ever you're in this country on your own." (Prichard 1956, 51)

The "obstinate lines" of Hugh's frown testify to his indomitable stubbornness whilst Geary's bet underscores the power of the land: twelve months on one's own are enough to beat the best intentions. Once again, Prichard, by proving Sam Geary right, seems to back all the prejudices against the land. Before he marries Mollie and soon after his mother's death, Hugh succumbs to his desire and has sex with Coonardoo. However, even though the "dark evil forces" of the bush had constantly besieged Hugh in Wytaliba, his sexual encounter with Coonardoo is only possible when he is lost in the ultimate isolation of the outback. There the force of the land is so strong that his will finally succumbs. However, the author, in order to save the integrity of her hero, artfully creates a perfect excuse for this contravention. The pain caused by the loss of his mother causes the protagonist to lower his guard and, more importantly, he finally gives in only when he is *lost* in the depth of the bush in the sole company of Coonardoo:

"We'll rest here a bit," Hugh said. "Then you can show me the way back to camp again, Coonardoo."

She nodded, smiled and stretched to sleep on the far side of the fire. Hugh sat watching her. Years fell away between them. She was Coonardoo, the old playmate [...]. This was a childish adventure they were on. His gratitude as he thought of how she had followed and watched over him during the last weeks. It yielded to a yearning and tenderness. Deep inexplicable currents of his being flowed towards her.

"Coonardoo! Coonardoo!" he murmured. Awakened, she came to kneel beside him, her eyes the fathomless shining of a well in the shadows. Hugh took her in his arms, and gave himself to the spirit which drew him, from a great distance it seemed, to the common source which was his life and Coonardoo's. (Prichard 1956, 71)

The reminiscing about youth indicates the return to a sort of pre-symbolic order and, as further proof, the author specifies that it is "a childish adventure they are on" (Prichard 1956, 71). Freed of the moral constraints imposed by his schooling in Perth, Hugh is capable of indulging in what he had sworn never to do: he "takes a gin." However, the text is also careful in limiting the protagonist's agency to the negligible taking of Coonardoo in his arms, while blaming the rest of the action on the force drawing him to her. From this perspective, in the most explicit Orientalist fashion, Coonardoo's innate sensuality and uninhibited sexuality are to blame for this casual sexual encounter. Clare Corbould, working on this idea from a feminist perspective, clarifies the significance of this symbolism:

> Coonardoo's sexuality is constituted differently from the white women in the text. While she shares their basic need for sex, as 'the well in the shadows'('coonardoo'), she is also the white-man-made source of relief, like water to land. [...] the Black woman is designated as a human mediator between white man on the one hand and nature [...] on the other. In other words, Coonardoo is defined from white phallocentric viewpoint. (Corbould 1999, 421)

The scene of Hugh's and Coonardoo's sexual encounter is the principal exemplification of the mediating role native women play between white man and nature. Through Coonardoo, Hugh abandons himself to a third agent and, in fact, the text specifies that the protagonist gives himself to 'the spirit which drew him from a distance' and that was 'their common source of life'. What is suggested here is that, apart from having sex with a 'gin," the protagonist is here entering in metaphysical contact with the territory. There is no further doubt that, seconding the tradition that construes the new colonies as virgin lands waiting to be "taken" by the colonial authority, Coonardoo is the key that gives access the land. As Terry Goldie argues, "sexual ownership of the indigene seems to fill in the spiritual – and sensual – gap left by the legalistic fact of white ownership" (Goldie 1989, 73). It is for this reason that the heroine is so strongly desired and contended by Sam Geary, and it is also for this reason that as soon as she leaves the station, the land becomes sterile with drought. Here the novel reveals its twofold complexity: on one hand, nature and the native woman are stigmatized as the classic dentate-like forces that consume the white man in the outback, on the other hand, Coonardoo is absolutely necessary to the spiritual survival of the land.

As Anne Brewster explains, because of Hugh's obstinate refusal to form a stable relationship with Coonardoo, the novel becomes an "intensely 'personal,' domestic and everyday [...] drama [...] locat[ed] within a strictly bounded private sphere" (Brewster 2002, 155). The protagonist's psychological dilemma exemplifies a cultural dilemma artfully induced by the Discourse and significantly reproduced by the author. Laura Ann Stoler, in her critical study *Sex and the Education of Desire*, suggests that the colonial enterprise was a sublimation of the colonizer's sexual drive (Stoler 1995, 171). The colonizer, by immersing himself in a highly eroticized region (eroticized by the western Orientalist Discourse), with his virtue, managed both to express his superiority and to satisfy his "urge" Thus, as Ronald Hyam extensively argues in *Empire and Sexuality*, the empire "provided 'sexual opportunities' for European men when those in

Britain where severely reduced" (Stoler 1995, 175). However, at this point the artificially created image of lasciviousness, by becoming real, turns to the advantage of the Discourse. The Englishman who debases himself by "taking" a native woman, becomes the living proof of both the native's corrupting force and the ensuing need for stricter control over this space. By inducing deviance in a purposely stigmatized zone, the Discourse proves itself right and can put in motion a repressive apparatus that reinforces its influence over the colony and reaffirms its current dominant position at home.

Sam Geary, as described by Prichard, is the embodiment of the white men who take advantage of the outback as an off-scene setting in which to indulge in repressed sexual fantasies. Hugh, on the contrary, is the paladin of the reactionary side of the Discourse who, by abstaining from sexual contact, reinstates the moral superiority of that same Discourse that had previously transformed the bush into an obscene scenario. Accordingly, in the foreword of the 1929 published edition of the novel, Prichard specifies that the person that inspired Geary has been prosecuted by the law. She also rejoices the passing of a legislation preventing white men from taking "gins" to hotel rooms. The dynamic is evident: the expansion of the "scene" proceeds with the progressive imaginative incorporation of marginal areas which are initially deemed obscene and are later reclaimed by the Discourse, which sanitizes them through a sweeping authoritarian action. Hugh is caught in the middle of this process and Prichard very daringly exposes the many facets of the dilemma he faces. As previously mentioned, Coonardoo is also the key to accessing the land and, therefore, the protagonist is confronted by the momentary contradiction of the Discourse. Hugh cannot possess the land because he refuses / he is prohibited to possess Coonardoo. It is in fact Sam Geary who takes over the station in the end. However, as suggested by the foreword of the novel and by the general dynamic previously exposed, this is only a functional transition. The villain of the story acquires the land only to be later punished by the law. As a result, the Discourse definitively reclaims the land and purifies it of all obscenity by definitively fencing nature off.

There is, however, an alternative possibility. Various details suggest that the actual pioneer is Sam Geary. This character, by treating his native wives decently, by introducing the first car in the outback and by allowing Sheba (his concubine) to drive it, demonstrates being a real innovator. Nevertheless, from the author's perspective, this still amounts to sheer exploitation as it is simple lust that draws Geary to "black velvet." On the contrary, Hugh, with his gallant heroism, subverts this scheme and, as his daughter suggests, takes his wife "like most men take a gin, and Coonardoo [is] always [...] a sort of fantasy with him" (Prichard 1956, 223). Cath Ellis, in her essay "A Tragic Convergence: A Reading of Catherine Susannah Prichard's *Coonardoo*," clarifies that this "is an acknowledgment that the marriage between Mollie and Hugh is based on sex-hunger rather than sex-love and that the relationship between Hugh and Coonardoo is based on sex-love, without the satisfaction of sex-hunger" (Ellis 1995, 70). This consideration clarifies Mollie's function in the colonial project: as Stoler suggests, "bourgeois women in colony and metropole were cast as the custodians of morality, of their vulnerable men, and of national character. Parenting and motherhood specifically, was a class obligation and a duty of empire" (Stoler 1995, 135). Stoler's feminist take on these circumstances indicates the way Mollie is unremittingly held captive: first, when she performs the transitory function of satisfying Hugh's sex-hunger and, later, when she becomes the remote custodian of his morality. Hence, by returning to the city and maintaining herself "pure," she is not only avoiding to "witness" Hugh's obscene debasement in his sex love relationship, but she is also subtracting herself from the never mentioned but implicit menace of black-male sexual partners. White women are thus banned from the ob-scene space of the outback.

Love is the key to the chimerical alternative suggested by Prichard: not only are Hugh and Coonardoo perfect mates, they are also united by a profound attachment to the land: "the common source which was his life and Coonardoo's" (Prichard 1956, 71). They both love the land and if Hugh, rather than embracing the bourgeois capitalist Discourse imposing him to marry white in order to have a legitimate heir, had really married Coonardoo, Wytaliba would have prospered and Winnie, the fruit of their union, would have inherited it. This is however an utopian dream; there is no place where this can happen. If Hugh's character represents what the new and true Australian should be – someone capable of loving the land – this prospect is immediately ruled out as his love for the land is stereotypically mediated by an Aboriginal women. As Ronald Hyam argues, even in the colonies it is absolutely impossible to love a native (Hyam 1990, 123). There is therefore no place for Hugh's love to flourish. As previously argued regarding Gemmy in *Remembering Babylon* – where he represents the unwelcome liminal figure suggesting an alternative solution – Hugh as well, as the victim of a dangerous hybrid situation, is psychologically destroyed by the Discourse. In the end, as Terry Goldie posits in *Fear and Temptation: The Image of the Indigene in Canadian, Australian and New Zealand Literatures*, Hugh's annihilation "simply fulfils the usual male fear of the succubus" (Goldie 1989, 75). In other words, the white male hero succumbs neither to Coonardoo nor to the harsh country of Wytaliba; on the contrary, he is defeated by the moral constructs investing native women with an aura of danger. The same danger which, projected upon the country, makes it treacherously obscene. Hugh strives till the end not to become prey of this fictional danger.

Wytaliba is doomed to ruin. Prichard's narrative offers no solution. From within the restraints of the Discourse nothing more can be done. The capitulation is only a matter of time and, as suggested by Corbould's idea that fertility of the land and sex are interrelated, Hugh's self-starvation during his sexless cohabitation with Coonardoo is only detrimental: "The drought begins after Hugh and Mollie stop having sex, and is broken only when Coonardoo gives herself to Geary" (Corbould 1999, 420). Hugh's "gallant" attempt of possessing Coonardoo by claiming her as his wife but not accepting her as his sexual partner is thus a non-viable solution. Thenativewomen must be sexually possessed, and as the objectifying epithet 'black velvet' suggests, "the normative sexual relationship of the white male with the indigene female is rape, violent penetration of the indigenous, although this is not the primary image of sexual intercourse" (Goldie 1989, 76). Accordingly, Geary, in Hugh's absence, takes what he had always wanted:

> Geary's voice bellowed, "Coonardoo! Coonardoo! Where are you, Coonardoo?" [...] Heavy and drunken, in the doorway, his eyes glazed, Geary stood, swaying, an old man with his hair on end, his face red, swollen and ugly. [...] [M]ale to her female, she could not resist him. Her need for him was as great as the dry earth's for water. (Prichard 1956, 203)

Geary's calling "Coonardoo! Coonardoo!" even suggests a parallel with her sole sexual encounter with Hugh. In both cases, she passively responds to the call of the white man and has sex with him. Possibly, in spite of all the justifications used in Hugh's situation, it is exploitation of "black velvet" in both cases. What is important is that the outcome is always productive to the Discourse as in one case she gives birth to Winnie and in the other the rain finally comes to quench the thirst of the land. On the contrary, after Hugh discovers Coonardoo's "infidelity" and banishes her from the station the drought is relentless.

As Sue Thomas suggests, this novel "is a tragedy and there is no comforting promise of restoration of moral order for its audience" (Thomas 1987, 243). The ethical boundaries drawn by the novel sadly retrace those proposed by the Dominant Discourse and the ensuing sense of tragedy is heightened by the unbearable position Prichard places her hero in. According to Ruth Morse, "if [...] Hugh had been able to make more than a mystical marriage with Coonardoo [...], salvation might have come. It lies to hand, completely out of reach" (Morse 1988, 93). The socio-topographic function of the outback intrinsically negates the possibility of a love-marriage between the heroes of the novel: the sexual exploitation of Aboriginal women and its corresponding moral condemnation are the principal instruments in the dispossession of the ancestral owners of the land. Not even Geary, who is so explicitly condemned as an immoral person, attempts the impossible: he does not love, he only "takes" Aboriginal wives. On the contrary, Geary fulfils his socially prescribed function by acquiring Wytaliba and thus reinstating the violent and immoral pattern of possession of the land. The outback is thus confirmed as an off-scene setting of Australian obscenity and the Discourse, in due time, is given the possibility of sanitizing it and incorporating it in the scene. Hugh's love, not fitting in this scheme, is close at hand but impossible to attain.

3.2.4 Capricornia

Xavier Herbert's *Capricornia* (1938), published almost a decade after *Coonardoo*, details even more clearly the socio-topographic configuration of Australia. The novel, written during the author's residence in London, was born out of his already deep knowledge of the Northern Territory and, as Sean Monahan points out, from the yearning he must have felt for his home country while enduring the "cold, wet, dreariness" of the British Capital and the rejection of his manuscript "Black Velvet" by British publishing (Monahan 1985, 16). The almost epic proportion of the novel – surpassed only by the encyclopedic one of *Poor Fellow My Country* (Herbert 1975) – is filled with near-Dickensian characters involved in a story which unravels in the characteristic way of the Australian yarn. Mudrooroo, in the introduction of the 1990 edition of the novel, goes so far as to say that "*Capricornia* might be considered 'The Great Aussie Yarn' in that it goes on and on like a river flowing towards the mythical inland sea, which in reality turns out to be a desert of ill-promise" (Mudrooroo Nyoongah. In Herbert 1990, xiv). Here, as in Lawson and Paterson's cases, the yarn confirms itself to be at the heart of the process of Australian cultural mythologization and literature, and with its pretence to objectivity, becomes the medium of its canonization. As Mudrooroo's evocation of the inland sea suggests, the Northern Territory, flimsily disguised under the fictional name 'Capricornia,' is firstly a land of fantasized expectations and opportunities. Russell McDougall in "Capricornia: The Bastard Son" defines this space in a very clear and synthetic way: "*Capricornia* gives the lie to "Christianity and commerce" as the twin *raisons d'etre* for the expansion of the Empire, adding copulation and concubinage: the Land of Opportunity heralded in its early chapters is clearly the land of sexual opportunity" (McDougall 2000, 25).

The Capricornian space, just like Sam Geary's station and the outback in *Coonardoo*, is a land of opportunity mostly because it is an ob-scene space, isolated to the point that moral laws cease to apply. The first few pages of the novel suitably portray the colonial enterprise: since the pioneers "were impatient of wasting time on people who they knew were determined to take no immigrants," the foundation of Port Zodiac – prompted by the discovery of gold – is dismissed in a simple and matter of factly way (Herbert 1969, 1). The fact that the resulting bloodshed is almost taken for granted in the narration – as the settlers "were impatient of wasting time" – is the first indication of the moral freedom enjoyed at the periphery of the empire. If the frankness concerning the brutality of the expansion of the frontier immediately sets the novel apart from Prichard's *Coonardoo*, the subsequent account of the foundation of Flying Fox – a trepang-fishing base – re-establishes a parallel between the two texts, yet within a new and more violent dimension: Captain Edward Krater lands on the island of Arrikitarriyah and, with his crew of natives from another tribe, immediately takes possession of both the land and its people, inevitably paying particular attention to women:

> Because they regarded Krater as a guest and a qualified person, the Yarracumbungas did not mind his asking for the comeliest of their lubras, [...] [b]ut they objected strongly when his black crew asked for the same privilege. They were definitely unqualified according to the laws. [...] The islanders said that the old order had passed; and to

prove it, one of them seized a lubra and ravaged her. The violent quarrel that resulted was settled by Krater, who hurled himself into the mob, bellowing and firing his revolver. (Herbert 1990, 4-5)

As in *Coonardoo*, control over the land is established through sexual intercourse with native women, once again suggesting that the immoral act of miscegenation is intimately related with the control over the newly conquered space.

The double nature of the frontier settlement is also brilliantly epitomized in the Shillingworths brothers: their arrival in Port Zodiac from Batman (alias Melbourne) and their sudden metamorphosis from simple clerks into posh upper-class citizens exemplifies the type of socio-economic opportunities offered by being so far away from the centre of the empire. Herbert specifies how, in a matter of hours, the two brothers reinvent themselves as entirely new persons:

> Hopeful as [they] were of improving their lot by coming so far from home, they had no idea of what opportunities were offering in this new sphere till they landed. [...]
>
> Within a dozen hours of landing they were wearing toupees. Within two dozen hours they were closeted with Chinese tailors. Within a hundred hours they came forth in all their glory of starched white linen clothes. Gone was their simplicity forever. (Herbert 1990, 13, 8)

In this new "sphere" Oscar Shillingworths sees and seeks the opportunity of reinventing himself a gentleman. In state of Capricornia a simple government official has a much higher standing than his equivalent in the south; in order to represent the distant centre of power his role is symbolically elevated and inevitably overemphasized. This is the first step to the dynamic fabrication of the identity of the cultural and racial Other: as Oscar and Mark Shillingworths seek this opportunity they become caricatures of their initial selves: they "drop the slangy speech that had pleased them formerly, [...] raised the status of their people when families were talked about" and Oscar, "[c]arried away by this magnificence, [...] added a walking stick to his outfit, though he had lately been of the opinion that the use of such a thing was pure affectation" (Herbert 1969, 7). It is in fact with pure affectation that the pretence of superiority is achieved: as a paladin of the imperial project in the new colony, Oscar takes this opportunity to reinvent himself in accordance with the role of exemplary moral figure in the colony. He thus rapidly marries a white nurse employed at the hospital under his control, buys a cattle station and becomes part of the landed gentry of the far North.

Mark, his younger brother by eight years and only twenty-two at that time, does not so promptly respond to the interpellation of the Discourse – or not to this particular one – and rapidly drifts away from the path of "righteousness" set for the "paladins" of civilization. His drifting leads him to the parallel world of freedom typified by Flying Fox but otherwise surrounding Port Zodiac and the limited reach of its power. This is the realm of sexual opportunity analyzed by Ronald Hyam in *Empire and Sexuality* and presented in the previous section in relation to Prichard's novel. As Krater himself explains to Mark, "it was actually the black lubras that had pioneered the land, since pursuit of them had encouraged explorers into the wilderness and love of them had encouraged settlers to stay" (Herbert 1990, 13). Again native women are confirmed as the prime medium of access to the land: objectified as black velvet, they are given in the task of attracting white men into the wilderness while intended to passively accept rape and bridge the "gap left by the legalistic fact of white ownership" (Goldie 1989, 73). Mark Shillingworths responds to this collateral interpellation of the Discourse: in the confinement and isolation of Flying Fox he finally indulges in his desire of black velvet and "takes a gin" named Marrowallua.

Capricornian society thus perfectly reflects the geographical displacement of obscenity which is depicted in its centripetal organization of civilization around Port Zodiac: on the outskirts of town Mark kills Choo See Kee; in the obscurity of the side streets people get drunk and forget their sorrows; a little out of town the Aboriginal people are confined in the Compound; outside of town and on stations people such as Tim O'Cannon and Peter Differ try to live morally with their Aboriginal wives; in the confinement of his houses and in the isolation of his stations Humbolt Lace succumbs to his desire for black velvet and subsequently marries off Connie Differ to hide his shame; in Flying Fox Mark begets a "yeller feller" and abandons him to become Nawnim (no name); Frank McLash, while hiding in the tropical forest after murdering a man, is killed while attempting to rape Tocky during a storm. Moving further from Port Zodiac and its ramifications of power, the Capricornian space becomes the stage of increasingly obscene events: socio-economic impersonation, miscegenation and murder.

Sexual lust and violence are an ever-present tension in the social life of Capricornia but these are concealed behind a pretence of respectability. This is the "other side of the coin" of the unblemished façade proposed by the discourse of economical opportunity, and Mark Shillingworths adheres to the corresponding subterranean project of the discourse: as Krater's remark on black velvet suggests, and the studies of Hyam and Stoler confirm (Hyam 1990; Stoler 1995), transgression at the periphery of the empire is used as a double-edged sword because, while expanding the borders of the empire, it activates the reactionary response of the Discourse which, while establishing itself at the periphery, also reinforces itself at the centre. Once again, obscene spaces are used first to expand the reach of the Discourse by discursively incorporating isolated areas, and later to enforce order on both sides of the frontier: thus, the obscene space, after due reformation, becomes a potential extension of the scene and the pretext to employ the repressive state apparatus on both the obscene space and the scene – which might otherwise be contaminated. Mark is therefore part of this scheme as much as his brother is: with his boat The Spirit of the Land he represents the complementary opposite to his brother's rigid formality and to the rules he embraces. According to Sean Monahan, Herbert continuously contrasts "the Australian way of the swagman and the colonial way of the squatter and trooper" and, by "demonstrating in Capricornia and Capricornians the swagmen's freedom, brotherhood and vitality, [he] is celebrating what he sees as the characteristic Australian virtues" (Monahan 1985, 17). To present this idea the novel quotes Banjo Paterson's *Waltzing Matilda* and dedicates an entire chapter to the analysis of the potential of the swagman. Chapter 23, with its indicative title "Do You Remember Black Alice," peremptorily recalls the eclipsing of Marrowallua (Norman's mother). In this chapter, Andy McRandy explains to a now adult Norman the importance of his ancestry: "in this defining myth, the Swagman represents those white Australians who have accepted the potential of their adopted land, a potential already actualized in the Aboriginal way of life with its stress on freedom and brotherhood" (Monahan 1985, 16).

Mark is the embodiment of this provoking Emergent Discourse and, despite the fact that the author clearly celebrates this figure and invites the reader to identify with him, it is still clear that this contrast can be put to use by the Dominant Discourse. According to Monahan's definition itself, the swagman is "jolly because free of responsibility. He roams where he will, never tying himself to a job, never becoming a rich man, simply surviving – and happy in his freedom" (Monahan 1985, 17). This is a clear threat to the Dominant Discourse, whose main assumption (see section 3.1) is that, living in a fallen world, men must work to make the earth flourish. From this point of view, both the Aboriginal people and the swagman, with their carefree and nomadic lives, represent the absolute negation of civilization. For this reason the colonial discourse sets to annihilate and displace the Aboriginal people. However, this idea is not solely at the basis of the appropriation of the territory, but, as Lydia Weavers explains, also at the heart of the identification process of the colonizer:

> Throughout *Capricornia* Aboriginal people are linked to the landscape in a way that simultaneously signifies their dispossession and their possession. As the settlements and stations, railway lines, telegraph systems and mineral companies spread over Capricornia, charting and measuring and dividing up the country, the Aboriginal people are driven to the edges of society, in the Compound or the mission;

abused and underprivileged they are nevertheless always there, the black outline to the white map of civilization, the other by which civilization knows itself. (Wevers 1995, 39)

The image of the "black outline to the white map of civilization" eloquently describes the relationship established by the colonial enterprise with the colonized; one of almost mutual dependence. From this perspective, it is possible to infer a similar relation between squatter and swagman and therefore to uncover their mutual relationship. If, as Weavers suggests, the full-blood Aborigines "are what is being repressed, or contained, they are the Other whose presence gives meaning to civilization," (Wevers 1995, 40) then the swagman is the reinsurgence of that otherness within the boundaries of civilization. This reveals the carefully hidden truth surrounding the colonizer's identity and its being split between white Self and black Other: the connection between white swagman and black colonized subject demonstrates the real origin of the iniquity and vice projected on the racial Other. In *Capricornia* Aboriginal people are doubly appropriated: their depiction as despicable savages or as role model swagmen entraps them in opposing but interoperating discursive strategies. This ultimately confirms the necessity of the Dominant Discourse to produce an easily identifiable other in terms of mimicry:

> Colonial mimicry is the desire for a reformed, recognizable Other, *as a subject of a difference that is almost the same, but not quite.* Which is to say, that the discourse of mimicry is constructed around an *ambivalence*; in order to be effective, mimicry must continually produce its slippage, its excess, its difference. The authority of that mode of colonial discourse that I have called mimicry is therefore stricken by an indeterminacy: mimicry emerges as the representation of a difference that is itself a process of disavowal. Mimicry is, thus, the sign of a double articulation; a complex strategy of reform, regulation and discipline, which 'appropriates' the Other as it visualizes power. (Bhabha 1994, 86)

The process of identification induced in the colonized is inherently and forcefully incomplete; this produces subjects that are "almost the same but not quite" and therefore the dark mirror-image of the colonial self. As Bhabha argues, the sole presence of mimicry in a text disrupts the colonial Discourse by doubling it; in Herbert's *Capricornia*, however, the disruption is heightened by the presence of the white swagman who, with his dispersal in a space ideally set apart for black Otherness, and with his identification with the racial Other, blurs the black contours of the white map of civilization.

Characters like Tom O'Cannon and Peter Differ, both decent combos, and Chook Henn and Mark Shillingworths, two amiable larrikins, create a halo effect over the frontier; the borders between probity and incivility are blurred in an over-layering of possibilities. Herbert thus suggests an alternative vision to the idiosyncratically Manichean one of the Colonial Discourse. According to this perspective these people are not inveterate sinners but representatives of the Spirit of the Land, and forerunners of a new kind of Australian: the true Capricornians. However, the parallel drawn by Andy McRandy between Aboriginal culture and the idealized Australian swagman spirit betrays another type of cultural appropriation. McRandy extensively praises native culture yet his emphasis only serves to reiterate the distinction between colonial Discourse and its mirror image:

> [Aborigines] simply preserve their game and fruits and things by drawing on 'em carefully and so save 'emselves the labour of havin' to till and sow and the trouble of gettin' all mixed up financially over their stock as we do. You might call it primitive. But lookin' closely and comparing' it with our system of sweat and worry and sinfulness, I dunno but what it aint quite as good. (Herbert 1990, 325)

McRandy's appraisal places the Aboriginal way of life within the colonial authority's sphere of influence. It is not a real commendation of an-Other culture. On the contrary, it is an over-simplified rationalization of the other culture in terms which make it acceptable to western society. He covertly describes the Garden of Eden, an arcadian dream of past bounty of the land. What betrays him is his attitude towards hisnativeMissus – "Sugary Black Plum. […] I call her Velvet. Lovely name ain't it? I call 'em all that. Lovely creatures" (Herbert 1990, 313) – and his fantasizing about the "Great Bunyip" – the uniting divinity of "Binghis" and true Capricornians. These are blatant appropriations and distortions of the identity of the colonized subject; a way to gain a foothold in a land where one does not belong.

The white man's Spirit of the Land, symbolized in Mark's boat, is thus a new discursive layer overlapping the Aboriginal Spirit of the Land; the one that Norman briefly perceives in the song of the Golden Beetle, but that is immediately lost as soon as Bootpolish rescues him in the alluvial plains where he finds himself stuck during the wet season. Bootpolish's speech to Norman denotes his mimicry of the Dominant Discourse: "Proper good country dis one. Plenty Kangaroo, Plenty buffalo, plenty badicoot, plenty yam, plenty goose, plenty duck, plenty lubra, plenty corroboree, plenty fun, plenty ebrytings" (Herbert 1990, 307). Mimicking the white colonial discourse, Bootpolish offers his master Norman "plenty lubra" and, in the true swagman spirit, "plenty fun." In spite of Herbert's good intentions – one must remember that this is the first novel where white readers are asked to identify and sympathize with a half-caste protagonist – the text presents instances of cultural misinterpretation which, as in this case, betray the true intentions of the encompassing discourse: "a complex strategy of reform, regulation and discipline, which 'appropriates' the Other as it visualizes power" (Bhabha 1994, 86).

The Aborigine is thus doubly appropriated, firstly when individuated and marginalized as the cultural Other and secondly when reshaped in the form of a mock alternative to the Dominant Discourse. Of course the Swagman and his hybrid Spirit of the Land are an unviable possibility. Mark, even when outliving his industrious and well-behaving brother, is spared the ruinous destiny of the other swagmen only by accepting reintegration into society with the cunning help of the Shouter. His jesting response to Heather's question "you wouldn't do a bunk with the cash, would you, dear?" demonstrates his definitive and contented conversion to the tranquil life of the law-abiding citizen: "Me? [...] and leave a treasure like you behind?" Mark's carefree spirit is won over by the appeal of a well-off life within the bourgeois boundaries that he had so keenly evaded. Norman as well, supposedly the true ambassador of the social alternative represented by the half-caste, ends up embracing his uncle Oscar's cultural inheritance: at the end of the novel he triumphantly returns to Red Ochre and waits for the "boom" to hit the cattle market. Even though a half-caste, he is accepted in society for his whiteness; not even in Herbert's Capricornia is there space for hybridity, as demonstrated by the novel's closure with the finding of the skeletal remains of Tocky and her baby – Norman's baby. Norman is welcomed into white society at the price of the disavowal of his Aboriginal heritage. Tocky's death – like that of all other unmentioned, forgotten, prostituted and discarded Aboriginal mothers – proves this idea by reinstating the trend by which Aboriginal women are obliterated by the Dominant Discourse and literally expunged from the text (cf. Lawson 1987, 39). Implicitly, Aboriginal women are denied the possibility of an existence outside of the role of Black Velvet.

In the end, the Capricornian space is efficiently held in check by the dominant discourse through a wise socio-topographic configuration of the land. Wevers writes that "[c]ivilization is charted as a series of socially significant locations, mostly gendered and race specific" (Wevers 1995, 40); among them she enumerates the railway (destined to connect the far north with the civilized south), the compound, the mission and the courthouse. These locations actually form the operational framework over which the broader subdivision between scene and obscene space is organized. Mark's and Norman's return to the scene emblematically represents the domestication of the Spirit of the Land – in his hybrid Aboriginal/swagman form – and the consequent rehabilitation of the obscene space that, in their roaming, they have exposed to the imaginative and reforming gaze of the Discourse. The swagman's rebellion against societal rules is thus profitably controlled by the Dominant Discourse, which uses it to take control of new territories. Using a lexicon made popular by New Historicism, it can be said that in Capricornia, as well as in the other novels analysed in this section, deviance is typically marginalized, contained and reformed through a discursive strategy that imposes the western arrangement of power-knowledge relations to a socio-topographic space. In the end, the scene prevails over obscenity, the land of opportunities – obscene space of sexual and economical exploitation – is transformed into yet another extension of the western scene. Therefore, the North is destined to rapidly become a replica of the cities of the South (Batman, i.e. Melbourne) while obscenity is pushed even further away.

3.3 An Aboriginal Perspective

The texts analysed in sections 3.1 and 3.2 clearly present the process of socio-topographic transformation of Australian space from a white perspective. These novels, which differed from one another in literary period and intellectual attitude towards the land, were arranged in a thematic, rather than a chronological, order so as to draw attention to the strategies used by the Dominant Discourse to seize and control the Australian space. Each novel, consciously or unconsciously, drew attention to a specific historical phase with its corresponding attitude or a tactic contributing to the expansion of the scene and the retrocession of a frontier, which contained the ingeniously constructed otherness of the ob-scene space beyond it. However, as clearly stated in *Remembering Babylon* (1993) and suggested in *Voss* (1957), there is another side to the story narrated in their pages. As Henry Reynolds proves in his seminal text, there is also *The Other Side of the Frontier* (Reynolds 1990) to be considered. Silenced for two centuries, the Aboriginal perspective has finally begun to emerge in the outstanding works of native authors who can legitimately talk about the experiences of being colonized and marginalized.

The perspective disclosed in novels such as Mudrooroo's *Doctor Wooreddy's Prescription for Enduring the Ending of the World*

(1987), Kim Scott's *Benang* (1999) and Alexis Wright's *Plains of Promise* (1997) challenges the legitimacy of the assumptions at the basis of the colonial conquest: the Aboriginal, used by the colonial discourse as the recipient of its own "Otherness," is here re-presented from an internal and independent perspective which strives to liberate itself from the grasp of the Dominant Discourse. As Adam Shoemaker argued in his influential work *Black Words White Page*, this task is not an easy one when the only medium available to re-address the problem is the one imposed by the coloniser. The novel, a product of bourgeois European culture, is thus reinvented as a means of expression of the culture that it initially helped to subjugate. Thus, the adaptation of the native oral culture to written prose and poetry stands as a reminder of the changes imposed by the colonizer. On the other hand, the appropriation of a tool from the colonizer's culture indicates a constructive form of hybridization.

White discourses on hybridity propose the hybrid as the solution to the illegitimate ownership of the land; a way of re-establishing harmony by claiming a share of the subjugated culture. However, in doing so, they also posit a functional obliteration of the Aborigine. The Aborigine is once again reduced to being an instrument used to gain access to the land, and once transformed in a deliberately re-formed hybrid, the original indigenous identity is postulated as subjugated and definitively lost. In contrast, from an Aboriginal perspective hybridization is a process endured at the cost of an excruciating pain that engenders a loss that is also the origin of a potential for new existence.

The alternative perspective proposed in the following novels will therefore focus on both the transformation of the Australian space and that of the identity of its native people. The point of view presented on "the other side of the frontier" undermines the assumptions postulating the obscenity of the unexplored Australian landscape and the Otherness of the Aborigines, but it also once again evidences the ruthless implementation of the strategies of the dominant Discourse. *Doctor Wooreddy*, due to its explicitness in the subversion of the colonial cultural tropes, is the first novel to be considered; by also dealing with the first contact period and with the brutal extermination of the Tasmanian Aborigines it effectively introduces thenativeAustralian perspective. The following novels tackle the issue in different settings and at different times, but the intent is the same: to contest the official history of the settlement of the continent and expose the subaltern voices oppressed throughout the colonial struggle.

3.3.1 *Doctor Wooreddy's Prescription*

Mudrooroo's *Doctor Wooreddy's Prescription for Enduring the Ending of the World* is a novel that openly confronts a very delicate theme weighing on the conscience of white Australia, the extermination of the Tasmanian Aborigines. In the past decades this topic has been focus of great attention and in 1976 two novels were published on the subject: from very different standings Robert Drew's *The Savage Crows* and Nancy Cato's *Queen Trucanini, The Last of Tasmanians* addressed the issue of guilt in white conscience and the necessity of reconciliation before a sense of closure could be achieved. Almost thirty years later Keith Windshuttle's allegations against the Black Armband historians[8] and his highly controversial *The Fabrication of Aboriginal History* (Windshuttle 2002) demonstrate how sensitive the subject still is to the Australian conscience. The almost rhetorical question of whether the extermination of the Tasmanian Aborigines

---

[8] 'Black Armband Historian' is a term coined by Geoffrey Blainey in his 1993 *Sir John Latham Memorial Lecture*, in which he tried to illustrate his point of view regarding the current attitude of historians towards the past. In this lecture he explained that, from his point of view, Australian history had swung from the "Three Cheers" view of history, celebrating the past as unequivocally glorious, to the the diametrically opposite "Black Armband" view of history, which saw the past as daunted by innumerable faults committed against several minorities and in particular against the Aborigines. (Blainey, Geoffrey A. (1993). "Balance Sheet on Our History." *Quadrant* 37.7-8: 10-15. Blainey hoped the time was ripe to settle upon a point of view which would conciliate both "factions" of historians, however, the term has been ever since used in a pejorative way by neo-conservative politicians and scholars.

was a genocide or not is thoroughly analysed in Henry Reynold's *An Indelible Stain? The Question of Genocide in Australian History* (2001). In this study the celebrated historian endeavours to give an impartial account of the events resulting in the demise of a people. An at least partial awareness of Reynold's findings is important in order to comprehend the significance of Mudrooroo's work.

The historian's meticulous analysis discloses the complexity of the mutual relations which ended so tragically: Governor Arthur was intimated not to exterminate the natives, as their extinction would have left an indelible stain on the English Crown; at the same time, the guerrilla warfare started by the natives disproves the common belief that the Aborigines were passive to white colonization. Their resistance to invasion was conducted in the most effective and accessible manner: the attack of isolated shearers and farmers. Considered as being treacherous assaults, these attacks were countered with vicious zeal by the pastoralists who, making no distinction between guilty or innocent parties, hunted down the natives with murderous retaliatory expeditions. In the end, extermination was generally regarded as a viable and desirable solution. Some parties went so far as to openly discuss the idea in the papers (cf. Reynolds 2001, 53, 54, 55). The overall picture unmistakably confirms the colonizer's responsibility but it does not prove the existence of a state sanctioned policy promoting genocide. Henry Reynold's work presents a colonial society where guilt cannot be blamed uniquely on a class of people or an institution; what emerges is the shared responsibility of individuals who, living and acting within the relevant discourse, became agents of the extermination of the Aborigines, even when trying to prevent it.

Similarly, Mudrooroo wrote a biting novel that focuses its attention on the obtuse cruelty of the acts of individuals. Thus, the rape of native women at the hands of simple convicts, or the policy for the protection of the natives conceived by The Chief Protector of Aborigines George Augustus Robinson, fall into the same type of imperceptive obedience to the over-encompassing Discourse. As Jodie Brown implies in an essay on *Doctor Wooreddy*, it is "in the form of narrative inversions and the subversion of ideological structures by a series of simple reversals of black and white attitudes" (Brown 1993, 75) that the author operates his mocking contestation of the colonizer's Discourse. Individuals such as Robinson thus become the focal points of this almost carnivalesque (cf. Brown 1993, 74) parodying of history with the ensuing implicit challenge to the centralizing forces driving their actions.

The first and most strikingly relevant of these inversions takes place in the first few pages of the novel: the Aborigines of Bruny Island have a particular socio-topographic conception of space which embodies all the evil of the world into Ria Warrawah and confines this entity to the sea: "He, or she, or it was the sea and lived in the sea from which it sent manifestations as well as tidal waves to harm the land and those who lived on the land. But try as it might, it was held at bay by great ancestor" (Mudrooroo 1983, 2).

This founding myth is bound to clash with the Eurocentric structuring of western culture: if the colonizers presumptuously regarded themselves as dispensers of culture and civilization, the natives, on the contrary, viewed the invaders as evil manifestations of the sea. Ironically, the Aborigines fail to recognize the invaders as fellow human beings and initially consider them "nums" (ghosts). Only after having studied their bewildering savagery and considered their greed for women do they realize that they are humans. This unfortunate sociocultural misunderstanding is the cause of young Wooreddy's fascinating revelation; when he sees an English vessel for the first time, he realizes that the world is about to end:

> Nothing from this time could ever be the same – and why? Because the world was ending! This truth entered his brain and the boy, the youth and finally the man would hold onto it, modifying it into the harshness or softness as the occasion demanded. His truth was to be his shield and protection, his shelter from the storm. The absolute reality of his enlightenment took care of everything. One day, sooner rather than later, the land would begin to fragment into smaller and smaller pieces. [...] Then the pieces holding the last survivors of the

human race would be towed to sea where they would either drown or starve. (Mudrooroo 1983, 4)

This incident provides Mudrooroo with an excuse to create his almost completely anaesthetized protagonist: from that moment onward, Wooreddy detachedly observes his world coming to an end. However, this almost prophetic image also holds the key to understanding the conflict between natives and colonizers: what is at stake in this battle is the socio-topographic control over the land. Wooreddy foresees the way the colonizers, by imposing their spatial configuration upon Van Dieman's Land, will literally seize control of the territory by first breaking it apart – with roads, settlements and sheep stations – and by later incorporating the spaces therein contained with the expansion of the settled areas. The Colonial Government – Ria Warrawah – will in the end take the last natives to Flinders Island – tow them to sea – where they indeed die of consumption.

Brown claims that Mudrooroo's interrogation of a genocidal past "help[s] to heal the cultural fracture within contemporary Aboriginal communities" (Brown 1993, 72), and that he achieves this by proposing alternative representations to the white stereotypes debasing Aboriginal people. In *Writing From the Fringe* (1990) Mudrooroo himself explains that this is one of the most significant characteristics of Aboriginal literature: "Aboriginal writers are very conscious that history is a white construct in that a past *truth* is maintained, and are eager to redress the balance. In a sense when we talk of history we are talking of *myth* masquerading as objective history" (Mudrooroo 1990, 169 – emphasis in the original). "Myth" masquerading as "history," or more generally as "knowledge," is in fact what conveniently discriminates Aboriginal people and confines them to the socio-cultural fringe of society, a purposely constructed ob-scene space. In *Writing from the Fringe*, Mudrooroo explains that this dislocation is at the heart of what distinguishes fringe literature – with its peculiar de-centred and alternative take on reality – from the white Australian one. When the authors manage to resist the interpellations of the Discourse – embodied in white editors demanding conformation to western tastes – their writing will reflect a cultural standing which is both different and intrinsically unsettling for the white narrative (Mudrooroo 1990, 165-178). In *Doctor Wooreddy*, this implies to undermine all the cultural tropes that facilitated the socio-topographic transformation of the native's land: the othering of the Aborigines (cf. Reynolds 2001, 129) and the denial of their right to live on the land they possessed (cf. Reynolds 2001, 121). It is thus that Wooreddy, with a scientific detachment fitting a real doctor, becomes the personification of this marginal perspective; his attentive study of the *nums* will subvert all the prejudices discriminating Aboriginal people.

Initially conditioned by the belief that the white invaders were manifestations of evil, Wooreddy questions their humanity:

> They where under the dominion of the Evil One, *Ria Warrawah*. They killed needlessly. They were quick to anger and quick to kill with thunder flashing out from a stick they carried. They kill many, and many die by the sickness they bring. [...] A sickness demon takes those that the ghosts leave alone. (Mudrooroo 1983, 11)

The failure to recognize the invader as human reflects the insistence of the colonizers in regarding the Aborigines a pre-human species or, after Darwin, the missing link between apes and humans and, in any case, a doomed race. Significantly, the natives of Bruny Island can only explain the savagery of the assailants by denying them a common humanity. When they later realize that the white ghosts are humans after all, they will doubt their intellect. Watching a group of white men rape a native woman, Wooreddy considers "with interest the whiteness of the ghost's penis" and as he quickly "begins to find the rape a little tedious" he starts to wonder "about the grammatical structure and idiosyncrasies of their language" and concludes that "perhaps it wasn't even a language" (Mudrooroo 1983, 20-21). The superiority of the white discourse is tragi-comically undermined by Mudrooroo's inversion of the most common cultural stereotypes: allegations stigmatizing the native language as inarticulate are paralleled by similar claims made against English; likewise, accusations of Aboriginal disorderly sexuality are unequivocally countered by systematic rape and violence at the hands of the western invaders. Adam Shoemaker, in his essay "Sex and Violence in the Black Australian Novel" explains that Mudrooroo "clearly implies that Black Australians were traditionally masters of the art of love-making and only the invasion of the brutal Europeans extinguished this talent" (Shoemaker 1984, 50). In the novel, this superiority is reaffirmed when, later in the novel, Wooreddy is confronted with Trugernanna's inexperience:

> Wooreddy did not know that Trugernanna had only endured the rough embraces of ghosts, and so many older women had died that she had remained ignorant of the different sexual positions. [...]
>
> Each day Wooreddy made love to his wife but her lack of response began to bore him. After all he was a doctor with a knowledge of love-making and he had already been married. Now it seemed for nought. Finally, he accepted that they were together, not for love, but for survival. (Mudrooroo 1983, 46-48)

The protagonist's resignation is a form of adaptation to the conditions imposed by what he considers as being the ending of the world. However, Mudrooroo's stress on sexuality reminds one of the importance of this theme in the discourse transforming and appropriating Wooreddy's homeland and, when the doctor considers that "the nums were overgreedy of women as they were overgreedy of everything" (Mudrooroo 1983, 20) he discloses that connection between native women and conquered land. As Shoemaker clearly reminds us, in the novel "whites rape not only women, but, in a symbolic form, practically everything else with which they come in contact" (Shoemaker 1984, 50). Hence, the novel does not simply affirm the sexual superiority of the natives and the depravity of the colonists, but it also contests the discourse's use of sexuality as a means of control of the territory. If in *Coonardoo* and *Capricornia* Aboriginal women are almost naturally accepted as being the figurative access to the land, in *Doctor*

Wooreddy this trope is carefully deconstructed. It is George Augustus Robinson that becomes the expedient of another of Mudrooroo's inversions; the Chief Protector of Aborigines, or The Great Conciliator as he likes to be called, is a small and base man assailed by the same urges as the vilest of convicts:

> Robinson's mouth went dry and his ruddy face paled as the women rose like succubi from hell to tempt him with all the dripping nakedness of firm brown flesh. [...] The man with the ghost was more interested in the weight and content of the women's bag. It bulged with oysters, and pocking up from the bottom a large crayfish quivered spasmodically. (Mudrooroo 1983, 43)

Shoemaker regards this passage an exemplary illustration of the "carnal urges" driving Robinson – and with him the entire colonial enterprise – which are also "those 'animal urges' which European commentators of the time associated with native peoples" (Shoemaker 1993, 53). The strategic othering of the natives is thus continuously revealed throughout the narration and the attention is focused on the discursive construction of reality. It is thus that, as Justin MacGregor argues in "A Margin's History," later in the novel Wooreddy's consideration about the written page of a funeral service "reveals the relationship between physical and written oppression" (MacGregor 1992, 113): "He held the sheet of paper low in his trembling hands, he was getting over an attack of the coughing demon, and stared at the letters forming words and sentences that stood at attention in line like the red-coated soldiers" (Mudrooroo 1983, 145).

Letters, words and sentences, just like soldiers, are used as "a weapon [...] to repress alternative cultures, interpretations and perceptions" (MacGregor 1992, 113). As the plot of the novel progresses, it becomes clear that this topic is at the heart of the author's research; after all, since he uses the English language, Mudrooroo has to compromise on using the very weapon that the colonizer used to subdue his people and to write the victor's version of truth. This paradox is addressed at a very early stage of the narration, when Wooreddy participates in a strike against an isolated hut inhabited by a white man: "Was it advisable or even permissible to use *num* weapons? This was a never ending dispute and Wooreddy's carefully considered opinion met other carefully considered objections. The debate had dragged on for years and would drag on until no one was left to take sides" (Mudrooroo 1983, 145).

This is of course, just as the precedent one, a metaphoric consideration on the nature of language and its usage; the meta-narrative question is whether it is legitimate or not to use an alien language and genre which have been used as tools of oppression. For Mudrooroo the answer is obviously yes, and with the careful use of this foreign medium from the marginal position imposed by the colonizer he is capable of subverting that system and reclaiming a position of discursive authority.

The reality emerging from the pages of *Doctor Wooreddy* is an entirely obscene one: not only has the discourse imaginatively constructed an image of Van Diemen's Land as a place of otherness in order to justify its conquest and reformation, it has also exploited its isolation from the scene – Sydney, London – to unleash the passions projected upon the land and its natives. The ob-scenity of this space – spatial and discursive – became the excuse that permitted the obscene treatment of the natives at the hands of the colonizers: rape, murder, transportation, near-starvation and, as a result, genocide. It is this construct that is patiently refuted in the narration. With this novel, through the reification of history, Mudrooroo attempts to piece back together the land that Wooreddy had prophetically seen disintegrate and literally fall apart under the discursive pressure of the colonizer. The final goal of this project is to restore a cultural space, or a new and alternative scene, where the descendants of the native people of Tasmania will be able to stand in dignity – with a past that belongs to them – upon their own land.

Another fundamental subtext to the novel is the constant attention to time. Although apparently unrelated to the spatial theme of this research, time is an important dimension to the socio-topographic construction of a place since, as will be later explained (section 3.3.2 and particularly in chapter 5), the past can be isolated into certain ob-scene locations. In this case it is particularly interesting to notice the totally different conception of time that the Aboriginal people had and the result of the disruption of this reality of theirs. Wooreddy's early realization that "the times" are changing constitutes the basis of his acceptance of the fate of his people and, eventually, the key to the birth of a new reality: "The old ways were losing their shape and becoming as the cube. [...] no one had any trust in the future and they accepted a prophecy that passed among them [...]. [I]t was the times. [...] [I]t was because the world was ending" (Mudrooroo 1983, 9). In a similar way to that described by Tzvetan Todorov in relation to the conquest of Mexico and the ensuing demise of the Aztecs (cf. Todorov 1984), the arrival of the Whiteman in Tasmania caused the cyclic structure of the native's mythic time to collapse when confronted with the inexplicable appearance of a disturbance: an invader. As a consequence, as Kateryna Arthur argues in her paper "Fiction and the Rewriting of History: A Reading of Colin Johnson,"[9] the natives of *Doctor Wooreddy* "are displaced not only from their land and all that sustained them there physically and psychically, they have also been transposed into an alien time scheme" (Arthur 1985, 59). The entrance into the colonizer's linear time would initially seem to warrant a grim fate for the natives who, unsettled by the changes in the immutable pattern of existence set by the Dreamtime Ancestors, contemplate for the first time a future differing from the past and as a consequence the possibility of an ending: "fewer babies to be born, to be weaned, to die – and this meant fewer mature adults to keep and pass on the traditions [...]" (Mudrooroo 1983, 9). However, it is Wooreddy's ready

---

[9] Mudrooroo changed several names before settling on 'Mudrooroo': he started his writing career as Colin Johnson and later changed his name to a tribal one (a common thing to do for native writers of his generation), Narogin Mudrooroo, only to later change it to Mudrooroo Nyoongah. After the Narogin tribe disowned him and his Aboriginality was put in question, he shortened it to the plain Mudrooroo.

acceptance of this new condition that seems to hold the key to the enduring of the ending of the world: Frank Kermode in *The Sense of an Ending* explains that "apocalyptic thought belongs to a rectilinear rather than cyclical views of the world" and that "History is purely intellectual discourse which abolishes mythic time" (Kermode 1967, 5). In other words, the millenary vision inherent in the belief of the coming of the apocalypse and God's new kingdom on earth literally directs time towards a future event; this reformulates, or even creates, the past. Mythic time, being cyclical and repetitively similar to itself, does not offer such a clear distinction between present, past and future. The arrival of colonizers abolished mythical time not only by intruding its immanent present – a simple intrusion would have been dealt with a reformulation of myth – but also with the active imposition of the discursive construction of history in present, past and future terms.

The protagonist's acknowledgement of this new condition allows him to take the first steps towards the adaptation of his life in function of a survival technique which, while not saving him from his fate, will lay the foundations of future Aboriginality: hybridization. By hypothesizing the ending of the world, Wooreddy unconsciously enters the linear time scheme introduced by the colonizer, and becomes involved in the analytical investigation of the potentials of this new condition. The attentive examination of the enemy and his world, however, is not enough to spare his life; it is his sacrifice that sets the possibility of a new form of existence and identity for the Aboriginal people. When taken to the Australian mainland by Robinson and after fleeing with a local tribe, the Doctor finally comprehends the limitations of his world view. When the chief of the rebel tribe leads him to a sacred cave, the protagonist is confronted with an inspiring vision:

> Great spears fell from the roof. Great Ancestor casting down his spears to keep Ria Warrawah at bay – but other spears rose from the floor to join them in a oneness. They met and there was no conflict as he had always thought that there should be – that there had to be! [...]

3 The Outback 151

Ria Warrawah and Great Ancestor came from a single source which he had been seeking in his dream. (Mudrooroo 1983, 197)

It is this realization – probably owing to Mudrooroo's time as a Buddhist monk – that leads the protagonist to foresee the disclosure of a new reality, one that is not simply based on the Manichean opposition of good and evil, but one where it is possible to exist within the interstitial spaces of the Discourse. Justin MacGregor argues that at this moment Wooreddy "begins to understand reality," one where "negotiation is possible from the interstitial space between cultures only when the binary classifications of good and evil, civilized and savage, are rejected" (MacGregor 1992, 116). This indicates the acceptance of the colonizer as not simply something that belongs to a world that is other (something out of a reciprocally ob-scene space), but as something that is integrating part of the cosmogony disrupted by its arrival. At this moment, Wooreddy seems to grasp the fictional nature of Otherness and ob-scenity. It is therefore inappropriate to say that the doctor starts to understand reality; what he sees is a new reality, one that is alternative to both thenativeand the western realities. In a way he is already one step ahead of the colonizer who still views the world in Manichean terms.

The positive outcome of this form of hybridization comes, however, at a very high price; the text makes clear that to enter this new world the natives must endure the ending of their world. Hope is consigned to the last page of the novel precisely when Wooreddy dies and his body is buried in a shallow grave:

> They clung to each other and let the tears roll down their cheeks as they watched the shore and the storm clouds clearing away. The yellow setting sun broke through the black clouds to streak rays of light upon the beach. It coloured the sea red. Then Lawaya Larna, the evening star, appeared in the sky as the sun sank below the horizon. Suddenly a spark of light shot up from the beach and flashed through the dark sky towards the evening star. As it did so, the clouds closed again and the world vanished. (Mudrooroo 1983, 207)

Wooreddy's death marks a moment of ritual transfiguration: the sky, the sea and the sun outline an immense Aboriginal flag dominating the landscape. The apparition of this symbol – representing the forthcoming pan-Aboriginal unity – implies the continuation and not the ending of Aboriginal culture. Wooreddy's and all the other natives' sacrifice is not in vain: as Mudrooroo himself explains, "when Wooreddy dies his spirit ascends to the sky to become part of the Aboriginal flag. [...] [This way] he lives on forever in his community and he is a source of strength to them" (Mudrooroo 1990, 177). With his death Wooreddy fulfils the fated destiny he had prophesised for himself and his people; however, modern Aboriginality is also born at this moment. What the text seems to suggest is that the contemporary sense of Aboriginality is a form of hybridity born from the contact with white culture. This painful but inevitable process caused a double displacement, one in time and one in space, as to enter into Apocalyptic time implies to abandon the mythic construction of the world. The novel relates the birth of this new condition, that of living, thinking and writing from the fringe. For Mudrooroo, being displaced and ostracized in an ob-scene space at the margin of society becomes a vantage point: the alternative perspective enables the observer to discern between "myths" and "truth" and thus to challenge the dichotomial distinctions imposed by the Dominant Discourse. As Justin MacGregor argues, Mudrooroo's aim is not to "rewrite history" or to "represent the past accurately" but to "break the long-standing stereotypes" of the colonial Discourse (MacGregor 1992, 116). As a result, Aboriginal writing proposes an-other history which reminds us of the partiality of the victor's history. Marginality, as a site of alterity, thus becomes a most important location, as, with its mere existence, it intrinsically challenges the dominance of the hegemonic discourse by making it "an/Other in a world of Others" (MacGregor 1992, 116). This alternative perspective clearly overturns the conception of scene and obscene space: marginality – clearly belonging to the colonizer's obscene space – becomes the site of a new scene, one purified of the discursive constructs previously debasing it to obscenity, and returning these themes to Discourse from which they originated. In order to do so, Mudrooroo had to reform both history – which actively dismantled the native's conception of the world – and space.

3.3.2 *Benang*

With an aim similar to Mudrooroo's contestation of time and space, Kim Scott's *Benang, From the Heart* (1999) tackles white history and strives to re-write the story which shapes both the identities of the native tribes and the space where they live. Obviously this takes the author into the recesses of white Australian culture and leads him to the exposition of the ob-scenity therein concealed. Written after long archival research, Kim Scott's novel explores the Australian space from an Aboriginal perspective and provides an appalling account of the settling of the south coast of Western Australia. As Gerry Turcotte appropriately declared, *Benang* is a "sweeping historical novel" that will surprise its readers "for the originality of the voice that speaks [there]" (Turcotte 1999, 9). This comment underscores the significance of the narrative structure proposed by the author: Scott, drawing from the experiences of his own family, managed to create an imposing meta-historiographic saga which redefines Australian history by recounting it from an alternative and marginal perspective. "The voice," or rather the voices, speaking in the text belong to those that Gayatri Chakravorty Spivak – after Antonio Gramsci – would call the subalterns of Australia; these emerge from history into the text in the form of intertwining Aboriginal life stories which, with their plain brutality, give the non-Aboriginal reader a chance to witness what has been hidden in the ob-scene spaces at the margins of Anglo-Australian culture.

At first, the most disconcerting and obscene things in the narration are the number of killings, the ruthless reprisals and the undifferentiated brutalization of Aboriginal men, women, elders and children.

However, at a second stage, what becomes more disquieting is the viciousness with which these acts are perpetrated:

> Fanny glanced about, thinking of how [...] these Dones had no respect for who they took, or how they treated them. Such thoughts left her, suddenly, when she saw an old man at the woodheap. He must've been lying there the whole time, in the sun, among the timber, and had only now raised his head. Less than a dog, he had no bowl of water, and a chain was looped around his throat. (Scott 1999, 174)

The savagery of the acts related throughout the story exemplifies the cultural inversion taking place on the frontier. In accordance with the attitudes generally accepted at the time, the native chained in the sun is treated as savage; as if he was not part of humankind. Such episodes demonstrate that the absence of an official justice – the police force – or in many cases its complicity, contributed to the creation of an ideal ob-scene scenario wherein the pioneers could abandon themselves to the most immoral behaviours:

> Mustle, as did so many others, held trials in his homesteads. People were chained up on the veranda, and given their chance to speak in whatever English they may have had. [...]
> A gavel striking our wood; rap rap rap. Tap tap tap. Hollow sound of wood on wood. [...] Old Mustle sat there with the coils of a silver wig falling over his shoulders. He was enjoying himself, was grinning to an audience which contained, besides his own brother, a Moore, a Starr and a Done. There was enjoyment, certainly; but it was malicious, and angry, and the laughter was cruel, even its restraint.
> 'Send them to the islands.' (Scott 1999, 469)

The pleasure with which the settlers mimic an official trial reveals both their need to reinforce their own righteousness in the face of manifest moral corruption and the pretence of being the bearers and dispensers of moral and civil enhancement. The Aboriginal perspective on the outback thus reveals the true origin of the alleged obscenity of this space. Unambiguously the corruption is born on the white side of the frontier, as demonstrated in the cases of *Remembering Babylon*, *Coonardoo* and *Capricornia*. Morality is not only exclusively defined in western cultural terms, but white immorality is also purposely projected, unleashed and confined in an area which is actively shaped through a discursive effort of the dominant power-knowledge structure.

For this reason, Kim Scott's aim was not only to dig up an obscene past that white Australia has so keenly tried to obliterate; his major objective was to respond to and challenge the white Australian Discourse which continued to discriminate against Aboriginal people, confining them to the ob-scene margins of society. *Benang* manages to do this by underpinning all instances of injustice and miscomprehension that occurred from the moment of the first encounter to the present. These events, the backbone of which is constituted by happenings concerning the protagonist's family line, are reconstituted in a network of significant locations and moments that reframe the Aboriginal experience and identity. These inter-related connections provide a framework for the creation of an independent historic and socio-topographic structure which redefinesnativeAustralia and redeems it from the taint of the discursively imposed ob-scenity. As a result, Kim Scott's narrative, by blending meta-historiographic fiction[10] with "life stories," successfully re-maps Australian history and geography and hence to "con-text" white Australian Discourse that imposed the arbitrary distinctions between scene and obscene spaces. By subverting the coordinates of this moral constructs, just as Mudrooroo did in *Doctor Wooreddy*, Scott succeed in relocating Aboriginality on a reformed scene from which it is possible to create the basis for an alternative native Discourse.

---

[10] Linda Hutcheon defines historiographic metafiction as one kind of postmodern novel "which rejects projecting present beliefs and standards onto the past and asserts, in strong terms, the specificity and particularity of the individual past event." It also "suggests a distinction between "events" and "facts" that is one shared by many historians" (Hutcheon, 1988, 122).

The novel's plot is driven by the protagonist's growing awareness of his Aboriginal ancestry and his resulting quest for personal identity. Harley, raised by his white grandfather, has been plucked from the native side of the family according to an unforgiving project of human breeding. Adopting Auber Octavius Neville's ideas and methods for the dilution of the native race into the white one,[11] Ern Salomon Scat – a fictional character Kim Scott created around his own grandfather – devotes himself to the procreation of a white offspring out of successive inter-breedings between Aborigines and white Australians:

> The black will go white. It is exemplified in the quarter-castes, and by gradual absorption of the native Australian black race by the white.
> The position is analogous to that of a small stream of dirty water entering a larger clear stream. Eventually the colour of the smaller is lost (Auber O. Neville, "Black May Become White: Work of Elevating the Natives," Daily News. In Scott 1999, 7)

As a result Harley's narration begins from an extremely marginal standpoint: as his grandfather's eugenic and cultural project intended, almost every trace of his Aboriginality has been wiped out. Trying to escape the pauperization caused by his grandfather's social and racial engineering, Harley studies Ern's documents and discovers an astounding universe of racism and under-privilege. The files classifying his family on the basis of skin colour, somatic features and fractions of native blood, betray a detached attitude common not only to his grandfather but to an entire nation:

---

[11] Serving from 1915 to 1940, Chief Protector of Aborigines A. O. Neville was convinced of the possibility of breeding out the natives in as few as three generations. This could be made possible by keeping the "half-caste" from having children with "full-blood" blacks. The need to eliminate the blacks as soon as possible was induced by the fear that half-castes could increase in number and eventually become a threat for the white community – full-bloods, in contrast, were considered doomed to extinction. For this reason the forcible removal of children became an accepted policy that lasted until the end of World War II and beyond. (After signing the Universal Declaration of Human Rights in 1948, Australia had to refashion this policy so that it could last until 1970).

> I paused to read from a book which had passages underlined on almost every page. There were a couple of family trees inscribed in the flyleaf. Trees? Rather, they were sharply ruled diagrams. My name finished each one. On another page there was a third, a fourth. All leading to me. (Scott 1999, 29)

Harley, the intended outcome of his grandfather's eugenic project (the "first-born-successfully-white-man-in-the-family-line") begins a reciprocal process in which the branches of the diagrams are retraced at the discovery of each relative's life story. Harley's investigation, through his grandfather's files and later through the accounts of two uncles, allows more than one century of family history to be retraced all the way to the present and to take its rightful place into an otherwise heavily censored – and obscene – Australian history.

Accounts of individual lives are thus bound together in an imposing saga that reminds of South American prose, but that stems from "life stories." This genre, made popular by contemporary Aboriginal authors such as Sally Morgan, celebrated the transfiguration of individual experience (a person's life) in universal knowledge (that person's life narrated into a book and made exemplary of innumerable others). As a result, autobiographies evolve into narratives that, without renouncing their uniqueness, stand for an entire people. Branching off from this genre, Kim Scott's semi-autobiographic novel simultaneously evades the rules of realist narration and carefully weaves an intricate family history. This combination of distinctive approaches produces a meta-historiographic narration that explicitly challenges white Australian history. First inhabitants, first explorations and first dwellings are exposed as counterfeit locations of culture that deliberately usurp Aboriginal antecedents. The word-play with the title of Homi Bhabha's *The Location of Culture* stresses the fact that timelines and maps actively "locate" culture in time and space. The scene, as the implicit centre of the Dominant Discourse, is therefore invalidated as the sole location of culture through the rediscovery of the Alternative Discourse concealed in the obscene space beyond it. Kim

Scott became aware of and interested in proving this discourse wrong when researching his family history:

> [I]n lots of local histories that I read in the region that my family had been moving for thousands of years, lots of local histories tried to talk about who was the "first white person born" in such and such an area. It seemed to me that in doing that they were trying to impose a story on a landscape and jettison the pre-existing stories. (Buck 2001)[12]

In accordance with Hayden White's view that "history is the collection of narratives we tell ourselves in order to create a past from which we would like to be descended" (Robert Markley, "History, Literature, and Criticism," in Con Davis and Finke 1989, 878), *Benang* demonstrates that the colonizers' recording of the past is nothing but a deplorable attempt at gaining a foothold in the territory while simultaneously trying to efface the antecedent Aboriginal history. For each first white man born, the novel provides an alternative story, the wilfully discarded one, reminding us that Aboriginal people were there first, had always been there and never ceased to inhabit that territory.

Australian history is therefore literally "re-mapped." The co-ordinates of its authentication are displaced, cancelled and reverted to a long forgotten socio-topographic structure where the scene and the ob-scene space did not exist – not in the terms imposed by the white Dominant Discourse. Thus, official accounts are re-told and the obscene past is finally liberated from the depths of the land where blood has inexorably seeped:

> They crept to the natives camp deep in the night, gently raised their weapons and fired an earth-shattering volley over the heads of the sleeping natives. The natives rose as one man, and as one demented man they screamed and fled through the bush with more frightful roars behind them. Their bewildered pet dingoes yelped and ran in a

---

[12] No longer available on the internet.

wide circle – one of them was shot dead to show what those noisome weapons could do. (Scott 1999, 185)[13]

The official account of this episode – which hides the truth about near complete extermination of Harley's great-great-grandmother's tribe – betrays a prejudice and racism that inherently invalidates the reconstruction of the event. The image of the natives rising and moving as a pack of wild animals is only too obviously a concession to the need to de-humanize the victims of the massacre. The loathing was nonetheless genuine and, as Henry Reynolds demonstrates in his study of genocide in Australia, it has been a common tendency to consider the natives less than human and thus to shoot them just as if they were dingoes:

> If it is wrong to hold the country – give it up; if it is right – hold it as of old, peaceably if possible but when such terrible proof is given of the impossibility of peace, treat them as they deserve; [if] it is useless to tame them, then destroy them, as you would any other savage beast, men they don't deserve to be called. (The Sydney Morning Herald, May 19 1858, In Reynolds 2001, 122)

What occurs here is a typical case of "pseudospeciation." In his study of human aggression and war, Irenaus Eibl-Eibesfeldt explains how the biological norm "Thou shalt not kill thy own kind," which is characteristic of all vertebrates, can be easily overcome by human beings through the use of a cultural norm filter:

> The vital role is played here by cultural pseudospeciation. The fact that the other party is often denied a share in our common humanity shifts the conflict to the interspecific level, and interspecific aggression is generally destructive in the animal kingdom too. Over the biological norm filter that inhibits destructive aggression in man as in other creatures, a cultural norm filter is superimposed that commands

---

[13] Kim Scott paraphrased these events from an article from *West Australian Royal Society: Journal and Proceedings* (1954).

us to kill. [...] The important point to bear in mind is that destructive war is a result of cultural evolution. (Eibl-Eibesfeldt 1979, 123)

It was thanks to a "frame of mind" convincing them that they were not about to confront fellow human beings but only non-humans, that punitive parties could set out to kill. Thus the "culturally imprinted" cannot only inhibit the inborn aggression controls and "perfectly suppress the constitutional" but can also "dispose of the relic of bad conscience" (Eibl-Eibesfeldt 1979, 169). Therefore, with unblemished candour, the Australian Discourse upholds an unlikely story of weapons gently raised to fire a demonstrative volley above the camp. Due to this type of self-confidence western history now betrays itself and proves to be a collection of implausible stories.

The novel, by revealing these ob-scene spaces, stresses the importance of the clashes/encounters between the two cultures as crucial moments of cultural alteration: every blow struck by white Australians only partially demolished its target, as the Aborigines responded by stubbornly adapting to every new situation. In *The Other Side of the Frontier*, Reynolds considers that "like the white colonists the blacks were pioneers, struggling to adjust to a new world of experience and one even stranger and more threatening than the Australian environment was to the Europeans" (Reynolds 1990, 2). *Benang* offers a reciprocal perspective to Malouf's *Remembering Babylon*, which celebrated the courage of the underprivileged settlers who were placed at the frontline of the imperial struggle. However, as the celebrated historian points out, the trauma caused by colonization was even greater on the Aboriginal side:

> The fortitude and courage of Aboriginal clans which experienced the massive impact of European invasion demand our attention and respect. They may eventually earn as much, perhaps even more admiration, from future generations of Australians as white explorers, pioneers and other traditional heroes of nationalist mythology. (Reynolds 1990, 2)

Accordingly, Scott overtly pays tribute to the sacrifice and courage of his forefathers. In the novel, this relentless "hacking away" at Aboriginal culture spawned an infinite number of what Edouard Glissant, borrowing from Gilles Deleuze and Félix Guattari, would call rhizomic roots: "The single root is the one that kills everything around itself whereas the rhizome is the root that stretches towards other roots."[14] As the colonizer's single-root culture strived to eradicate its competitors, the Aborigines were forced to take the role of the rhizome which, by moving horizontally, side-steps obstacles, circumvents hindrances and finally resists eradication. The novel therefore proposes an image of history in which the survivors of white Australian politics of annihilation and absorption can be considered "affiliative offspring" (cf. Said 1983, 17) of both former cultures. This peculiar position, otherwise described as that of the barbarian in Mario Vargas Llosa's *García Marquéz: Historia de un deicidio*, enables its holders "to have the best of both worlds" (Scott 1999, 292) and to be predatory in the face of the culture that subjugated them. As a result, an immense cultural richness and freedom of movement is granted to those who have been plucked from their culture:

> The absence of a cultural tradition implies an emptiness that also involves an extreme liberty; due not only to the fact that the barbarian, that orphan, can loot with equal ease all the cultural reserves of the earth (something that the 'civilised' person cannot do, limited as he is by the mental picture that his own civilisation imposes on other cultures), but, most especially, because his Adamic condition, that of a pioneer in the domain of creation, constitutes an incentive for his ambition: it permits all sorts of excesses and enhances the impetus and audacity of innocence.[15]

---

[14] My translation from French: "La racine unique est celle qui tue autour d'elle alors que le rhizome est la racine qui s'étend à la rencontre d'autres racines" (Glissant 1996, 59)

[15] My translation from Spanish: "La falta de una tradición cultural significa un vacío que es también suprema libertad. No solo porque el bárbaro, ese huérfano, puede saquear con igual comodidad todas las reservas culturales de la tierra (lo que el 'civilizado' no puede hacer, limitado como está frente a las otras culturas

Harley takes full advantage of this position and in typical postmodern fashion constructs his narrative by jumping back and forward in time, shifting from the present of the narrator to that of the focalizer's time, and dealing freely with the stories of the family members. This systematic disrespect for chronology stands as a symbolic reframing of the idea of time and evolution; a subversion that echoes Adam Shoemaker's allegations against the role that "chronological time" had in imprisoning the Aborigines in a subaltern position by stigmatizing them as a fossil Neolithic culture (Shoemaker 1998, 9). The native life-stories that resurface in the pages of the novel prove this wrong. They counter the winner's history by weaving together individual experiences into story that defies the concept of chronology itself.

Kim Scott's narration is therefore also a nomadic one. Following the routes traced by Harley's journey in the discovery of his family history, it visits white Australia's ob-scene spaces and tracks down a series of "relevant locations." These can be considered rhizomic roots, where the present sense of Aboriginality was forged and which coalesce into an alternative scene. Hence, the narrator visits the places where his people lived, were born or were killed and, with a quasi-magic relationship with the land, re-enacts fragments of his ancestors' lives. Harley's performances are startling: he literally hovers over the campfires and "sings" about things that he should not know, things that the land itself reveals to him through the crackling of the fire. This kind of privileged relationship with the land challenges the idea that being airborne means to be disconnected from the land. In Harley's case, it is in fact the deep connection to his tribal country that provides him with a far-reaching aerial vision. This is entirely different to the one acquired by western people when flying over the ground

---

por la visión que de ellas le impone la suya propia), sino, sobre todo, porque su condición adánica, de pionero en el dominio de la creación, constituye un aliciente para su ambición: autoriza a ésta todos los excesos, el ímpetu y la audacia de la inocencia." (Vargas Llosa 1971, 208).

or when looking at maps. For Simon Ryan, maps are imperial technologies intrinsically crippled by the perspective distortion and inherent politicisation that are employed in the construction of a "universal space" which is intended to supplant all other world-views:

> Space has usually been categorized in one of two ways. There is the absolute space of geometry, cartography and physics, and there is the relative space of individual cognitive mapping and landscape appreciation. [...] The imperial endeavour encourages the construction of space as a universal, measurable and divisible entity, for this is a self-legitimizing view of the world. (Ryan 1996, 4)

If maps encouraged the use of Cartesian space, settlers wholeheartedly embraced this unilateral perspective that emptied the land of its original inhabitants by superimposing a blankness that was perceived as unknown, unsettled and, consequently, ob-scene territory. Scott's novel challenges this conservative concept. Harley's viewpoint is proposed as a resurrected "individual" model of space in contrast to the "geometric" one that was used to conquer and topographically create Australia. Hence, Harley's elevated position – flying like a hot-air balloon – bears no relationship to the perspective distancing of the ideal viewer postulated in maps. It is the profound connection to his tribal territory and the consequent knowledge of all its elements that gives Harley the capacity to fly over the land and to expand his gaze across it. Whilst the point of view of the explorer map-maker is assertive and egocentric, the protagonist's elevation is perspective-free and genuinely descriptive.

The manner in which Harley's grandfather looks across the territory from a similarly elevated position exemplifies this difference: "Ernest Salomon Scat was up in the air, back then, and looking around. He had touched jetty, railway, electrical and telegraphic wires, sealed road. He had rarely touched the land. Ernest Salomon Scat floated all his life, in a different way to myself, and never even realised it" (Scott 1999, 85). Ern's gaze is that of a pioneer: from the height of a roof he "explores" the territory searching for signs of likely economic growth and the inherent change in status of this obscene space to that of scene. By looking at the land he is already laying a claim on it and, as he predicts the arrival of the railway, he can also envisage the profits he will make by selling it. Harley's grandfather never descended from the metaphorical "elevated position" from which he thought he could control the land – a position induced by his presumptuous western attitude towards a land which was described as empty and full of opportunities. Ironically, this implies that his "floating," even though symbolic, is in fact a sign of factual disconnection: he never belonged to the land, he only tried to possess it. This means that Ern becomes an instrument of the imperial ideology claiming that "the Aborigines do not have a different space to that of the explorers; rather they under-utilize the space" (Ryan 1996, 4). Caught in the mechanism of colonial space-creation, Ern is "elevated" to a position that is merely a fictitious stance used to take control of the recently fabricated sets of socio-topographic referents imposed on the land. What Harley sees from a very similar point of view is a set of completely different signs:

> I studied the pathways and tracks which ran across the coastal dunes, and saw the white beach as the sandy, solidified froth of small waves touching the coast. I noted how rocks and reef and weed lurked beneath the water's surface, and saw the tiny town of Wirlup Haven and how Grandad's historic homestead – as if shunned – clung to a road which was sealed and heading inland. (Scott 1999, 165)

This set of landmarks is chosen from a set of symbolic locations evidencing Harley's connection to the land. As a result, the protagonist/narrator's point of view is not set above these places but, in a sense, within the story there inscribed. The place where the sea and the land mass meet, the grandfather's house which seems to hold on tight to a road heading inland and the tiny town which is even further inland, seem to suggest the existence of a path. Therefore, as the novels previously analyzed testify, the creation of scene and obscene space, and the later expansion of the scene, proceeded according to a precise trajectory: the white men arrived from the sea, initially settled on the coast and later expanded their dominion to every inch of the interior. The ocean and the Australian land-mass – as in *Doctor Wooreddy* – seem to become the symbols of the two relevant cultures: that of the conquerors and that of the natives. The aerial perspective that Harley consciously wishes to acquire when flying over the coastline allows him to embrace this encounter:

> In the mornings I would attach strong fishing line to a reel on my belt, anchor one end of it to the house and, stepping out the door, simply let the breeze take me. I rose and fell like a wind-borne seed. The horizon moved away so that the islands no longer rested on its line, but stood within the sea, and it seemed that the pulsing white at the island's tip was not mere transformation induced by collision, but was blossoming and wilting at some fissure where sea met land. (Scott 1999, 165)

Those islands, like outposts of the mainland, are the first places where the sea meets land. Isolated in the midst of the water, they are not only detached from the "motherland" but also independent. The pulse at the tip of the islands, or rather the 'blossoming," as the narrator suggests, iconically represents the site of the colonial encounter. Encouragingly, this produces a continuous flourishing. These islands, although part of an obscene setting, are key locations in Harley's family history. It was there that his ancestors were taken to be "imprisoned," and it was also there that a whaler took Sandy One's grandmother and kept her captive as his slave-wife. It is, therefore, on one of those islands that the first "fruits" of the colonial encounter were born. The daughter of William the whaler and his captive Aboriginal woman was handed over to an ex-convict to whom she gave a son, Sandy One Mason, the protagonist's great-great-grandfather. Therefore, for Harley flying is neither a simple symptom of uprootedness nor a position of control. It is too detached and peaceful to be either of those. Rather, it represents the spiritual connection granting him a point of view independent from the distinctions between scene and obscene space. From there, with his gaze, he fully embraces the land, he recognizes it, knows it, narrates it and sings it.

Again, it is the freedom of those who live between cultures that enables the narrator to hold the strings of an untidy narration. As in the case of chronology, the spatial movement reforms the white Australian Discourse: individual lives, through their relevant locations, create nets of stories that sway across the land and chart it as they meet, intersect and part again. It is not by chance that this alternative cartographic structure is highly reminiscent of the system of songlines that once mapped the entirety of Australia. Aboriginal mythology codified the territory according to oral narratives recounting the travels of the dreamtime ancestors who travelled across the land and shaped it in the course of their adventures. Ceremonies were celebrated in the most important locations and the territory became a homely environment without ever being altered by human intervention.

Thus, Harley's growing sense of belonging finds its roots in locations – regardless of the whether they are part of the scene or obscene space – where blood has encrusted the land, where amniotic fluid has seeped into it or where tears of desperation have been spilled. The process of socio-spatialization[16] through which the social imaginary of the territory is re-constructed is a blend of the western one – using manmade landmarks to establish a sense of belonging – with the Aboriginal one – which is uniquely imaginary. In this manner, Kim Scott substitutes the fabricated white Australian socio-topographic construction of the territory – and therefore scene and ob-scene space – with

---

[16] The term 'socio-spatialization' is here used as defined by Rob Shields in *Places on the Margin: Alternative Geographies of Modernity*. The geographer clearly defines the term as follows: "I use the term *social spatialisation* to designate the ongoing social construction of the spatial at the social imaginary (collective mythologies, presuppositions) as well as interventions in the landscape (for example, the built environment). This term allows us to name an object of study which encompasses both the cultural logic of the spatial and its expression and elaboration in language and more concrete actions, constructions and institutional arrangements" (Shields 1991, 31).

one based on the locations that have become relevant during the daily struggle for survival of ordinary Aboriginal people. These constellations of places where new rhizomic roots have been sunk into the ground, are therefore modern ceremonial sites interconnected through a network of lives expanding freely into time and space.

Having established that *Benang* simultaneously reframes history and geography, we could also regard this novel as a modern epic (cf. Glissant 1996, 35). After all, what it does is to set its people back into the territory by providing them with a deep sense of identity and with a collective history functioning as a generative discourse. However, *Benang* not only offers itself as the foundation of a new Australiannativecultural "context," it also actively responds to the White Australian Discourse by proposing itself as a "con-text" (cf. Thieme 2001, 4-5). As a counter-text, Kim Scott's book does not rewrite any specific novel – as is the case of Peter Carey's *Jack Maggs*, Jean Rhys' *Wide Sargasso Sea* or J. M. Coetzee's *Foe*. More generally, *Benang* responds to the official histories dispersed throughout the Australian archives and to the politics of assimilation conceived and promoted by the chief protector of Aborigines, A. O. Neville, in his treatise *Australia's Coloured Minority: Its Place in the Community*. Hence, at times, the subversive action of the novel takes place thanks to direct quotations from Neville's book and from official community histories. At other times, the contestation of the "pre-text" – or in this case we could say pre-Discourse – is implicit in the genre of historiographic meta-fiction. It is the entire novel that rewrites the story that white Australians have proclaimed to be Australian History.

This novel proposes an original solution as the network of stories re-mapping history and geography do not coagulate into a solid-state Discourse. On the contrary, the Aboriginal Discourse invoked here would lay its foundations on the dispersal of identity and on the common but differently endured experiences of resistance to systematic annihilation. This, as Deleuze and Guattari argue in *A Thousand Plateaus*, is the distinctive condition of the rhizome, a condition that against all odds enhances the plasticity of Aboriginal culture because "the rhizome connects any point to any other point, and its traits are not necessarily linked to trails of the same nature; it brings into play very different regimes of signs, and even nonsign states" (Deleuze and Guattari 1987, 21). The uniqueness of this system is that by being a "non-hierarchical" and "a-centred" structure – but essentially a non-structure – which "has multiple entryways and exits, and its own lines of flight" (Deleuze and Guattari 1987, 21), it can be approached by anybody at any given point. Through this system the Aboriginal people, be they "full-bloods" or "part-Aboriginals", fringe-dwellers or integrated, stolen or underprivileged, traditional people or urbanized citizens, can always follow a trail leading back to a common origin. By reclaiming this complex and often incoherent past of endurance and forced alteration they can all consider themselves as Aboriginals with no distinctions. As an ultimate consequence, every nodal point dispersed throughout the net of inter-relations between people, places and time, also becomes a 'de-centred site of in-betweeness' from which each individual can beneficially look at the world from the perspective of an ever-deferred point of view. This condition, which Mudrooroo recognized as a defining characteristic of fringe literature and which is nothing more than a heightened manifestation of Bhabha's figure of the migrant (Bhabha 1994, 4-5), again offers itself as a vantage point from which to view the world with an intrinsic critical perspective.

Kim Scott's re-mapping and con-texting of Australia therefore creates a dynamic discourse that, as theorized by Deleuze and Guattari, is embodied in a 'nomadology' that opposes the "history [that] is always written from the sedentary point of view and in the name of a unitary State apparatus" (Deleuze and Guattari 1987, 23). This nomadology is conveyed through the rhizomic nature of the novel which is a consequence of its affiliative relation to the oral Aboriginal tradition. As Adam Shoemaker pointed out in an essay published just one year before the publication of *Benang*, a distinguishing feature of Aboriginal storytelling is that its narratives "are stories in which journeys take place, in which journeys themselves are the story"

(Shoemaker 1998, 9). In *Benang*, life stories, with their life-long journeys, intertwine with each other and defuse the socio-topographic construction imposed upon the territory. The obscene spaces of the Dominant Discourse are revisited and reshaped as each life story is put in relation to historical events that, through the reader's perceptions, move away from the domain of fiction and become active constituents of our social imaginary (cf. Shields 1991, 31). Finally, the rhizomic nature of the novel is further borne out by its continuous internal movement, which once again is a distinctive characteristic of indigenous storytelling: "Indigenous Australian Storytellers: lay down tracks which are typically circular; which journey forward and backwards; which involve transformations, metamorphoses, changes" (Shoemaker 1998, 9). *Benang*'s main characteristic is, therefore, that it neither begins nor ends. As the narrator himself says, it is a story of perpetual "billowing, one of return, return, and remain" (Scott 1999, 497). Kim Scott's accomplishment is especially significant because, through the blending of traditional culture and western culture, he has succeeded in creating a rhizomic narrative which is capable of upholding an inclusive Discourse – one without ob-scene spaces of seclusion – that embraces both Aborigines and white Australians.

3.3.3 *Plains of Promise*

Benang's socio-historiographic reconfiguration of white history from colonial times to the present exposes South Western Australia's ob-scene spaces. In a similar way, Alexis Wright's *Plains of Promise* (1997) recounts a family history that has been affected by all the policies which have governed Aborigines during the past century. However, this story is one that mostly concentrates on silences and isolation. The reader, rather than being confronted with a deluge of words – as in the case of Harley's stories – is challenged by what remains unsaid. The obscene is here locked in a past that has been silenced in order to escape hurt and guilt. Alexis Wright's care in speaking without exposing old wounds is an outstanding illustration of how the problem of having an obscene past now affects both the white community and the Aboriginal one. *Plains of Promise* tactfully confronts this problem by disclosing a reality that needs to be revealed – to present its obscene side – but also by interpreting silences that, no matter what happens, cannot be broken.

The novel tells the story of four generations of women who, caught in the white man's process of assimilation, are torn apart from each other and ruthlessly deracinated from their culture. In this novel, the pain suffered by mothers and daughters stand as an indictment of the cold and calculated policies that ruled the lives of the Aborigines during the second half of the twentieth century. The novel, predominantly set in a remote mission on the Gulf of Carpentaria, begins when Ivy's mother sets herself on fire after her daughter has been taken away from her. It is the beginning of the 1950s, and the assimilation policy is at its peak. The text provides very little information about the time before the narrative present. Ivy's mother past is mentioned almost casually:

> Ivy was all the woman had left. The child she gave birth to when she was little more than a child herself. The child of a child and the man who loved her during the long, hot nights on the sheep station where she had grown up. She had not seen the likes of a mission before. That was where bad Aborigines were sent – as she was frequently warned by the station owners who separated her from her family, to be an older playmate-cum-general help for their own children. (Wright 1997, 12)

Ivy's mother, who remains un-named throughout the text, is the first of the many broken links in this family line. Yet, even less is known of Ivy's grandmother's past. This character is lost to an unbridgeable past that sets her descendants apart from their tribal heritage. Ivy and her own mother have been uprooted from their land and traditions and, as a consequence, are denied access to their ancestor's culture. Indeed, soon after giving birth to Ivy, the young mother is returned to the native camp, however, despite being back among her own people, she remains an outcast:

> [T]he woman was often abusive to everyone. It was said that none of her own people wanted anything to do with her. She was too different having grown up away from the native compound in the whitefellas' household. And having slept with white man... "That makes them really uppity," they said. [...] "You know what she went and did? She went and chucked hot fat over one of the fellas when he was trying to be nice to that child. [...] Anyway, she's got to go – this sort of thing only gives the others bad habits ... if you don't deal with it properly." (Wright 1997, 12-13)

The voices speaking at the sheep station expose the prejudice of the settlers' perspective. The lack of sympathy for the woman's condition shows how, in most cases, Aboriginality was considered to be a genetic trait rather than a culture. Hence the woman's incapacity to re-integrate into Aboriginal society is mistaken for pride, rather than being acknowledged as unbelonging.

The incommunicability between Ivy's mother's worlds – the western one, where she was raised, and the Aboriginal one, to which she was returned – is confirmed by the lack of information regarding her mother's fate. Such stories, being too painful to be recalled, are not passed on. Thus, they are lost in the rift left by cultural displacement.

From the beginning, silence creates a powerful tension which holds the plot together. The unspeakable past thus becomes an obscene space and, as a result, what remains unsaid is often as important as what is revealed. So, the reader is left to wonder about stories and times that have been literally removed from the narratorial present. The stage of this plot, marked by the shifting opposition between the obscene-past and the present-scene, differs from Benang's topographic equivalent by lacking physical markers. Silence, which deliberately conceals the past and its untold stories, becomes a concrete presence in the novel. Hence, the reader is asked to participate in the sense of exclusion and is left to wonder about the past of Ivy's tribe.

This gap can be bridged with some historical research and a bit of imagination. As Michael Slack argues in a paper on the frontier period in the Gulf of Carpentaria, the Queensland Native Police and its brutal methods were imported to the gulf in an attempt to defeat the resistance of the native tribes: "Violence, murder and rape were given a measure of legitimacy under the auspices of this largely autonomous force" (Slack 2002, 78). With a quotation from a letter dated 1880 to the Colonial Secretary, Slack gives testimony of a past that could have easily been that of Ivy's tribe and family:

> It has been customary for several year[s] past and also up to the present time for Sub-inspectors and their troopers to go into the bush, round up the blacks and shoot them indiscriminately and kidnap the gins and little boys and take by force either to the stations or the township of Normanton and there make them slaves and if any attempt to escape is made they are shot down like wild beasts. (I. Watson, in Slack 2002, 78)

In *Plains of Promise*, the violence of the frontier period is mentioned only once in a scathing and heart-wrenching comment that, with a split in the curtain of silence, offers a glimpse of the past:

> The history of these cattle stations was forged by Aboriginal people who lived in slavery, bound to the most uncivilised and cruellest people their world had ever known. Those who were enslaved were those who had escaped the whiteman's bullet, his whip, his butchering and trophy collections – the sets of severed ears decorating the lounge room wall. (Wright 1997, 133)

Apart from this instance, that pain is respectfully left unmentioned. For this reason, the past becomes an off-scene space where the "objects" of the past – just as if they were psychological objects removed to the unconscious – are removed to the cover of silence.

Alexis Wright, in a speech given in September 1998 at the Tasmanian Readers' and Writers' festival, explains the difficulty and significance of talking about the past:

> There are taboos about breaking the codes of conduct. This includes the relationship to one's elders, to other people and their land, and what is considered good manners. So, in the context of my culture, I do not break taboos. The taboos I do break are to do with the way this country generally views itself in its relationship with Aboriginal people. I do not like the way we are being treated by successive governments, or the way our histories have been smudged, distorted and hidden, or written for us. [...] I want the truth to be told, our truths, so, first and foremost, I hold my pen for the suffering in our communities. (Wright 1998)

So, in spite of this commitment to truth and even when working with fiction, the author avoids breaking the taboos of her community. Hence when "[t]here are stories [she] know[s] about people from [her] homeland that cannot be spoken about outside of closed doors" that silence is respected and truthfully represented in the fiction. In this case, the silences come to represent both the white man's psychological repression of guilt to the level of the unconscious and also the Aboriginal way of the dealing with the past. As a result, in the narration of the novel, what remains unsaid or only vaguely mentioned acquires an uncanny characteristic: the past is a tangible presence haunting the main characters.

Once removed from the station and transferred to St. Dominic's Mission for Aborigines, Ivy's mother is once again an outcast. Here, tribes that should never have met have been packed together in a space where the ancestral territorial territories have been adapted to blocks and huts. In this situation Ivy's mother is not – and cannot be – offered any sympathy; even when Ivy is taken away from her. After her mother dies, Ivy inevitably becomes the second broken link in the family line and an outcast in the community.

The Aboriginal community of St. Dominic's does not take the death lightly, as a death is always an important matter. The shadow of a deceased person must depart without hindrance whilst the community gathers in ceremonial mourning. In Ivy's mother's case, things go differently:

> No one up to this moment had known how the woman had achieved her aim of killing herself. That question had become enmeshed and lost in other issues – the reason why and who was to take a share of the blame. The method was simply a secondary matter until Old Donny mentioned it: now everyone was dumbfounded, realizing how bad the woman must have felt to go and douse herself in Maudie's kerosene then set herself alight. (Wright 1997, 10)

For the reader the reason why the woman committed suicide remains veiled in mystery. The stories about men descending with ropes from the sky to persecute her and of crows attacking her in the middle of the night create a haunting atmosphere that will persist throughout most of the novel. These untold stories are part of the obscene past struggling to resurface. As a matter of fact, it soon becomes apparent that Ivy's mother leaves a curse behind. Soon after her death a series of suicides by fire plagues the community. Alexis Wright's emphasis on the difficulty of talking about these events proves that to establish the nature of the suicides is only of secondary importance. The Aborigines of the mission seem to believe that they are caused by magic, whereas the western reader, with his/her scepticism is led to think that the cause is sheer despair. Both interpretations demonstrate that suicide is the only "sure free way of leaving St Dominic's without permission" (Wright 1997, 22). The multilayered text can thus be read at different levels of understanding and, at times, the plot is archipelagic: the clues dispersed throughout the text give the reader a first hand experience of the difficulty of gaining an understanding of the intricate dynamics which link together the bare-bone facts initially disclosed.

On a different plane, irrefutable evidence is given of the extreme racism of the assimilation policies that the Northern Territory enforced in the 1950. Missions were places of confinement where the natives lived under a regime comparable only to apartheid (cf. Colin Tatz *Genocide in Australia* 1-2). The isolation of such places makes it possible for those entrusted with the Aborigine's lives to treat the natives as an inferior race doomed to extinction. Colin Tatz explains how missions and settlements run by the government came to play a crucial role in the "pacification" of the frontier as:

> Law would keep whites out and Aborigines in protective custodianship. Geographic location would see to it that no one could get in, or out. Government-run settlements and Christian-run missions were established in inaccessible places to protect the people from their predators; to encourage, sometimes to coerce, Aborigines away from the "centres of evil"; to allow for the Christianising and civilising process in private and away from temptations; to enable better ministration – in the quiet of a hospice, so to speak – to a doomed, remnant people.(Tatz 1999, 19)

The government, by portraying the outback as an obscene space, posits that the Aboriginal people are now under the threat of unscrupulous white man – the so-called predators and their own moral weakness – hence the need to keep them away from the centres of evil. Conveniently, the solution to this problem is to isolate the natives and to surrender authority into the hands of a few individuals:

> The missionaries did not simply supply a nursing service for "incurables", or a burial service: they became active agents of various governmental policies, such as protection-segregation, assimilation, so-called integration and some of the latter-day notions like self-determination and self-management. More than agents, they were delegated an astonishing array of unchallengeable powers. Uniquely – in terms of modern missionary activity in colonised societies – mission boards became the sole civil authority in their domains. (Tatz 1999, 19)

Under these circumstances, places like St Dominic's Mission for Aborigines become ob-scene spaces par excellence. Supported by the backward mentality of the people working on the mission and the isolation of the community, the unchallenged power of the pastors transforms these institutions into highly secluded places where anything can happen without the rest of the world's knowledge. Following this trend, at St Dominic's, Errol Jipp uses his authority to cover up his mismanagements and wrongdoings, because: "Then, heaven help us, it will get in the newspaper [...] and every southern bleeding heart will be up here breathing down our necks" (Wright 1998, 27).

The silence surrounding the mysterious deaths that, after five years, still plague the community becomes a riddle that the reader is left to solve alone. Respecting the silences maintained around these facts, Alexis Wright encourages the reader to draw his/her own conclusions. This attitude also reflects the process that led the author to write fiction:

> I also learnt to imagine the facts about our family. [...] We in fact have a saying in our family – Don't tell anybody. So I learnt to imagine the things that were never explained to me – the haunting memories of the impossible and frightening silence of family members. Throughout my life, I have learnt how to piece the mysteries together [...]. I can only now feel I can tell the story of our family revealing the voices of loved ones who never, ever told a story that they felt was too shameful to tell. [...]
>
> I felt literature, the work of fiction, was the best way of presenting a truth – not the real truth, but more of a truth than non-fiction, which is not really the truth either. (Wright 2002, 10, 12)

The reader is thus forced to experience the frustration of being denied the full picture while also being invited to use his/her own imagination to understand the complicated dynamics behind such horrible happenings.

The mission's best kept secret is Errol Jipp's sexual involvement with the school girls. Even though it is widely known throughout the community that the pastor uses the girls for sex, there are a number of factors which ensure that the secret is maintained: the isolation of the mission, Jipp's tight control over it and, most importantly, the silence kept by victims and all other involved parties – including the pastor's wife. Pride, prejudice, guilt and shame are enmeshed in an entanglement of feelings that strangles the entire community. When one evening Beverly discovers her husband's infidelity, she is silenced by the pastor's vehemence: "You have made me taste the filth. Get out of my sight" (Wright 1997, 29). Jipp's self-justification is astonishing: "He had previously spent years discussing this matter with God. He told himself (and God) that his situation was different, the use of black flesh a necessity. God knew he would never reduce himself to their level" (Wright 1997, 31). In such an isolated community moral and religious laws loosen and change according to the needs of individuals. Hence, in the pastor's mind, fornication is reduced to an irrelevant bodily need, mostly pardonable because satisfied through "black flesh." The objectification of the schoolgirls is a convenient adaptation of the idea that the Aborigines were an irredeemable race. Thus, Jipp even becomes a suspect in the deaths of the girls of the mission. It is the unspoken words of one of the girls that induce the reader to doubt the pastor's integrity:

> She had grown delirious when the missionary demanded she name the father. The perspiration ran from her body while she whispered that the spirit that looked like grey smoke was in the room, drawing the life from her and her baby. The next morning both the girl and baby were gone. The hut smelt as though it had burnt down. It was hours later before anyone could go inside because of the heat radiating from the destroyed bodies. (Wright 1997, 40)

Clearly two different realities confront each other in these events. Western logic encourages the reader to interpret the girl's reticence to name the father as a clue to Jipp's guilt and involvement in the mysterious death. Conversely, the native interpretation of the events invokes a realm that transcends rationality and that, in western terms, can only be classified as magic. It is in fact these two realms that constantly challenge each other at St Dominic's. Aboriginal immemorial time culture still defies the western institutions by adapting to the new conditions and striving to remain alive. Thus, the authority of the elders silently parallels Jipp's apparent control over the community:

> [The elders] have nothing to say to one another about their institutionalised life. The old ones gave up talking about it long ago [...] They sit separately, and sniff the freshness of cut grass [...] Errol Jipp sweats as he pushes the rotary mower up and down. He is determined to stop himself glancing up to the open ground [...] He is angry they are sitting there in the dirt in the heat. They always do it. Sit there in the sun for nothing [...] They sit silently, separately until midday. Then they get up and walk back again over the scorched dusty track. Empty handed. Independence intact. Another successful protest against whiteman's time. (Wright 1997, 20)

As Suvendrini Perera suggests in his article *Futures Imperfect*, what is represented here is "a conflict of temporalities: the time of the old ones resisting whiteman's time confronts colonial stereotypes of shiftlessness and 'walkabouts'" (Perera 2000, 14). The inactivity of the elders hence becomes a meaningful and effective *action* challenging the constraints imposed by western time and culture. The text here illustrates not only the suffering endured by the Aboriginal people but also their silent and uncompromising resistance. The symbolic self-determination of the elders is one of the means used to contest colonial dominance. Although much more drastic and dramatic, Ivy's mother's suicide too is a mean of resistance.

At St Dominic's, however, Ivy's life is caught between these two opposing worlds to which she fails to belong. There, it takes the elders five years to make a decision regarding her problem and, when Elliot returns from his second trip to her country with the news that "she must be returned," Ivy is already pregnant with Jipp's child. As a matter of fact, the pastor chooses her as a lover precisely because of her lack of connections in the community. Ivy lives outside every grouping in an ultimately obscene social space. After a hasty marriage to El-

3 The Outback 179

liot – who brutally vents his frustration on his unwanted prize – her baby is secretly given for adoption, and Ivy's stay in the community comes to an abrupt end when the couple kill each other in one last violent conjugal fight. From this moment onward, the girl is dominated by successive institutionalizations that slowly cripple her mind.

After Ivy is dispatched to an asylum with a note saying that she must not be returned home, the narration delineates the successive policies (assimilation, integration and reconciliation) that paternalistically ruled Aboriginal people's lives. At Sycamore Heights, rather than being a patient treated for her condition, Ivy is most clearly a prisoner in the institution. The idea of the mental institution being a place of seclusion and organization of society has been thoroughly explored by Michel Foucault in his seminal text *Madness and Civilization* (1961). The French philosopher's analyses are particularly helpful in unmasking the collusion between the government's need to confine and control the Australian natives and the institutions supposedly established to rescue the outcasts of society from their misery. Foucault traces the birth of the asylum back to the founding of the Hôpital Général in 1656 in Paris when the homeless, shiftless and unemployed where gathered in one institution instead of being left to roam at the margins of society. This change was induced by the need for a reorganization of space and power:

> In its functioning or in its purpose, the Hôpital Général had nothing to do with any medical concept. It was an instance of order, of the monarchical bourgeois order being organized in France during this period.
>
> Before having the medical meaning we give it, or that at least we like to suppose it has, confinement was required by something quite different from any concern with curing the sick. What made it necessary was an imperative of labour. Our philanthropy prefers to recognize the signs of a benevolence toward sickness where there is only a condemnation of idleness. (Foucault 1967, 40, 46)

Ivy's experience is an example of the scheming endured by the natives at the hands of the various governments and their institutions. Both the Mission and the mental institution have nothing to do with the well-being of the inmates; on the contrary, they are structured so that the outside world may find a confirmation of the need for their existence. Those confined therein, as Foucault argues, are branded as "idle and shiftless people" unfit to live in the so-called civilized world. Foucault clearly presents the cultural matrix behind this Protestant logic: "If it is true that labour is not inscribed among the laws of nature, it is enveloped in the order of the fallen world. This is why idleness is rebellion – the worst form of all, in a sense: it waits for nature to be generous as in the innocence of Eden" (Foucault 1967, 56). It is so that the elders' silent protest acquires an even more prominent importance: by resisting the scheme of integration in the idle/productive categories imposed by western society, the elders vindicate the validity of their alternative social structure. Ultimately, this confrontation is a claim of ownership of the land and a contestation of the premises on which Australia was stolen from its people. This simple silent act powerfully contests the concept of Terra Nullius and the idea that the Aboriginal culture was a primeval fossil culture. Jipp, perhaps not even fully aware of the political meaning of this stance, dreams of putting an end to this protest: "He'd make them feel the hurt, even if it took transportation to the island penal colony for lepers and unmanageable blacks a thousand of miles away. It would take only the stroke of a pen – 'for their own good' " (Wright 1997, 31).

If the mission can be seen as a first level of seclusion – which becomes an obscene setting due to its isolation – the penal island and the mental institution are both configured as a second and more secreted space of social segregation. The island, as evidenced by the pastor's remark about the "unmanageable blacks," is explicitly used for the sole purpose of getting rid of individuals who are deemed unfit for social integration. Conversely, the mental institution masquerades as a charitable institution offering shelter and treatment to those who are particularly vulnerable and in need. The reality behind this façade is once again only sketchily depicted. Ivy, traumatized by the kidnapping of her baby and by the fight with Elliot, loses her memory and withdraws into an almost autistic silence. Within this physical and psychological confinement, her life is once again transformed into a nightmare. Both the treatment inflicted on the patients – "Pants down, lie down. [...] Feet together and drop your legs" [...] "Get dressed now. Quickly!" (Wright 1997, 171) – and the further abuse of her body, are all muted by the walls around her and by the complicity of the staff:

> It was Ivy's case that gave Penguin his ultimate power. [...] The verdict was a botched abortion, without witnesses or evidence, followed by a cover-up completed by the former administration. The victim was, of course, unable to talk about her ordeal. A detailed confidential report gave the name of the suspect and option for appropriate courses of action to be taken. [...] A one-sheet summary was given to each member of the board at a special meeting and collected again afterwards. All written evidence was then destroyed in one gulp of the shredding machine in Penguin's office. (Wright 1997, 171)

The asylum described by Foucault, intended as a structure of socio-political control, reveals the importance of this space as one of power. In this case power is exerted on this place via repression and isolation, creating the conditions for the emergence of an ob-scene space. Ob-scene once again suggests off-scene, but in this case the mental hospital, which is obviously an artificial space, reveals the centrality of the Discourse in the creation of the dynamics linking transgression to repression. Penguin's takeover of Sycamore Heights is an exemplary case: transgression "providentially" calls for disciplinary action, the seizing of additional power and the reinstatement of the deepening of the definition licit and illicit. Ivy, along with all the other institutionalized Aborigines, is caught in a mechanism that manipulates her existence in order to justify the need for its authority.

After a surprising recovery resulting from an experimental treatment based on belly-dancing, Ivy is sent home when Sycamore

Heights – as well as many other institutions – is finally freed "of those powerful arms [...] imposing missionary zeal on voiceless minorities" (Wright 1997, 180). At the start of the 1970s, the new government policies tried to set themselves apart from the previous methods of strict control over minorities. With "Integration" the charges of the system are suddenly disowned and, with no further facilitation, "granted" self-management. According to this trend, Ivy is sent "home" to the Gulf of Carpentaria to live with an elderly woman who has offered to take her in. For Ivy this is no liberation. This new-found freedom is nothing more than a new type of confinement. Ivy, whose mental health has been compromised by a life of successive institutionalizations, is not capable of interacting with the outside world and is therefore forced into self-seclusion. Paranoid about being spied on by the neighbours and secretly poisoned by her hostess, Ivy lives for several years without ever leaving the house, in constant fear for her life. When one day lightning strikes the roof, setting off some hidden boxes of gelignite, the house is blown to pieces and the two women are thought dead. Surprisingly Ivy survives the explosion and, in one final act of mistrust against all other human beings, she takes to living with the goats by the river.

The effects of the government's efforts to extricate itself from Aboriginal administration – resulting in the so-called policy of self-regulation – are best appreciated in the last part of the novel. Ivy's daughter is the last of the broken links in the chain of forced separations. Mary, like many other representatives of the stolen generation, discovers her Aboriginality only in adult life. She therefore has to strive to bridge the gap left in her life. In an attempt to cross the cultural barriers separating her from her new identity, she quits her highly remunerative IT job and takes up a low paying position in an Aboriginal organization promoting self-determination and self-government. This new work introduces her to both a new Aboriginal partner and to the overwhelming maze ofnativepolitics. In spite of this central position, Mary remains an outsider to the events unfolding around her.

3 The Outback   183

Just as she starts feeling grounded in her new Aboriginal identity and soon after giving birth to her daughter Jess, the police raid her office searching for clues connecting the organization and her boyfriend, Buddy, to the riots taking place in the streets. This incident comes as a reminder of her lack of insight in the roles and associations of the organization – all of which remain unexplained. As a result, in order to protect her from the police, Mary is hastily dispatched to work in isolated native communities. The state of abandonment of these places is sometimes appalling:

> The vicinity of the old reserve became obvious to Mary as they passed broken-down car bodies strewn on either side of the road and left to rust. Some showed signs of temporary habitation: green garbo bags flagging in the wind had been used to provide privacy for the occupants from outside elements. Perhaps young lovers looking for time out from overcrowding, with twenty or more inside whatever housing existed on the reserve. (Wright 1997, 263)

Very often lacking the most basic needs, the Aboriginal communities have remained obscene spaces. Being isolated, they fail to attract the attention of the white community, which remains blissfully unaware of the third-world-like conditions plaguing the lives of the native people. The hasty change from total control over government run institutions, such as missions and reserves, and the subsequent neglect of Aboriginal affairs, lead to the state of general destitution of these communities. Hence, Aboriginal people are once again pushed to the side. The social disadvantage forcing them into poverty is used as a tool to keep them off-scene. Alexis Wright's novel counters this attitude by disclosing these realities and by portraying them in her narration:

> It was obvious from the extensive rust patches that the fence was originally a part of the protectionist era of a few decades ago. Its purpose to keep Aboriginal people inside and white people out. Both. One could never be too careful. The voices of authority, for the sake of decency, for the good of the town, for the prevention of disease,

184 Obscene Spaces in Australian Narrative

> would have been well pleased when the fence was brand-new. Such were the echoes of the good old days – when you could do something about your blacks being an eyesore around town. Now the fence was left standing to keep white people, small-town yobbos, outside, particularly at night when the young hoons like to imagine themselves gung ho as Ku Klux Klansmen, trying out things like throwing petrol bombs into the houses where children slept. Or firing an odd round or two of rifle shots for practice or the sport of it on their drunken way out, driving their revved-up Falcon utes, flashlights blinding, to go and shoot up the roos. (Wright 1997, 265)

This passage shows how tense the situation is between the two communities. The artificially created ob-scene space served the sole purpose of secluding the white self's Other. A change in government policy has made no difference to this state of affairs. Obscenity is still located on both sides of the fence; one side suffocated by its own bigotry and racism, the other almost perishing as a result of its crushing disadvantage.

Mary's work consists in helping communities improve their standard of living. Over a period of a couple of years, she visits several isolated areas where she tries to establish connections between the communities and her organization promoting pan-Aboriginal self-government. Per-chance, one of the communities she is appointed to is St Dominic's. There, apart from trying to broker a deal with the elders, Mary also re-embarks on her personal quest for identity. Sadly, both her goals fail miserably. On one hand, she is betrayed by the top representatives of her organization who, in a sudden change of policy and against the ideals of self-government, use her report on St Dominic's community to support collaboration with the Federal Government in Canberra. On the other hand, although Mary actually meets her mother, she never realizes who the woman is. Ivy, after being discovered living with the wild goats, is returned to St. Dominic's. There, still being unwelcome, she is set up living in a shed by an isolated creek. The frightening meeting happens during a daytrip to the creek, when Mary, Jess, the now elderly Elliot and his son, Victor, seek shelter in the shed during a thunderstorm:

> At first Mary thought it was an animal. A wild animal cowering in one corner. A roo' or emu, with long matted fur or feathers. She screamed for Victor. [...] Suddenly the door burst open. Elliot's large frame stood in the doorway. [...] [Elliot] grabbed the old woman by one of her bony arms and pulled her to her feet. She was like a small child beside him. Curled up like a diseased leaf, not much bigger than Jessie. She was so frightened of Elliot that her growls stopped instantly. [...] "Ivy, you listening to me?" Elliot barked at the woman "I want you to meet Mary and little Jessie here. They are *our* family." (Emphasis mine Wright 1997, 293-295)

Elliot will be blamed and much reproached by the elders for this unplanned meeting: "He had made a promise to them not to re-unite Mary and her mother. [...] they had told him *only one*, now the power would be too strong" (Wright 1997, 299). The belief in Ivy's mother's curse still clutches the community. As a result, upon Mary's arrival, Ivy is removed from the community so that the reunification of the family may not eventuate in an awakening of the curse. The meeting, though brief and confusing, is a meaningful moment for Mary:

> "Just say hello to her, Mary," Victor said, yawning, wanting to get back to bed.
> "Hello, Ivy." Mary did what she was told. And she was surprised to find herself rewarded by a gentler look from the old woman, peeping over her folded arms position.
> "This is Jessie," Mary went on, but the child had gone back to sleep in her arms. The woman peeped out again then turned away. Mary felt a sudden surge of disappointment and depression which she could not explain to herself. (Wright 1997, 295)

As Elliot says, this is their family reunited. However, Mary's disappointment is reminiscent of how the optimistic title of the *Bringing Them Home* report did not account for the fact that reunions were not to always easy or happy homecomings. The experience of returning home is often complicated by the unearthing of the pain and home is often complicated by the unearthing of the pain and grief of the families who had lost their children and, as in Mary's case, by the shock caused by facing realities that are too bleak to be immediately internalized. The lack of closure makes the process an open ended one. Jess is the key to this open-ended future. In spite of the elders' scepticism, the events which occur after the family is at last brought together, seem to imply that the future may offer regeneration for Jess and Mary, as well as for the land they come from. Although Mary has to hastily abandon the community – she believes on account of her boss' betrayal but, in fact, it is because of the encounter with Ivy – what looks like a failure acquires a very different meaning when considered from a different perspective:

> The twin-engined plane flies over Elliot's outstation. Mary looks down and sees the old woman sitting under the shade of a tree. She is busy with something on the ground, perhaps playing with a stick. It is impossible to see. But Mary can feel her contentment. *"Besides, she's happy here ..."* She hears Victor's kind voice. (Wright 1997, 301)

What initially appeared to be plain segregation can also be seen as a positive alternative to institutionalization – where, apart from being secluded, she would also be kept away from home. The elder's distrust of Mary's organisation symbolizes a new socio-topographic arrangement where the outback and its isolation imply emancipation from the Dominant Discourse: "We don't want anyone's conscience by prescription, Mary. We will do it ourselves" (Wright 1997, 301). Victor's words stress the real meaning and need for self-determination and self-government. As Mary discovers, even the organization she works for and devotes herself to is not immune to the influence of power. However, as they fly over Ivy's native land, the pilot calls the passenger's attention to a beautiful sight:

> "It's a beautiful sight. A beautiful sight." The pilot's voice interrupts the multi-channel inflight and entertainment. The big plane jives to one side. "Everyone look down the right, if you please," he says. No

one could fail to do this when the plane is flying side-on. "This is pure magic, ladies and gentlemen. What you are witnessing is the water once again coming to the surface of what we call the 'Disappearing Lake.' It has been dry for at least thirty years. A rare sight, and it is my privilege to show it to you." (Wright 1997, 302)

Soon after recovering from the fright provoked by the sharp turn, Jess declares that she wants to go to that lake. At that moment, Mary remembers that Elliot once told her a story about a disappearing lake. It is thus that the importance of the return of the water is suddenly revealed: the waterbird's story is Ivy's, Mary's and Jess' story.

> The young bird left behind had been able to devise a secret way to make water flow. [...] The secret was passed on to the child, this meant that they should always live by the lake. But the crows, greedy and evil, needed to live in new places. Their magic was so strong that [...] they made the little waterbird and its child's child and so forth go with them. [...] Over time, however, the waterbird's children's children's child went mad, because she lost her daughter in a terrible place. And the secret of the lake was lost because the crows were too interested in evil things and could not control the waterbird's madness. So the great lake dried up and is no more. (Wright 1997, 303-304)

The return of water to the Disappearing Lake demonstrates that the reunion of Ivy, Mary and Jess is very significant: despite there being no immediate remedy for the fracture created by the government policies, the waterbird's secret has been unlocked once again. Here, Wright suggests that the mechanism controlling the flow of water to the lake is a metaphor for the passing on of culture and belonging. The delicate cultural equilibrium that "the crows" had disrupted is restored in a final moment of recognition: Mary instinctively promises her daughter that one day she will take her to the lake. Jess' future is still open. Being the first unbroken link in the family line, she enjoys the security of being born within her own culture. This is the meaning of the water resurfacing in the lake: culture being passed on and flourishing once again. The lake represents a space that is not obscene any longer but that is the site of a possible alternative scene: that of Jess' future.

By exploring unmentionable spaces and past stories, Alexis Wright's novel, symbolically delivers hope to otherwise unreachable places. The novel deliberately explores these ob-scene spaces; not in a morbid search for the sensational but, rather, to provide an alternative to the traditional interpretation of Australian history. As Alexis Wright puts it:

> Solzhenitsyn believed he had a duty to write for all those who would never be heard – an obligation to the people who did not survive, and because he believed that writers and artists could conquer falsehoods. He thought that literature could succeed in imprinting upon a bigoted, stubborn human creature the distant joy and grief of others.
>
> Another great writer, Günter Grass said, a writer is someone who writes against the currents of time. We too have bad history and must write against the currents of our times. For example, who in Australia wants to read our sad stories when we now have academics writing that the cause of our disadvantage is our own culture and traditions? We have a total colonial history of genocidal acts which spurs on our desperate need to write to give this country a memory. (Wright 2002, 4)

The author's agenda is very clear: to provide her people with an independent perspective on their history and, perhaps most importantly, to force her white Australians to face up to the fact that they are, in a large way, responsible for contemporary Aboriginal disadvantage. *Plains of Promise* succeeds in doing so by subverting the stability of the scene. By exploring the obscene spaces concealed by the façades of the scene the novel subverts the socio-topographic construction that still confounds Australia's identity.

4 The City:
The Crumbling Bulwark

The stereotypical representation of the city as the dichotomized opposite of the bush has been shaped during the entire course of Australian literary history. Lawson and Paterson's exchange in *The Bulletin* discussing whether the bush – as we would say nowadays – was either a utopian or a dystopic space can be seen as a critical moment in this process. At that time, as Australian literature came of age, its internal themes crystallized in a unique form that would later influence the nation's literature. The goal of this chapter is to examine the outcome of this legacy through a selection of contemporary novels. The assumption is that the Australian city has been built as a bulwark of civilization facing an immense frontier, the outback. This chapter will contend that this moral haven has progressively disintegrated and that the lines of demarcation between the two socio-topographically distinguished areas have become blurred. The city succumbed to an internal dilemma. Taking on the role of bulwark of civilization required disowning the negative drives born in society and displacing them into the outback. This established a double estrangement which persists nowadays. The Australian city distanced itself from both the land and its people, thus making it possible for otherness to thrive at its heart.

The best way to understand how this occurred is to trace its origins in the cultural tradition that was imported from the old continent. From the beginning of European colonization the interior of the continent was perceived as "other" and hostile. The vast spaces occupied by the natives could not be considered home. Their otherness was intimidating and thus, for a long time, white Australians lived as if in a state of siege. This unease is best portrayed in David Malouf's *Remembering Babylon* (1993), where the inhabitants of a small settlement of tropical Queensland try to come to terms with their new environment:

> Out here the very ground under their feet was strange. It had never been ploughed. [...] And around, before and behind, worse than weather and the deepest night, natives, tribes of wondering myalls who, in their this way and that all over the map, were forever encroaching on boundaries that could be insisted on by daylight – a good shotgun saw to that – but in the dark hours, when you no longer stood there as a living marker with all the glow of the white man's authority about you, reverted to being a creek-bed or ridge of granite like any other. (Malouf 1993, 9)

This passage points to the sense of deracination involved in the experience of migration and exile; the settlers are bewildered by having to confront a completely un-made landscape. The land has never been tilled, the small clearings opened in the forest might be the first ones since the time of Gondwanaland, and in this hostile environment the natives embody the opposite of Rousseau's noble savage. Malouf, in an interview with Nikos Papastergiadis, clearly explains this sense of unbelonging:

> When those early European settlers came to confront the Australian landscape, it wasn't the hostility of extreme drought and rain that was most frightening to them, rather it was the sense that the landscape reflected nothing back of their own humanity. They would look at it and remain something separate. It had not been shaped by them and they could not see their humanity in it. That in itself is a very frightening thing, to be faced with an entirely unmade landscape when the very notion we have of landscape is of something made. (Papastergiadis 1994, 85)

It is this highly interventionist application of the process of socio-spatialization that has seen western society become a highly urbanized one. According to the geographer Rob Shields, "[socio-spatialization] points to the ongoing social construction of the spatial at the level of the social imaginary (including collective mythologies or presuppositions) and in the form of intervention in the landscape" (Shields 1991, 31). According to this theory, "space" is first created by knowing it

4 The City: The Crumbling Bulwark 191

and naming it. Then, once it has become part of a collective sense of place, it becomes institutionalized as an abstract geographical place.

The first European settlers, finding themselves in a land completely void of both substantial and mytho-poetic signs, actually arrived in a space that appeared to be undefined. This was not the case of the Aborigines who, without altering the land, had constructed a universe immensely rich in topographic referents, all of which were full of meaning. The settlers, blind to this type of socio-topographic construction of space, did not interpret their new environment according to the illuminist ideas proposed by Rousseau in *A Discourse on Inequality* (1754). In the virgin land they did not see a luxurious garden of Eden populated by noble savages, but a threatening wilderness ready to swallow them.

Robert Pogue Harrison, in his book *Forests: The Shadow of Civilization* (1992), gives an account of how the perception of the forest (which in Europe is the archetypal form of untamed nature) has changed and influenced our society from classical times up until the present. The starting point of this analysis is Giambattista Vico's *New Science*, in which humanity originates in the forest. After the flood the descendants of Noah "lost their humanity over the generations and became solitary, nefarious creatures living under the cover of branches and leaves" (Harrison 1992, 3). These creatures, the Giants, were bestial beings who territorially occupied the forests:

> They became bestial "Giants." Abandoned early on by their mothers, they grew up without families or consciousness, feeding on fruits and searching for water. They were shy, brutal, restless, incestuous, and lacked any notion of a higher law than their own instincts and desires. They copulated on sight, aggressively and shamelessly, exercising no restraint whatsoever over their bodily motions, and they roamed the forests incessantly. (Harrison 1992, 4)

The Giants' "bestial freedom" is extremely suggestive in psychoanalytical terms. Their disorderly and incestuous sexual habits are permitted only because the giants grow up in the absence of a father.

Living under the thick foliage of the post-flood forests, they are not only unaware of who their fathers are but also of the existence of the "Law of the Father" – be it either God-given or imposed by the super-ego. The forest, with its thick coverage, provides shelter from the prying eye of the central moral authority. In this private space the human being can become devoid of morality and a pure expression of its unconscious. Vico theorizes the existence of an ob-scene space; a location that the process of socio-spatialization has set apart from the scene with the construction of borders, façades and walls (Lefebvre 1991, 36). These locations, being separated from the prying eyes of society, seem to be granted special freedom.

In this space, the last taboo is also violated: the offspring, abandoned to a state of complete social anarchy, can encounter their parents and have sex with them. In terms of Lacanian psychoanalytical theory, it can be said that, in the forest, the *Nom du Père* is absent. Here, the French equivalents of the English "Law of the Father,"[17] apart from playing with the ambiguity created by the almost homophonous French words *nom* (name) and *non* (no), could also be seen as directly alluding to *the* Name of *the* Father: God almighty. Once the *Nom du Père* has been forgotten, human beings can revert to a state of nature. In this case, to be ob-scene is both a consequence of and a motivation for being off-scene; the obscene only surfaces in off-scene settings.

According to Giambattista Vico, the village and the city developed when the Giants, after hearing the first bolt of lightning and probably caught in the act of copulating, become aware of the existence of the sky:

> And because in such a case the nature of the human mind leads it to attribute its own nature to the effect, and because in that state their nature was that of men all robust bodily strength, who expressed their

---

[17] The literal translation would be the "Name of the Father," but the term has been translated into English with a rendition of the concept underlying the French word-game.

4 The City: The Crumbling Bulwark 193

violent passion by shouting and grumbling, they pictured the sky to themselves as a great animated body, which in that aspect they called Jove, the first god of the so called greater gentes, who meant to tell them something by the hiss of his bolts and clap of his thunder. (Harrison 1992, 4)

Villages thus developed in the clearings of the forests which were later extended to make space for the cities. Humanity, by choosing to live in a space where they could worship god and live abiding to his rules, also submits to a condition of perpetual exposure to the prying eye of the collective moral authority. This condition is reminiscent of Bentham's panoptic prison where the guards, standing in a tower placed at the centre of a circular building, could see the prisoners without being seen. Bentham's prison economized on the costs of guarding by enhancing visibility: anyone at anytime could be watching everyone from the central tower. Foucault, in his seminal text *Discipline and Punish* (1979), explains how visibility comes to be a much more efficient means of control than simple seclusion:

> The panoptic mechanism arranges spatial unities that make it possible to see constantly and to recognize immediately. In short it reverses the principle of the dungeon; or rather of its three functions – to enclose, to deprive of light and to hide – it preserves only the first and eliminates the other two. Full lighting and the eye of a supervisor capture better than darkness, which ultimately protected. Visibility is a trap. (Foucault 1979, 200)

In *Discipline and Punish*, Foucault also gives details of how this principle becomes the main mode of control through which the state disciplines society. Morality and civilization seem therefore to be based on visibility while, as Pogue Harrison suggests, the forest remains a shadowy and haunting presence in the European conscience.

Before accepting this theory, the Arcadian tradition that pervades English literary production, must be also taken into account. In his seminal study *The Country and the City* (1973), Raymond Williams clearly illustrates how the connotations of these areas came to be and how they slowly changed in time. The contrast between country and city crystallizes around the idea that, on one hand, the city is a *centre* for businesses, knowledge and culture but also an oppressive site of anonymity, crowds and confusion. On the other hand, ever since classical times, the countryside can either represent primitiveness or simplicity and ease of life (cf. Williams 1973, 1). It is the recipient of the longing for a past condition that continuously shifts back in time. As a result, this kind of idealized condition never reflects the actual way of life of the peasantry. The Golden Age is always out of reach:

> I remember a sentence in a critically influential book: Leavis and Thompson's *Culture and Environment*, published in 1932. The 'organic community' of 'Old England' had disappeared; 'the change is very recent indeed'. This view was primarily based on the books of George Sturt, which appeared between 1907 and 1923. In *Change in the Village*, published in 1911, Sturt wrote of the rural England 'that is dying out now'. Just back, we can see, over the last hill. (Williams 1973, 9)

Williams goes on enumerating a series of authors and quotations that take us two centuries back in time: "Thomas Hardy's novels, written between 1871 and 1896, and referring back to rural England since the 1830s"; "Richard Jefferies, looking back from the 1870's to the old Hodge," and "George Eliot, in *Mill on the Floss* (1860) and *Felix Holt* (1866), looking back, similarly, to the old rural England of the 1820s and early 1830s" (Williams 1973, 8). But it does not stop here, for Cobbet looks 'to the happier country, the old England of his own boyhood in the 1820s' (Williams 1973, 9). The process is a never ending thread of yearnings that can be followed to the beginning of time; a process that Williams compares to an escalator moving all the way back to the state of lost grace that our civilization seems to innately long for:

> Must we go beyond the Black Death to the beginning of the Game laws, or to the times of Magna Carta [...]? Or shall we find the timeless rhythm in Doomesday, when four men out of five are villains,

bordars, cotters or slaves? Or in a free Saxon world, before what was seen as the Norman rape and yoke? In an Iberian world, before the Celts came, with their gilded barbarism? Where indeed shall we go before the escalator stops? (Williams 1973, 11)

Of course the answer is 'Eden,' but as Williams argues, before we can reach this point, "we must get off the escalator" and consider that "the witnesses we have summoned raise questions of historical fact, [literary fact] and perspective" (Williams 1973, 12). The key to the functioning of this process is its continuously shifting perspective. While lifestyles and landscapes endlessly shape and change each other, Arcadia inevitably slips back in time. The myth of an Arcadian rural England is like a mirage which continuously drifts away.

Arcadia is never a forest, it is a garden. Ideally it would be the Garden of Eden – a place of ultimate harmony between subject and space where "there is an immediate satisfaction of needs, to such an extent that to speak of needs is misleading" (Vernon 1973, 9) – but in substitution of this unattainable state – in a world where "a radical distance has been inserted between man and his environment" (Vernon 1973, 9) – the object of desire becomes what is just "over the last hill." The existence of historical perspective, the possibility of looking back to topographic and mythopoetic points of reference did not only make England one's home, but it also made its countryside a space with which the city could sustain a dialogue involving the growing contradictions and problems of modern society.

Australia, being at the antipodes of the globe and with an apparently bare and void landscape, did not favour this process. On the contrary, the city immediately turned into a fortress poised to defend itself from a non-Arcadian environment. To the first settlers, the untamed Australian nature must have appeared as Vico's ob-scene forest. David Malouf's description of Australia's wild, empty spaces and the early settlers' perceptions of those places, is now even more evocative. The inscrutability of what lies beyond the clearings triggers the process of socio-spatialization connecting wilderness to barbarity and transgression.

Socio-spatialization allocates specific social functions to distinct socio-topographical areas. The city becomes the bulwark of moral society while the outback turns into the recipient of the negative drives produced at the heart of that same society. It becomes a scapegoat. This notion has endured for more then two centuries of European colonization and has helped transform Australia into one of the most urbanized societies in the world.

4.1 The Ubiquitous Closet

After having analyzed the origin of the dichotomization between city and outback, it is possible to appreciate the significance of the schizoid representations of contemporary metropolitan space. Even though this polarization is still predominant in current Australian literature, the city is no longer a clearly marked moral haven. Corruption has seeped into the folds of society, and the urban landscape is read and used in different ways by the numerous minority groups composing multicultural Australia. *Loaded* (1995) by Christos Tsiolkas is a perfect example of this transformation. This acclaimed debut novel plunges the reader in the queer teenage life of a homosexual "wog" – the son of Greek immigrants – who, with his defiant behaviour, tries to escape the limits of his heritage and gender. Over twenty-four hours, the protagonist moves around Melbourne and, while visiting family, friends and going to pubs where he drinks astonishing amounts of alcohol, he consumes drugs and has casual sex with numerous men and women. As he attempts to create an independent identity, his whereabouts reveal Melbourne's shadowy areas of transgression and outline its socioeconomic configuration.

Loaded begins when Ari wakes up at his brother's house in the eastern suburbs. From the beginning his position is clear: he challenges the norm. At breakfast, Ari verbally attacks his brother's girlfriend accusing her of being a stereotypical Anglo-Celtic Australian: "Janet asks […] why I've got an image of Africa on my T-shirt. […] I'm all for racism, I tell Janet, moving slowly towards her, rolling my

4 The City: The Crumbling Bulwark 197

eyes and putting on a mean motherfucker sneer, dropping my voice very low. I think every white deserves getting it in the throat" (Tsiolkas 1995, 4-5). At this moment and in this place – which could be South Yarra or Prahran – Ari declares being a wog, a Greek, and not a white. For him in this case what is important is not skin colour (as one of the flatmates points out he is European and evidently white) but the social meaning of the stand he is taking. His position is almost a Marxist claim; he despises the bourgeois environment, lifestyle and girlfriend that his brother has chosen for himself. The East is rich, while Ari and his brother are wogs and as such they are supposed to belong to the North, where the Mediterranean immigrants settled. Later, these same immigrants moved to the eastern suburbs where they could show off their hard won wealth. Sometime, as in Ari's brother's case, they even repudiated their origin and culture by "marrying" the Anglo-Celtic one. However, it is not in defence of his Greek origin that Ari attacks Janet. On the contrary, he admits, "I say nothing because the conversation is boring. I'm just talking crap to get at her. I read the papers, I see the news, I talk to people; white, black, yellow, pink, they are all fucked" (Tsiolkas 1995, 5). What he is attacking here, is the bourgeois western culture that he sees symbolically represented in Janet.

Ari's strategy is not to belong. He does not only attack Janet, he attacks everyone and everything. Thus, his portrayal of Melbourne is relentlessly caustic:

> [The East,] the whole fucking mass of it. [...] the whitest part of my city, where you will see the authentic white Australian. [...] Television rules. School, work, shopping, sex, are distraction to the central activity of the Eastern suburbs: flicking channels on the remote control. (Tsiolkas 1995, 41, 42)

> [The North,] is where they put most of the wogs. [...] The northern suburbs are unrelentingly flat with ugly little brick boxes where the labouring and unemployed classes roam circular streets; the roads to nowhere. [...] [It] is a growing, pulsating sore on the map of my city,

the part of my city in which I, my family, my friends are meant to buy a house, grow a garden, shop, watch TV and be buried in. (Tsiolkas 1995, 81-82)

[The West,] reveals itself as an industrial quilt of wharfs, factories, warehouses, silos and power plants. And the endless stretch of suburban housing estates. The West is a dumping ground; a sewer of refugees, the migrants, the poor, the insane, the unskilled and the uneducated. (Tsiolkas 1995, 143-144)

Finally, the South is seen as a positive space because it is where the real outcasts end up living and where Ari can imagine, even if only for a moment, a future for himself: "To the South are the wogs who have been shunted out of their communities. Artists and junkies and faggots and whores, the sons and daughters no longer talked about, no longer admitted into the arms of family" (Tsiolkas 1995, 132).

The portrayal of Melbourne is not encouraging; the city is described as a social wasteland where the only hope lies in the marginal space of the South. With his insolent behaviour Ari is resisting the working-class logic that has created the suburban environment that he despises with such vehemence. Joan Kirkby. in her essay "In Pursuit of Oblivion: in Flight from Suburbia," constructs her analysis of *Loaded* around the assumption that "Suburbia is the 'hidden underbelly of modernity,' 'an excrescence, a cancerous fungus'" (Kirkby 1998, 3). Suburbia is therefore an ob-scene sub-product of the modern city. Industrialization created a state of disease that generated a new area of social malaise, a new receptacle for those same drives that were supposed to be confined in the outback. Once again, according to a centre-periphery gradient it is the outskirts of the city, the excrescence, that becomes demonized.

The protagonist of *Loaded* escapes this rough schematization by refusing to recognize and respect the borders established to cage and lobotomize the working class:

4 The City: The Crumbling Bulwark   199

> The worker is alienated from his own labour because it is external to him; it is imposed on him from the outside and 'does not belong to his essential being'. Rather than being confirmed in his work, he is denied. Hence the worker comes to feel that he is himself only when he is not working: 'He is at home when he is not working, and not at home when he is working'. [...] Moreover, Lefebvre argues, the result of alienated labour is that 'man (the worker) feels that he is acting freely only in his animal functions – eating, drinking and procreating while in his human functions he is nothing more than an animal'. While 'eating, drinking and procreating' are also genuine human functions, 'when abstracted from ... other aspects of human activity and turned into final and exclusive ends, they are animal'. (Kirkby 1998, 7)

The protagonist, however, redraws the map of Melbourne by skipping from one side of the city to the other, encroaching on its social boundaries and upsetting its social order by transgressing every possible rule. Mandy Treagus argues that "though Ari is potentially marginalized by both sexuality and ethnicity he refuses the position of 'boundary marker' in favour of dissolving those very boundaries which could render him invisible and/or peripheral" (Treagus 2000, 219). With this attitude he resists interpellation; he is commanded to choose to be either a wog, a bourgeois white Australian, straight, gay or an outcast in the South... he refuses all of this. Ari literally "fucks" it all. He does not have a job and does not want one, he despises his friend Joe who with girlfriend, car and house is preparing himself for a soporific life; he pities his parents for the unhappy life they content themselves with. Yet, he also disapproves of Johnny's open rebuke against the system. His friend, in order to best upset his chauvinist father, impersonates his deceased mother Tula. Ari is not a drag-queen; on the contrary, he gets really upset when Johnny calls him by a female name. He acts macho because most of the men he wants will not go with him unless he is a real man. So, he is a "fag" but also a macho capable of drinking, doing speed, ecstasy, LSD and amyl. He mixes all of this together and abuses society in the same way he abuses his body with an orgy of sensations. Transgression is an addiction as well as a social statement. At a club, when provokingly asked if he is "gay, straight or bi," he readily embraces his friend's mocking definition: "A slut aren't you, Ari" (Tsiolkas 1995, 93). He agrees, it is the most appealing definition, the slut does not belong, the whore goes with anyone and anywhere. Ari refuses to belong because to identify with preconceived ideas means to be caged.

The suburban map is thus subverted as well; the much despised North, the place of his origin and therefore the most dangerous place for a homosexual that has 'not yet come out,' is the place where Ari keeps returning. There he seeks beat sex with the real Greek or Italian machos. The orderly East is in itself a dumping-ground for people boring themselves senseless, working, shopping, going to brothels on the way home and then crashing on a couch in front of the TV. The West is the land of plain disillusion:

> There is no America. There is no New World. [...] There is a last, and very cherished urban myth. That every new generation has it better than the one that came before it. Bullshit. I am surfing on the down-curve of capital [...] There's no jobs, no work, no factories, no wage packet, no half-acre block. There is no more land. I am sliding towards the sewer, I'm not even struggling against the flow. I can smell the pungent aroma of shit but I'm still breathing. (Tsiolkas 1995, 144)

And again, finally, there is the South, where for a split second Ari dreams of a life in a house by the sea, with George. But he messes that up too. Even though he really cares about George, he manages to hurt the only person that seems to accept him the way he is, someone who loves him. In doing so he rejects the ultimate classification, that of the outcast who lives in St Kilda or Elwood to escape the constraint of society. Ari does not even belong to the South.

The question of whether it is Ari's behaviour or the society around him that is obscene remains open. Ari has no doubts: society is at fault.

4 The City: The Crumbling Bulwark 201

> Pol Pot was right to destroy, he was wrong not to work it out that you go all the way. You don't kill one class, one religion, one party. You kill everyone because we are all diseased, there is no way out of this shithole planet. War, disease, murder. AIDS, genocide, holocaust, famine. I can give ten dollars to an appeal if I want to, I can write a letter to the government. But the world is now too fucked up for small solutions. That's why I like the idea of it all ending in a nuclear holocaust. If I had access to the button, I'd push it.
> As we got into Princes Bridge station I was imagining the apocalypse. I was getting so excited it was making my dick hard. (Tsiolkas 1995, 64)

This nihilistic vision is the result of a socio-spatialization that has failed to create socio-topographic spaces in which its inhabitants can fully experience their existence. From this point of view, the strict schematization of landscape is an infinite source of deprivation and at last of seclusion. Ari, who is aware of this and knows he does not belong anywhere, just hops from one area to the other, gorging himself with whatever he can get from each one.

Here, again, Raymond Williams' view of the city is particularly relevant. In *The Country and the City*, the chapter dedicated to London and the other metropolises grown during the industrial revolution, illustrates a situation not at all dissimilar to the one presented by Tsiolkas. In England, with reckless urban migration of the 19th century: "East London became in effect an industrial city [...]. A social division between East End and West End, which had been noted by some observers from early in the century, deepened and became inescapably visible" (Williams 1973, 221). The city, with the staggering class divisions that generated the slums, was depicted as a maze: "Conditions in the East End were being described as 'unknown' and 'unexplored' (that is by those with access to print) in the middle of the century, and by the 1880s and 1890s 'Darkest London' was a conventional epithet" (Williams 1973, 221). In less than a century the urban landscape had changed from Wordsworth's shining London to Conan Doyle's city of "labyrinthine obscurity and lurid fascination" (Williams 1973, 227).

The social fractures in the city fabric create boundaries that reiterate the dichotomization between city and country. Once again, space is constructed in order to contain both people and moral behaviour. The East End and South Melbourne coincide and become spaces of licentiousness, transgression and immorality. Australia's case is, therefore, neither unique nor original. In their struggle, cities strive to remain untainted in order to oppose themselves / exploit the ob-scenity of the outback. Ari's transgression goes beyond such broad definitions of space. His principal offence – homosexuality – belongs to a third space, that of the closet. Hence, it is important to notice that the protagonist's sexual encounters always occur in dark alleys, back streets, smoky and dim lit clubs, public urinals, or even simple rooms away from the crowd. Ari, with his belligerent attitude, manages to create closet spaces in each and every part of the city. This allows him to upturn the social fabric that would otherwise marginalize him to one closeted area.

The romantic image of pre-industrial London and its sudden metamorphosis in the grey metropolis represented in Victorian literature evokes Robert Louis Stevenson's *The Strange Case of Dr. Jekyll and Mr. Hyde* (1886) and its use of space in accordance with social norms. Dr. Jekyll's laboratory is a closet space where transformation and transgression are made possible: there the Doctor becomes the dreadful Mr Hyde. From a queer studies perspective, it is easy to presume that what is hidden in the laboratory and in the apartment in Soho is not just the "other" of the respectable doctor but his queer side. Dr. Jekyll's story ends tragically. In the end, in order to hide his secret (Mr. "Hyde"), he is obliged to kill his own self (Je- "kill") and therefore to commit suicide.

Ari's decision not to belong originates from the need to resist the norms that would otherwise lead him to choose an identity (queer, straight or bi) and marginalize him in an appropriate space. In this instance the closet acquires a different connotation. By being displaced to one place or another, it avoids marginalization and produces interstitial spaces where identity is not imposed through the dichotomizing rules of the heterosexual Dominant Discourse.

Michael P. Brown, in his book *Closet Space*, is interested in proving that the closet should not be seen exclusively as a metaphor but also as a real strategy which, by confining transgression into specific areas, aims at holding people under control through space:

> What would happen, though, if we spatialised the *closet* metaphor? By that I mean using space as a dimension of all social relation by which power/knowledge gets materialised in the world. What would happen if we made explicit the implicit geographic dimensions of the closet metaphor? We would have to acknowledge that the possibility that the closet is not always *just* a rhetorical flourish; that it is a manifestation of heteronormative and homophobic powers in time-space, and moreover that this materiality mediates a power knowledge of oppression. (Brown 2000, 3)

Michael Brown's analysis, being that of a geographer, is particularly valuable in the analysis of *Loaded* because it focuses specifically on the power relations created by the Discourse between society and space. Quoting Savran (Savran 1999), Brown argues that "the normalcy of heterosexuality depends to an extent on the very presence of homosexuality as other. In other words, the centrality of the *room* is premised on the architectural marginality of the *closet*" (Emphasis mine Brown 2000, 8). Ari's behaviour clearly challenges the marginality of the closet. In his peregrination around the city the protagonist actively creates his own closet spaces wherever he happens to be. Undeniably, the closet remains located in the dark sides of the city and it is therefore marginally located. However, its influence stretches far beyond the marginal function imposed by the Discourse. Ari does not renounce the closet because he knows that if he did "come out" he would be immediately spotted and classified as a "fag." What he is resisting is the rigidity of a social structure that would entrap him in the role of the scapegoat used to maintain the purity of mainstream society. If the closet and its marginality are supposed to justify and reinforce the "normalcy of heterosexuality," Ari's attitude subverts this tendency and transforms the closet into a widely dispersed space where identity can be fluidly reinterpreted. The protagonist of *Loaded*, by refusing to be gay, straight, bi, wog, proletarian or bourgeois, refuses to yield to the power that the socio-spatialization of space exerts on society. The closet is thus transformed from a space of seclusion to one of emancipation. Ari's interpretation suggests that, in the modern city, the closet can be displaced into the innumerable folds left in the urban fabric. In this case, the city of "labyrinthine obscurity and lurid fascination" originates a revolt against the confinement of transgression and in favour of the liberation of space from the socio-topographic construction imposed by the Discourse.

4.2 The Vanishing of the Scene

In a different setting and in a very different style, Peter Robb explores almost the same obscene spaces. In *Pig's Blood and Other Fluids* – which is a collection of three novellas – the author provocatively challenges Australia's chaste image. The postmodern/pulp portrayal of Sydney given in "Pig's Blood" and "No Sweat" mercilessly, but also nonchalantly, presents the drawbacks of modern society.

In "Pig's Blood" the exploration of this space begins with the flight of Pasquale Giannone from the scene of a vicious crime. In an unfinished villa near Naples, in Italy, he and two other gangsters are torturing a traitor to death:

> What about the fuckn information? What about the fuckn money? Pasquale thought again. A terrible anxiety came over him. He was part of this. The dumb cunts. The fuckn dumb cunts. What are they here for? The whole thing was now quite pointless. Pasquale had been through it all before. These guys might be his oldest and his dearest friends but without Don Mimì's guidance they were total fuckwits. Pino included. Especially Pino. Look at him now.
> Umberto had opened the zip of his dove grey designer strides and pulled out his hardening cock. He slowly stroked his prick and stared at Pino with moony lover's eyes. A smell of jasmine floated in on the

night air mingled with the ammoniac smells of sweat and urine and the acid smells of vomit and the fecal stench of Pino's drying shit. Umberto swayed slowly as he stroked. A slight crust had formed at the edges of his open mouth. Pino stared back at him over the sock in his own mouth until Enzo slipped on the wire and sharply twisted it and Pino's eyes went glassy. Umberto started pulling faster. (Robb 1999, 5-6)

That night, while Pino is so brutally and viciously executed, Pasquale decides to leave this obscene life forever and runs off to Australia taking with him only his mother and the recently acquired bag full of money.

After conducting a quiet life in Sydney for twenty-two years, Pasquale's Italian restaurant becomes renowned and because of a review in a newspaper, word of Pasquale's whereabouts reaches Naples and his old boss. Don Mimì gives Salvatore, who was born in Australia, but raised in Naples, the honour of settling the Pasquale Giannone account. Here the reader's first impression would be that Australia is threatened by Pasquale's past; Italy seems to be a looming presence about to contaminate Australia. Sal's arrival proves this assumption to be wrong. Australia is not an untainted space and during his brief stay the young and inexperienced killer will discover many facets of the country he visits.

Fayette and her story are the most explicit and direct example of the almost ordinary, but extremely acute malaise in society. Sal meets her by the trailer park of a military camp. He has just stolen a Porsche and he is testing his gun when she and her brother appear from nowhere and start chatting to him:

– Shot, said a thin and expressionless little voice behind him.
– Quite good anyhow, said another. Two outta three.
Sal swung round gaping. A small boy was squinting at him under the faded red of a reversed baseball cap. His tee shirt was too tight for him and his baggy shorts too baggy. The crotch was at his knees. The kid seemed to have no colour in his hair or eyes or skin at all. He was practically transparent. Next to him was a taller girl in cutoff jeans and

a halter top. She seemed to be in the earlier phase of post pubescence [...]. She was showing a lot of pale and coltish leg. Pale in an interesting way. (Robb 1999, 26)

As if there was nothing strange about it, the boy leaves his sister by a dead end road in the company of an armed man. Here, at the far end of civilization, normalcy has shifted its meaning. So, while the kid goes searching for dead bodies by the river, Fayette starts bartering for a ride on the Porsche which she obtains in exchange for sex.

This first glance at Australian suburbia proposes a very dreary picture: the two neglected and almost transparent kids, the military camp and the trailer, and the father who, being away training with the Black Hawks, is immediately substituted by a lover, are all elements blending into a scene where anonymity is the only façade covering up the obscenity of this condition. Coming from this state of affairs, Fayette's perspective in life is particularly down to earth: while the teenagers around her are obsessed with sex and drugs – which we could take as a normal condition – for her sex is a common thing and she uses it as a way out of her boredom.

> Fayette was slim and lithe and agile and eager and a lot more experienced than he had been expecting. After a while Sal decided he wanted to flip her over and have her that way too. He was ready for resistance and excited enough to be prepared to force matters a little if necessary but to his surprise Fayette eagerly complied and it was no big deal at all. She said everyone did that in army families. She's been used to it from an early age. Then they had a shower and some more cola and Fayette demanded that Sal came good on his promise of a ride in the Porsche. (Robb 1999, 27)

Peter Robb's biting style is not simply a conformation to the pulp literary genre; his fiction is the uncompromising depiction of a deeply corrupted society that somehow manages to still retain its vitality. The novella is thus imbued with a dark humour. It is the system that is diseased and, while Tsiolkas portrays the decay of urban society through Ari's aggressive revilement, Robb dispassionately describes that same reality through the actions and the life stories of his characters. As a result, the social comment is both subtle, being conveyed through the grim and comical effects of the story, and overwhelming, because of the overall sense of social degradation. The most distinctive characteristic of Peter Robb's world is the haziness of the moral boundaries of this new environment. The situation is best explained when considering Henry Lefebvre's definition of scene:

> enclosures and façades serve to define both a scene (where something takes place) and an obscene area to which everything that cannot or may not happen on the scene is relegated: whatever is inadmissible, be it malefic or forbidden, thus has its own hidden space on the near or the far side of a frontier. (Lefebvre 1991, 36)

What becomes prominently evident in the story is the way society has developed a new level of tolerance. This has induced a retrocession of the "scene" in favour of an almost whole-encompassing obscene area. The frontiers and the borders delimiting obscene spaces have changed into more flexible types of façades: indifference and habit have become blindfolds that replace the façades and reorganize ob-scene spaces according to individual perceptions.

As Sal wanders around the city, Sydney's ubiquitous levels of degradation become more evident. The sites of this permissiveness are varied: Fayette's house in the military camp and her story, the five star hotel where the "suits wait for the girls booked on the internet (Robb 1999, 60), the pizzeria trattoria Sciuè Sciuè in Leichardt where Giannone lures his women customers into sexual encounters in the private function annexe or in the nearby darkened parking lot (Robb 1999, 34) and finally the Blue Mountains where the actual murders take place. It is, however, the ordinariness of these places that successfully conceals their dark sides. In the society portrayed by Peter Robb, the displacement of immorality in a precisely confined and possibly unreachable space is neither plausible nor desirable. The city and its periphery alike have spawned an infinite number of all too evident closets that for their privacy rely solely on the indifference of the community. Hence, to seclude, to hide and to closet the forbidden is not necessary any more, the scene has become the stage of a new ostentatious social order where off-scene spaces are not needed: the scene has become obscene in itself. Jean Baudrillard, in *The Fatal Strategies*, defines the "obscene" in society comparing it to the obese bodies of its citizens:

> [The obese people] claim a sort of truth, and in fact they do display something of the systems, of its empty inflation. They are its nihilist expression, that of the general incoherence of signs, morphologies, forms of alimentation and of the city – hypertrophied cellular tissue, proliferating in all directions. (Baudrillard 1990, 26)

Here, the obese body stands for the entire social structure that, driven by consumerist frenzy, has rapidly transformed what once was the "scene" – or the lean body – into an amorphous and cancerous mass that, driven exclusively by the logic of production, thrives on its own disorderly growth. One of the major consequences of the incoherent growth of the system is the loss of the coordinates ruling the construction of social space. In this kind of society, where everything is fabricated and put on display, signs as well become the empty inflation of their own referents and meaning tends to disappear. A new space is thus born where façades lose their function as niches and closets are loosened from their constraints of socio-topographic control, and they fade in the general confusion. As a result, deviance becomes indistinguishable: enmeshed in the superfluous growth of an "obese" society, the borders between moral and immoral become blurred:

> It is therefore not the obesity of a few individuals that is at stake, but that of a whole system, the obscenity of a whole culture. It is when the body loses its rule and its stage or scene that it reaches this form of obscene obesity. It is when the social body loses its law, its scene and its stakes that it also reaches the pure and obscene form we know it to be. Its invisible and too visible form, its ostentation, the investment and overinvestment of all spaces by the social – the spectral and

4 The City: The Crumbling Bulwark 209

transparent character of the whole remaining unchanged. (Baudrillard 1990, 27)

Reflecting this state of affairs, in *Pig's Blood* hyper-visibility has become a new form of disguise. Sal wears expensive clothes and steals a Porsche, Sal's informer drives a black Ferrari Testarossa and the Mexican killers wear tailor made suits. It is the conspicuousness of these custom-made façades of respectability that grants them a new form of impunity. With it, as if made invisible, they are free to act and move as they please. In this new ostentatious/obese/obscene setting, being noticeable has become the best way to go unseen. It is for this reason that Sal is able to take a barely-dressed teenager to his five star hotel room. The reception staff presume they are movie stars. In a similar way, as the different threads of the story start intertwining, the Mexican killers, who, just like Sal, are on their way to the Blue Mountains, go perfectly unnoticed as they murder Fayette's belligerent stepfather. Just as Sal is about to meet Damion, who desperately wants his "stepdaughter" back, the two Mexican men stop at the concrete horse beer-garden and run into him before Sal does. Damion, exasperated by the long wait at Fayette's favourite pub, picks a fight with the odd-looking couple who, in broken English, insistently asks for directions. In a matter of seconds he is on the floor with his belly slashed open. As this happens in the midst of a crowd, the killing goes momentarily unnoticed and the smartly dressed Hispanic men are able to quietly trail off. In Peter Robb's world, crowds and indifferent behaviour are the keys to attaining invisibility. On the other hand Damion's story proves society's hypocritical blindness to its own malaise. Damion met Fayette's mother at a beer-garden and very quickly he settled into the house as a lover and stepfather. There his life consisted in drinking his days away, being fed by his partner and having sex with both mother and daughter. The most startling thing about this situation is that nobody, either in the neighbourhood or in the family itself, notices there being anything wrong. The scene has vanished from suburbia as well: the all too well known problem of marginalization has been assimilated and rapidly forgotten. In this state of affairs, social debasement disappears behind its own self-evidence, and those living in these conditions become invisible and are soon forgotten.

The resulting ubiquity of the closet, in its new gigantic and all-encompassing form, does not however make Sydney an amorphous mass. Leichardt is the Italian suburb where immigrants grew out of their misery. The outer suburbs with the military camp and the trailer parks are the margin of the Australian civilization (Fayette's family significantly lives on a dead end road) and the huge beer gardens on the edge of town stand for a fictitious and legendary freedom:

> The Concrete horse was fuckn huge and it stood for freedom. And the drinking area was fuckn huge too. Lodda truckies, lodda sports fans, lodda local people, all the livelier elements of Sydney's outer west. [...] [Fayette] liked the concrete horse, she liked the size of the place. She liked the fact that it was so big and so far out that nobody started pissing her off about being underage. (Robb 1999, 71-72)

This is how in the everyday perception of reality the old centre/periphery dichotomy remains unchallenged. Freedom, represented in this case by the enormous pub, lies at the outskirts of civilization where there is a loosening of the moral constrictions imposed on society. Yet, this is an illusion, just another tale used to create the impression that a moral order still exists. There is no uncontaminated centre capable of opposing itself to the corrupt periphery and, vice versa, there is no creative periphery opposing the reactionary centre. The reality is that a general stagnation has overcome each and every quarter of this city and that even the periphery has lost its transgressive uniqueness. The Blue Mountains, which are described in gothic terms, are nothing of the sort. They are a perfect example of this homogenization. The rumour goes that in the mountains the hotel family owners "had been quietly inbreeding for generations in the rooms that lined up [the] endless corridors [...]. Ugly things had sometimes been discovered" (Robb 1999, 36). In Sydney it is also said that couples disappeared without leaving a trace: "They wanted to do some bushwalk-

4 The City: The Crumbling Bulwark   211

ing. [...] Never came back. They found some remains not far from the hotel last year. Nothing identifiable though" (Robb 1999, 36-37). The reality, however, is very different: "As Sal was expecting, more and more strongly the further they got, the Blue Mountains turned out not to be mountains at all. No snow. No distant peaks. They'd driven up to a plateau and straight into some kind of suburb or town. The air was slightly cooler" (Robb 1999, 83). Sal's foreign perspective discloses the truth; the Blue Mountains are yet another suburb generated by the endless sprawl of the city.

The gothic mode would suggest real mountains, a gloomy atmosphere and sinister presences. On the contrary, what will provide Sal and the Mexican killers the perfect setting for their murderous feats is the big crowd that arrives from the city to attend the televised gourmet Sunday lunch prepared by Pasquale Giannone, the Italian celebrity chef. In this setting Salvatore feels under control: "He'd located his quarry. Checked ID. Reconnoitred the location. Location was perfect. Sprawling, confused, management swamped by the big city crowd. Nobody seemed quite sure who anybody was, and that was how Sal liked it" (Robb 1999, 99). In this obscene type of confusion – obscene because, having the "scene" disappeared, the entire social space has become off-scene – a new type of anonymity is granted. In this space "the odd sugar daddy" feels confident enough to try his luck with Fayette while she is playing videogames in the hall (Robb 1999, 99). In that same hall Mr Torquemada, a Mexican businessman who recently purchased the hotel, is forced at knifepoint to follow his killers to the laundry. There, only metres away from the crowds, he is slaughtered, cut into pieces and packed in a suitcase. Thus, the Mexican hit men simply wheel the body through the hall. Nobody notices anything and later, when Pasquale's mother discovers a washing basin full of blood. Pasquale only rejoices at the idea of having found the main ingredient of his favourite Neapolitan dessert: sanguinaccio, pig's blood cooked with chocolate.

Sal too is favoured by confusion generated by the crowd: as the guests get ready for the Asian dinner, nobody notices when he slips out on the terrace and fires two shots in a man's head. The murder is perfect, the man, who leaning over the parapet, falls off the cliff and disappears in the darkness. Sal, satisfied with his effort, returns to his table and thoroughly enjoys his dinner. Unfortunately, the man he kills is the wrong one. In the darkness he mistakes one of the Mexican killers, busy disposing of the luggage containing Mr Torquemada, for Pasquale Giannone, who slips away from the terrace. A mistake caused by simple coincidence: the Mexican hit man and the Italian chef were wearing the same type of suit. Sadly for Sal this will be a fatal oversight. In a final twist to the story, Sal is shot dead in the cab taking him to the airport. The cab driver is his informer, another hired killer who was checking on him to make sure he completed his job. All we know about this unidentified character is that, again, he chose a very striking car – the black Ferrari Testarossa – and that, with the conventional ostentation, he fools everybody. Even Giannone is deceived. After witnessing what was supposed to be his homicide in the Blue Mountains and fleeing to Sydney, he meets his death in the parking lot near his restaurant:

> On a summer Sunday morning the car park was almost empty. As Pasquale sat there tuning the stereo a black Ferrari testarossa slithered into the space from Norton Street. Beautiful Car. Turned People's heads. That was the problem. People noticed you. [...] A young guy had got out of the Ferrari and was walking over to him. Pasquale had never seen him before. He wondered what the guy wanted. He came up to the driver's window.
> – Baz Giannone? The young guy asked. The celebrity Chef? [...]
> – Yeah, Pasquale said. That's me.
> The young guy pulled a Beretta from under his shirt, held it up carefully in both hands, spread his feet well apart on the ground and shot Pasquale in the eye. When Pasquale slumped sideways across the passenger seat, the boy leaned in and fired twice more, hitting Pasquale in the temple and the neck. [...]
> The boy turned around and walked back to the Ferrari. (Robb 1999, 107-108)

4 The City: The Crumbling Bulwark   213

In a world where the scene has disappeared under the pressure of an exaggerated emphasis on appearance, Pasquale's assumption is wrong: the black Ferrari, precisely because it is so obviously noticeable, is the perfect way to go unnoticed.

Big crowds, the broad day of light and indifference, have thus become the new sites of transgression. As hypothesized by Jean Baudrillard and demonstrated by Peter Robb, nowadays obscenity does not necessarily reside in off-scene scenarios and, as a consequence, a new type of obscenity comes into being: what is obscene is the way our culture has become anesthetized and indifferent to the exposure of its own truths. Although in different ways, Baudrillard's and Robb's writings try to evidence this new alarming situation:

> Everything obscene is a matter of surface. But there are no more secrets beneath these superficies. What was kept secret, or even what didn't exist found itself expelled forcibly in to the real, represented beyond all necessity and all resemblance. Forcing of representation. As with porn: an orgasm in colour and close up is neither necessary nor convincing – it is merely implacable true, even if it is the truth of nothing at all. It is only abjectly visible, even if it represents nothing at all.
>
> For something to be meaningful, there has to be a scene, and for there to be a scene, there has to be an illusion, a minimum of illusion, of imaginary movement, of defiance to the real, which carries you off, seduces or revolts you. Without this properly aesthetic dimension, mythical, ludic, there is not even a political scene where something can happen. (Baudrillard 1990, 65)

Baudrillard argues that our society has reached the stage where reality – due to the media, to the reproducibility of images, to the immense capacities of production and to the abuse of these means – has become an inert and transparent surface where everything is visible – and put on display – but nothing can be dreamed of. Morality, ideals, fantasy, and all that an individual experiences in an abstract and subjective way, have succumbed under the weight of the printed, broadcast, displayed and blatantly celebrated reality produced by the system. Considering this new state of affairs it could be possible to mistake "Pig's Blood" for one of the countless idle manifestations of the Discourse. The novel, however, is neither simply pornographic, nor mere surface. The clever depiction of its obscene world is not simple conformation and, therefore, capitulation; on the contrary, it is an in-depth analysis of the new bi-dimensional and transparent surface that society has become. With his dry irony, which could be mistaken for cynicism, Peter Robb tries to prove the disappearance of the scene. The homogenous abasement of all the areas traversed by Sal in his journey – from the city centre to the forests of the Blue Mountains – should seduce or disgust the reader, thus raising in him/her the awareness of the otherwise vanishing scene. Irony is Peter Robb's last weapon. As Sal's victim falls off the cliff and is swollen by the darkness of the forest, the old dichotomy pure centre vs. corrupt periphery is only momentarily reinstated. As the reader laughs about Sal's mistake, this ultimate off-scene setting is revealed to be an illusory one. Laughter, preventing the passive identification of the reader with the characters, stimulates the critical analysis of the events. The terrace, although maybe representing the furthest reach of civilization, is not in any way more obscene than the city centre or its periphery. On the contrary, the unconcealed corruption at the heart of society is far more sickening. "Pig's Blood" faithfully portrays this new condition.

4.3 From the Periphery to the Centre

In her novel *Steam Pigs*, Melissa Lucashenko depicts the dynamics of suburban disadvantage in a substantially similar way to that of Christos Tsiolkas. Then again, she offers a very different reading of the potentials for subversion. In this novel the protagonist is a young Aboriginal girl who successfully escapes, first, from a provincial existence in the far north of Queensland which would have condemned her to bearing many children and living on the dole; and, secondly, from a "self-arranged" den of domestic violence in suburban Brisbane. Her point of arrival is the city (the river and the bridge mark the border between these worlds) and university where she eventually finds a way out of the spiral of self-denigration induced by white Australian society.

Sue's liberating journey follows a highly significant trajectory, she moves from the periphery (Townsville, a small and racist city) to the CBD, or central business district, of Brisbane. The opposition between untainted centre versus corrupted periphery is initially reinstated in this socio-topographic arrangement. Nonetheless, the heroine's marginal identity shifts this perspective and demonstrates that the centre itself produces the unsatisfactory social configuration afflicting Australian society. Sue's growing awareness of her Aboriginality allows her to vindicate a space of her own not only as a woman fleeing domestic violence, but also as a native rediscovering her past and therefore the space she should occupy in white Australia. In her case moving to the inner city does not mean succumbing to the bourgeois logic that Ari much despises, it means to challenge it by seeking empowerment.

The heroine of the novel is only 17 when she moves from Townsville to her brother's house in Eagleby, one of the outer suburbs of the capital of Queensland. She is forced to take this step because after having interrupted an unwanted pregnancy, the pressure from her community becomes too much to be borne:

> The same aunts who drank every day till they were pissdrunk and chainsmoked endlessly trying to lose their own babies had turned on Sue with a vengeance for taking the clean way out. Babykiller she'd been called, and worse, till she had to flee to Dave's for refuge from the strain of fighting back. (Lucashenko 1997, 116)

Sue is confident in her decision: thanks to it she has managed to get her high-school diploma and possibly to secure a future for herself. From her point of view work is liberation, economic independence and the only way to fulfilment. When she arrives in Eagleby, finds a job in a pub, buys a second hand car and finds a boyfriend who studies at university she thinks she has it all. She thinks she has already escaped the vicious circle that made "every second Murri girl [drop] out of school, stomach bulging at fourteen or fifteen, ready for a life of welfare" (Lucashenko 1997, 116). But when with pride she thinks of the way she escaped all that, she is still tricked into self-denigration:

> Mothers at sixteen, grandmothers at thirty, thirty-five tops. Buncha bloody bludgers, she thinks, I don't care what Rachel says about underprivileged! There was something in what she said about racism, and lack of jobs, but still they're a lazy useless bunch ... look at me, eh, I didn't let it stop me ... (Lucashenko 1997, 116)

Here the Dominant Discourse is talking through and for her. Although Kerry, a social worker, and her friend Rachel gave her the political awareness that will eventually lead her to real self-respect, she still fails to recognize that she is still entrapped. As Lefebvre suggests, she is caged by her working class origin. However, she is also discriminated as an Aboriginal and as a woman. Melissa Lucashenko exhaustively describes this condition in her paper "Many Prisons":

> Many Aboriginal women, receiving the double inheritance of racism and sexism in their lives, believe themselves to be ugly, bad, poor, and stupid. Many Aboriginal women have lost hope. Many Aboriginal women have found short term comfort and longterm pain from alcohol, drugs, abusive partners, or other addictions. Many Aboriginal women have absorbed the materialism of the coloniser, believing that possessions will change their lives. These Aboriginal women live in a Prison of Disempowerment which they have built out of the lies of colonisation. (Lucashenko 2002, 143)

Sue has already won a battle, she has given herself a better chance and is working to make it pay. The job, the car, the flat she rents with her boyfriend, they are all steps out of a social state to which she was predestined. However, these consumerist achievements are not sufficient to liberate her from the "Prison of Disempowerment" holding her the captive of a white perspective on the world. Her liberation can only be effective after she understands these mechanisms.

After all, Eagleby is quite similar to Townsville: not as overtly racist but substantially as socially dysfunctional. Sue's brother Dave has been abandoned with two kids by his girlfriend and Roger, her boyfriend, lives with his cousin who has 4 kids, no husband and a pregnant daughter who will soon make her a grandmother. The social life of the suburb is centred on cars, meeting friends at the pub and getting in fights when drunk. Sue quickly finds out that the suburb is yet another space of alienation and that her charming prince with the shiny ute[18] turns out to be just another woman-basher. Roger and Sue meet at the gym where they practice karate. Here, martial arts are used as a survival technique rather then in self-defence. Violence dominates the scene around Sue, fights are a common sight at the pub where she works. Roger decides to take a job as a bouncer if only to prove his own virility, women get bashed all around her and, finally, she gets bashed by Roger. Martial arts are just another attempt to reach empowerment in the terms imposed by the Dominant Discourse: brute force and physical confrontation. Sue, on this ground, is doomed to succumb.

It is the encounter with a social worker specializing in domestic violence that slowly opens her mind to the way out of this disempowerment. Kerry is an emblematic figure, her attitude, her motorbike, her house are all symbols of an emancipation that Sue experiences with her for the first time. "[T]he whole place with its wrap around verandas has an inviting feel to it that the local brick boxes can never attain, never mind how many Eagleby lounges – vinyl car bench seats – are splayed in the front yard. Kerry's red Evolution 1200 stands majestically in the dirt drive" (Lucashenko 1997, 67). Sue takes it all with a sense of awe and surprise. She has just been shown an entirely different universe. The shock is not produced by what she materially observes, but rather by its function. The verandas around the house stand

---

[18] A ute is a small pick-up truck with a very low profile that makes it look like a sport car. Short for utility truck.

for an open space, a shelter where women are always welcome. Verandas are an interstitial space between a misogynist world and the refuge Kerry has created. However, the house is not open to everybody. Not to men. Kerry's Harley Davidson is another clear statement of gender-role subversion. Riding a symbol of masculinity is a way to dismantle the binary opposition confining women in a defenceless state. Appropriating the symbol of power (and a bike is a symbol of phallic power because you ride it) is a way to take that power away from men's exclusive control. The acceptance of this gynaeceum is gradual; as Sue becomes aware of Kerry's homosexuality and of her living with her girlfriend she cannot stop herself from looking at her as a weirdo, surely not as a role-model. However, this perception changes as she is revealed a world ruled by blindfolding sexual politics.

The protagonist's path thus traverses different regions, areas, houses and districts; it is a journey of liberation that culminates with her arrival into the city. However, before reaching this stage, she has to go through her brother's house, Roger's cousin's house and her own flat in Eagleby. If this last accommodation was meant to be a real home, a nest for her love but also a space that she wants to be her own, she soon discovers that cohabiting with her boyfriend she has no space at all. There, she feels imprisoned by the anonymity of the suburb, by the walls of the apartment that seem to be closing in around her, and by her culturally-induced lack of self-respect. Kerry's role is that of deconstructing this virtual prison in the minds of women and to help them find a way out of domestic violence. Lucashenko, in an article written with Odette Best, specifically addresses this problem:

> The first step has already begun. Murri women have started to name the violence for what it is – not a trivial side-effect of alcohol abuse, not the legitimate response of powerless Black men to oppression, but as the cowardly, brutal bashings of physically weaker women by Aboriginal men who could choose not to abuse their Aboriginal families. So long as the violence is tolerated with the ideas that we should blame the grog, or the white society, or the women (!) for their behav-

iour, or any other of the many excuses, the violence will continue. (Lucashenko and Best 1995, 21)

What Sue needs to realize before leaving Roger is that she is not responsible for the beatings she is receiving and that there is no justification for it. As Kerry points out "It's a cycle [...]. He bashes her, and they make up, it's all like honeymoon again, and then a few days or weeks down the track the tension starts to build up" (68). After a final and very serious bashing Sue leaves her house and finds shelter at Kerry's place. In this space, by preventing Rog from stepping onto the veranda, she discovers that she can be in control and, more importantly, that men are not omnipotent. Talking to Kerry she says: "I know you do not want men in the house so I made him stand on the front yard, I had the dogs on the verandah with me" (Lucashenko 1997, 208). By enforcing a rule that Kerry has set to protect her women guests, she realizes that it is possible to create a space of one's own.

The following step leads Sue to West End, a suburb in the inner city of Brisbane. The Big Smoke as Sue calls it, was till then just a symbol of consumerism, the place where she went shopping on important occasions but also an unreachable destination. Her perspective finally changes thanks to a short story she reads in a book that belongs to her flatmate. At this point she becomes fully aware of her and the city's Aboriginality: "You can afford to look in vain for Brisbane, for what you can find? The blood on your great-grandfather's hands, perhaps? The bones under the kitchen, the Bora in the Backyard?" (Lucashenko 1997, 233). This vindication helps Sue find a sense of belonging in a city that would have otherwise remained an alienating space. Thus, as Margaret Henderson argues in her paper "Subdivisions of Suburbia," "[w]hile Sue's escape to 'bohemian' inner-city West End may resemble a classic bourgeois trajectory of self-improvement, [...] what she occupies is not only the white feminists' or yuppies' Brisbane, but Yuggera country" (Henderson, 78). The blood-stains and the bones in the backyard haunting the city become empowering symbols for her and her people. The centre, deprived of its alleged purity, loses control on the socio-topographic organization based on it. From this subverted standpoint Sue's "reclamation of an Aboriginal space and memory is an unsettling marker and reminder of those left out of white master-narratives of progress or liberation" (Henderson, 78).

4.4 Ostracized From Society

The protagonist of *Steam Pigs* successfully challenges white Australian Discourse and surpasses all the niches of confinement set on her way as traps hampering her progress towards self-determination. At the end of the novel Sue is a university student with a future open in front of her but, most importantly, with a place of her choice in the community. Different is the story of other Aboriginal people in Australia and particularly interesting is that of Doug, the protagonist of Archie Weller's *The Day of the Dog* (1981). This novel, set in the 1970s, is the story of a young Noongar from Perth who, after having spent eighteen months in prison, returns to his friends and relations to find the same sense of alienation that led him to despair and subsequently to jail. Again the organization of urban space is central to the text, however, due to a different point of view, its arrangement is mostly hazy and almost diametrically opposite to that of Melissa Lucashenko's novel.

Doug's first impression of the CBD of Perth is highly significant:

> It's a Tuesday night, too, so the streets are almost empty and only the towering buildings seem alive with their flashing, blinking lights. And when he came out, he had intended to walk these streets proudly, to get a job and show all the unbelievers what he really could be. Perth has changed. For a moment he is afraid and huddles in a corner along with the spiders and old butts and other unwanted things. (Weller 1981, 4)

4 The City: The Crumbling Bulwark

In this spectral vision of the city the majestic buildings of the CBD only reflect Doug's feeling of failure. The skyscrapers are cold and unfeeling, the empty streets resemble highways and the passers-by are indifferent, sometimes scared. The environment is totally indifferent to the Aboriginal youths who roam the streets and find refuge in its dark corners, in the side streets and in the few bars that tolerate them. They are riotous, violent and particularly loud; drunk most of the time. Clearly the indifference of the city, its coldness and emptiness are signs of the ob-scenity of this space. Like cigarette butts they are discarded by society and prevented from integrating. For the Aboriginal kids the city is almost no-place, an off-scene setting where they wander during idle hours, shoplift and commit other petty crimes.

By contrast, the degraded suburbs become equivocal homely environments. Their squalid apartments become cosy shelters where Doug finds repair from the sense of alienation felt in the centre. However, it is this social segregation that primarily contributes to the despair afflicting the protagonist. Even though in one of these houses he finds love and in his mother's house he finds nourishment and good advice, he still feels trapped in a self-reproducing mechanism of degradation. Doug does not find the means to counter this state of affairs and he soon resumes the position assigned to him by the Dominant Discourse. He lives in the suburbs during the day, and at night he walks the streets of a city which dies at night and that is only patrolled by Aborigines on foot, cars passing by and the police bullying the young natives. The violence used by the police against the kids (because they are little more than kids) is astonishing and it only causes further grief and anger. This violence is in fact possible only because of the overall indifference – or silent connivance, we could say – of society.

The Perth described by Archie Weller is extremely different from Tsiolkas' Melbourne or Lucashenko's Brisbane. This difference can be accounted for if we consider the difference of setting in time. *Loaded* and *Steam Pigs* are set in contemporary times while *The Day of the Dog* is set in the 1970s. In spite of this, Doug's problems are not at all different, however, the solutions available to him are not the same as the ones proposed in the other novels. The society he confronts is a different one, and different will be his path and end in it. In an interview given to Annie Greet in 1994, Weller accounts for this difference:

> I wrote *Day of the Dog* when I was 23 years old. I had just come out of jail for three months and was probably a bit bitter in my way of thinking. No I wasn't bitter – I was sad [...]. It bothered me immensely that this man who is probably as old as I was, 23 or 24 years old, is telling me what to do and where to go and how to get home and he was beating the daylights out of me. (Greet 1995, 145, 146)

What Weller is talking about here (and therefore in the book) is the type of society that created the ground for the events investigated during the 90s by the Royal Commission into Aboriginal Deaths in Custody. At that time in Perth there was a struggle for the control of the streets of the centre; the police was trying to move the Aborigines away: "Aboriginal people are social people who meet everywhere, they must come into town on the train, to certain areas of Perth that were our areas of town, in fact nearly half of Perth was our part of town, in the old days" (Greet 1995, 145, 146).

Doug Dooligan, who is an intelligent and very sensitive boy, finds it hard to cope with the pressure that white society puts on him. Penny Van Torn, in her article "The Terrors of Terra Nullius: Gothicising and De-Gothicising Aboriginality," analyses this procedure in detail and she argues that "[b]y the process of projection, Australian frontier gothic conscripts Aboriginal people into the role of white society's 'darker self.' The Aborigine is made to stand for all that lies outside, or stands against, or is suppressed within the civilized world" (Van Toorn 1992, 87-87). Understandably, this process remained proficient as long as the socio-topographic splitting remained clear-cut but, with the blurring of the borders between these fabricated collective self and unconscious, society becomes a disquieting territory of confrontation.

At times, as Penny Van Toorn points out, the novel almost risks reproducing the gothic trope afflicting Aboriginal people. Yet, the at-

4 The City: The Crumbling Bulwark

tention to the socio-psychological dynamics working on and around Doug deconstructs the essentialist vision depicting Aborigines as a violent bunch. As Van Toorn declares: "Aboriginal or part Aboriginal people have no monopoly on irrational violence" (Van Toorn 1992, 92). White kids and the police, and in particular the special squad "boys from brazil" taking care of the natives, take a prominent role in the dynamics of this violence:

> Headlights lance across the near-deserted car park and jab into the boys' startled faces. [...] No one is around to see what happens [...]. 'Where's the rest of the money you stole, you black bastard?' 'I never stole nothin',' says Doug. He is punched in the stomach [...] so he stumbles and nearly vomits. He screams to the moon and the clouds and the city buildings watching impassively. [...] 'I don't like you, Doug,' the driver whispers. 'I'm going to take you down to the Central and make you eat shit, you understand?' (Weller 1981, 86)

It is this sort of brutalization and the acute stress put on him by society that ignites Doug's tempers; at moments he loses control and becomes irrationally violent. He is scared of these states – being aware of what he might do, he tries to stay away from danger zones. Yet it is difficult to do so when one has no place in society.

The Epilogue of this novel is tragic. After having been involved, all in the name of friendship, in a robbery with real guns, Doug and the other kids all die in an accident during a car chase. After being released from prison, Doug simply spiralled down a path which inevitably condemned him to this sort of bitter end. He did what society asked him to do and he did not find an escape route. Even the bush, which for him should be a safe space, one that belongs to him through his culture, does not heal his wounds and actually becomes a new space of alienation. If for a brief period the protagonist spends a quiet time with his sister in-law in the country, he soon runs in trouble with his brother in law for borrowing the car without asking and staying away all night. He thus moves with his friends who are working on a farm clearing the bush. Once again subjugated by the logics of the

Dominant Discourse, Doug proceeds to the desecration of his own ancestral land:

> Amidst the tortured screams of the dying trees, the chainsaw's teeth bite into their virgin bodies, and the rumbling of the old faded red dozer smashing into trees, knocking them senseless, and pushing them into broken pile, their raw yellow roots jagging obscenely into the air, and the thudding of the cruel axe – amidst all this Doug no longer needs the friendship of the bush. (Weller 1981, 151)

The Day of the Dog deals with the suffocating malaise leading too many kids towards paths of self-destruction. It is interesting to contrast this trajectory to the opposite one followed by the heroine of *Steam Pigs*; Sue takes a centripetal path that leads her to conquer the centre of white civilization while Dough follows a centrifugal path that expels him from that virtual centre of society. In this process he almost has no agency. He is being pushed around so that he may never appear again.

4.5 Gangs and the Significance of Subcultures

The sort of despair suffered by Doug in *The Day of the Dog* is not exclusively relevant to Aboriginal people. The Anglo-Celtic community too has its underclass living at the fringe of society and striving to find its way back into it. In *A Bunch of Ratbags*, William Dick presents to the reader a social space that has been forced in a state of self-perpetrating despair. In the suburbs around the gleaming city centre, the working class live dismal lives which lead individuals into hopelessness, rage and violence. The author portrays this phenomenon as a kind of disease, a psychological disorder which is born out of the social malaise clutching the white Australian proletariat. In fact, the suburbs where the working class lives are described as ob-scene spaces which stand as a sort of "other" side to the CBD. They are portrayed as true regions of the unconscious. *A Bunch of Ratbags* pro-

4 The City: The Crumbling Bulwark

poses this troubled human unconscious as the mirror of the social unrest brewing in the ob-scene regions of the city.

The novel, set in Melbourne during the post-war era, gives a dispassionate portrait of the harsh living conditions endured by a large portion of the metropolitan population. The opening of the novel immediately frames the context of the story:

> The city of Melbourne is Australia's Second largest city. It has a population of about two million. Like every city it has its upper-, middle- and lower class suburbs.
> This story is about a lower class suburb – but more so about its people. (Dick 1984, 1)

Terry Cookie is the protagonist and narrator of the novel. Starting from his early age when he works as a labourer at the rail yards – he unloads wood-trucks in exchange for firewood and a small weekly salary – his life in Goodway constitutes the main thread of the story. This tale sets itself as exemplary of both the way downwards to social marginalization and of the way towards redemption from poverty and under-privilege. Terry Cookie's path out of disadvantage (but also most importantly out of his suburb) can be mistaken for a mere moral tale; however, there is more to the story as Goodway is an exemplary description of any of the lower-class suburbs of Melbourne. In this case, it is clearly identifiable with Footzcray (Bessant and Watts 1989, 196), one of the biggest, most densely inhabited and industrial suburbs west of the city. In Judith Bessant's and Rob Watts' words, Footzcray was "home to thousands of immigrants from Italy and Greece and to an even greater number of Australian-born working class women, men, and young people" (Bessant and Watts 1989, 196). There, the type of life experienced by these people is one of hardship and continuous battling against the odds of life. In this desolate environment most people struggle to simply meet the weekly bills.

> The houses are ageing, many built in the late nineteenth or early twentieth century. Most days there is an ubiquitous stench from the local

meatworks and a haze of smoke from the local foundries belching out sulphurous oxides and the ash which coats the washing hung out on the backyard clothes lines. (Bessant and Watts 1989, 196)

This environment, which reminds of a hell's circle from Dante's *Inferno*, is home to a vast portion of Australia's workforce. William Dick's novel tackles this complex setting and, through Terry's life, retraces all the phases in the average suburban life: unremitting poverty, domestic violence, hard work, gambling, drinking and finally gang violence. The strength of this book is its capacity of immersing the reader in the atmosphere and the logics that lead the protagonist to objectionable actions and decisions. Highly representative of the underlying logic in Goodway's social life is Terry's father's piece of advice to his son:

> He often told me that you don't get rich by using your hands; you get rich by using your head and being smarter than the next bloke. He said that there were only two kinds of people in this world: the ones that got pushed around, and the ones that did the pushing. He reckoned he was "gonna teach me real good how to be smart and not get pushed around". I often thought, what about you pushing me around yourself? but I was not game enough to say anything. (Dick 1984, 19)

In this lower-class suburb all its inhabitants are resigned to the idea of having to go through a bit of pushing around. Terry's father's interpretation of these living conditions is akin to the social Darwinist idea of survival of the fittest. In this case, fittest does not mean the same as in the definition given by Darwin in *The Origin of the Species* (1859), where natural selection means the "preservation of favourable individual differences and variations, and the destruction of those which are injurious" (Darwin 2003, 89). For Darwin, the fittest is only coincidentally the most well adapted individual. In Goodway, on the other hand, to be fit means to use either brute force or intellect to prevaricate others. As James Allen Rogers reminds us in his article "Darwinism and Social Darwinism," even a social Darwinist such as

4 The City: The Crumbling Bulwark

Thomas Huxley thought that the use of Herbert Spencer's phrase 'survival of the fittest' was a very unfortunate decision on Darwin's part. In Huxley's words, we "commonly use 'fittest' in a good sense, with the understood connotation of 'best'; and 'best' we are apt to take in its ethical sense. But the 'fittest' which survives in the struggle for existence may be, and often is, the ethically worst" (Allen Rogers 2000, 159).

It is exactly this sort of misinterpretation that leads people in Goodway to believe that to infringe the law does not make one a criminal but more simply a "ratbag." A ratbag is a rascal, a larrikin, someone that commits some sort of petty crime but who is also immediately forgiven out of sympathy. If initially the instances when this unwritten rule applies gain the sympathy of the reader – Terry steals mallee roots from the passing trains, empty lemonades bottles or a few lead ingots from the rail-yards – as the protagonist grows up, the induced moral relaxation becomes more worrying. As in the case of the father and son relationship, violence is often the only means of interpersonal communication. The "ethically worse" in Goodway becomes justifiable and so, when Terry's father bashes his wife until she falls unconscious, neither the neighbours nor the police are very concerned about it. As a result, the husband only gets told off.

In spite of all this violence, the story remains truthful to the actual ordinariness of these extraordinary lives. As a consequence, what seems to be outrageous and exceptional to the reader is actually acceptable and normal in this suburb. The author, conscious of this fact, uses a bit of irony to stress the peculiarity of this condition:

> If this story was a penny dreadful, then I suppose this part of the book would be where I started to plan to murder my old man, [...] but as it was real life I did nothing to gain vengeance – I just had to accept it, that my father liked to belt me up once in a while and that was that. After all, we where only normal people, and if every kid in Goodway murdered his old man after he got belted up, then there would have been no men left in Goodway at all. (Dick 1984, 49)

The inhabitants of Goodway are trapped in a vicious cycle that condemns them to fall prey to their own marginalization. As indicated by the narrator's meta-literary comment, "if this story was a penny dreadful," Terry fully understands this mechanism and manages to forgive his father for being an average frustrated man who becomes violent after losing at the races. In the end, in spite of all his defects, Terry even loves and somehow admires him. Nevertheless, the profound comprehension of this condition does not lead Terry to immediately be a better person; on the contrary, the necessity to survive in this intimidating environment leads him to the only available type of belonging: that of the mob.

Belonging to a gang becomes the only way to escape continuous prevarication, hence, as soon as in secondary school, he works his way up to the top ranks of a mob:

> Belonging to our mob made me feel fairly safe except for my hidden fear. Everybody wants to belong to something or someone, and everybody wants to feel safe. To pick a fight with me was to pick a fight with our mob. This went for any of our mob who got picked. This was the reason why there were so many brawls at our school. (Dick 1984, 88)

It is the unresolved sense of fear – fear of his father, fear of the schoolmates and mostly of the environment around him – that drives Terry, like many others, to find security in an organism that ends up sheltering individuals but heightening the overall tension in society. As the protagonist admits, fear remains while violence escalates. As a consequence, in the course of Terry's student carrier, the school is first almost blown to pieces by a student's retaliation against the chemistry teacher, and it is later half burnt to the ground. As the mob becomes the sole centre of belonging for its members, the rest of the world becomes estranged and as a consequence other and hostile. This is the origin of the irrational hate for the "dagos" (the Italians), for the police, for the gangs from the other suburbs and in the end for anything that falls outside the silent pact established between gang members.

Bessant and Watts, taking as an example William Dick's novel but working on the actual bodgie culture of the 50s, try to make sense of such violence and to explain it in analytical terms: "Do we treat it, as the respectable professionals of the day would have done, the 'child savers', the police, the journalists or the politicians of the day would have done, as reprehensible, as savagery, and as a sign of that delinquency that comes from failed parenting?" (Bessant and Watts 1989, 197). The perspective presented by the author of the novel already excludes the previous hypothesis. Parents have not failed their role. By doing their best in coping and teaching how to deal with the misery of life, they succeed in handing at least some basic respect for life. Thus, Terry and the other boys are not purely amoral beings, on the contrary, they are initially provided with a strong sense of morality, they start up with values which they prize. Through disillusion they later become rebellious and, rapidly, they completely go astray. However, they still follow a strong, even if independent, moral code. You always back up your mates and a real mate is one that you know will not let you down in a fight. This is more than just a code of honour; it is the reformulation of the definition of friendship.

Nevertheless, as Bessant and Watts argue, this bond of hostility against the world cannot simply be explained "as 'resistance' by the working class to changed conditions imposed on them by a careless rampant capitalist economy hungry for new raw labour" (Bessant and Cook 1997, 197). In the gang's antisocialism there is definitely not any sort of organized resistance against the system. The big mobs of the different suburbs are mostly busy fighting one other, fighting the immigrants and finally the police. The system, which sometimes sends the police to take care of the gangs[19], has more deceitful ways of control over these people's lives. To belong to a gang meant to follow a strict behavioural code. One could either be a square – dressed in plain

---

[19] It is here important to notice that, as in Doug's Perth, a special police squad is formed to cope with the violent youths.

labourer clothes – or a bodgie. The bodgie style, born in Sydney in the mid 50s (Bessant and Cook 1997, 189), required spending lots of money on expensive clothes chosen to match a rigid but continuously evolving dressing code. As a consequence, during the day money was gained through hard work, and later it was squandered in pinball parlours, on drinks and food or on clothes that mainly symbolized the belonging to a youth culture that strained to estrange itself from the parents' world. It is so, that youth rebellion falls into place within the strategies of consumerist society. Violence, aggression and vandalism are both the symptoms and the result of the general malaise reigning in lower class areas where the feeling of entrapment suffocates the youth's ambitions. The gangs, with their hatred, are the answer to the need of self-realization in a world where individuals would want to grow out of their destitute conditions but where they feel that they do not have the means to do it. As this novel suggests, the most readily available answer is to stand out as a gang and to release frustration through violence.

Terry's transformation happens when he fails to obtain the school prize normally awarded to the most gifted kids. The school, as a result of the fire that devastated part of the building, cannot afford a reward for all the qualifying students.

> Most of that night in bed I cried to myself and I lay there thinking: things never change for bums like us, not in this joint. Me and the old man, we are meant to get nothin' and be poor. We're just bums. Jeez, I wanted to show the old Mum and the old man my prize. Me and the old man against the world! That's what the old man reckons, and he's right.
>   Failing to get that book changed my whole nature slowly nut surely. I became mean and I was provoked easily into fights and I got pleasure in beating kids to a pulp because I hated everyone. I kept bashing them long after they had submitted. I hated them. (Dick 1984, 106)

Most clearly it is this sense of disillusion that fuels the protagonist's hatred. As he pounds into people it can be imagined that he is

4 The City: The Crumbling Bulwark 231

actually smashing his fists into what he feels are the obstacles that prevent him from realizing himself. Violence thus becomes both an expression of discontent and a symptomatic discharge of the accumulated stress. Bessant and Watts argue also that the criminal behaviour of the gangs was mostly motivated by the need to challenge the dreariness of the norm:

> It may be more illuminating to assume that there are a number of common ethical dispositions shared by groups of people normally more disposed to accentuate their apparent differences within a social setting than to accept that perhaps they share a great deal with the other. (Bessant and Cook 1997, 198)

Other, in this case, is the entirety of society, but most prominent is the need to set oneself apart from the despised world of the parents and to reaffirm at the same time a strong sense of belonging to the place of origin; hence the hate for the foreigners.

Terry Cookie is one of the very first kids in his suburb to become a bodgie. The transformation happens when he and two of his friends meet an old associate who after moving to Sydney has become a bodgie himself. The motivations given by Bootlace are highly indicative of the real motives of the transformation:

> Why don't you lot become bodgies – the cops hate us. It's terrific fun wearing bodgie clothes, man. You'd look better with a bodgie haircut [...] our Australian bloody haircut is rotten; it's like the rough end of a pineapple. [...] It's spreading like mad in Sydney so why not be some of the first in Melbourne? You'll kill sheilas, they really go for us, they are sick of the squares. (Dick 1984, 139)

The emphasis is definitely on anti-conformism. For this reason bodgies and cops (who are the embodiment of the norm) must necessarily counter each other to symbolize the distinction from normalcy. The striking and elaborate bodgie dressing code becomes the sign symbolizing exactly differentiation. Bessant and Watts, in their interviews with ex members of the bodgie movement, establish that

"Sometimes it seemed as if the bodgie clothes were a heaven sent opportunity to escape the inevitable fate of becoming like their fathers" (Bessant and Watts 1989, 205). For this reason bodgie style had such a wide success and the girls, as Bootlace proudly says, love it so much. In the end, the main aim for the youths of the time was to escape from the greyness of the existences they felt compelled to undertake. Then, quite obviously, Rock'n roll immediately came to play a huge part in the life of these youngsters. William Dick describes its rise in detail; from the first few songs heard on the radio, to the movies and finally to the growing of a fanaticism for Bill Haley and later Elvis Presley. Rock'n roll was just another expression of that desperate need to transgress, to be different and to feel free. Thus the new music and the new wild way of dancing immediately became part of the bodgie life. As Terry recalls: "we didn't know *then* that rock'n roll was born, but we did know that that music was meant for us, and we were going to have it" (Dick 1984, 246).

Then again, rebelliousness is not expressed simply through innocent exuberance; conversely, the most distinctive feature of the gangs is their indiscriminate violence. The main and easiest targets are the Italian immigrants that the government is helping migrate to Australia. In the novel the hatred sparks after a brawl between a few Italians and a group of Australian bodgie boys; then one of the best fighters in the gang gets stabbed several times by one of the terrorized dagoes. As the protagonist recalls, "from then on when we fought the dagoes it was no holds barred – bike-chains, coshes, fence-pickets, broken beer bottles, knuckle-dusters, anything, as long as they went down" (Dick 1984, 165). Beating up the immigrants becomes a past-time for Sunday afternoons and, at times, the crowd cheers the boys as they fight the foreigners "who were trying to take over [the] country" (Dick 1984, 163). Then again, the driving force of the aggressiveness of these youths is their consuming hatred for whatever comes in their way. An unconscious process of victimization leads the gangsters to always feel as if they had been wronged in the first place and so, when

4 The City: The Crumbling Bulwark 233

they set out to vandalize or belt an unfortunate victim, they think it is their right to do so.

When one day the police strikes back in retaliation for some crime committed by one of the gangs, Terry manages to escape the carnage:

> We looked down and watched helplessly as the coppers started punching into our boys and belting them up. Giving them rabbit punches, kneeing them in the stomach and then in the face, stomping their heels on a bodgie's toe and then punching him in the face. The sight was sickening. Just seeing the coppers in their true form made our blood boil. [...] "blokes against boys. Jeez, they're real tough! The coppers bastards. I'd like to have a machine gun here. I'd open it up on them bastards and kill the lot of 'em." [...] From that day we hated the coppers more than we hated the dagoes. We hated them more than anyone in the world. (Dick 1984, 181, 182)

Even if the cops' behaviour is surely reprehensible and not much different from that of the gangs, what becomes clear from this episode is the way Terry and his friends continuously fail to see any fault in their actions and therefore to identify the lesson imparted by the police as any sort of retribution for their past wrong-doings. On the contrary, the Goodway mob immediately sets out a scheme to retaliate against the police. However, as openly confronting the officers of the law is out of the question, the plan is to consistently wreck the park where the offence was committed.

Slowly, as the boys grow up into men, also the seriousness of their crimes escalates till, without them even noticing it, the supposed "ratbags" become real criminals. The novel describes this gradual change by reporting a number of alarming incidents. In one instance it is a newspaper article that gives an illuminating picture of the discordance between the gang's perspective and that of the rest of Melbourne:

> In one newspaper article concerning a raid on the Oasis after the raping of two girls, it was described as "a hangout for bodgies, criminals, thieves, perverts, prostitutes and all the rest of the city gutter trash.

"How's that? Fancy calling us gutter-trash, the dirty scabs," said Ape. "They must not like us or sumthin'?" We all laughed and Ape felt good. (Dick 1984, 193)

The gang members all fail to comprehend the gravity of their situation; as Terry recalls (here the narrator is speaking; the focalizer is therefore a much older and wiser Terry), the milkbar where the mob used to meet had really become "one of the toughest hang-outs in Melbourne" (Dick 1984, 192) frequented by all sorts of creatures of the underworld. Ape's mockery of the newspaper's comment reveals how little awareness of their position these people have; grown in such desperate conditions they have become blind to the degeneracy of their lives. In one case they all despise their friend Elaine because she is a prostitute and, when they discover that she had been having sex with her father, uncle and grandfather from a tender age, they fail to feel any sympathy for her. They only feel disgust.

As if oblivious of their origin and numbed by the endurance of a strenuous existence, Terry and his associates cannot see any wrong in their actions. Rape, due to the protagonist's involvement in a long term relationship based on love, becomes the first and later crucial point of disagreement between the main character and the other gang members. The narrator's voice recalls that "[i]t happened all the time, the boys raping some widgie or other, only [they] didn't call it rape; [they] just called it "forcing one out of her," or "making her give us one" (Dick 1984, 214). Rape is acceptable among members of the gang while it is unacceptable outside of it. The reasons given to support this claim are that a widgie would not go to the Police because she could always be reported for something she did. In addition to this, the police would not have believed she was forced to do something she did anyway most of the time. Probably, confounded as they are, the bodgies as well cannot accept a widgie's 'no' as true.

Terry, after meeting Caroline and starting to plan a future with her, reconsiders these positions and quickly finds himself estranged from his group and fighting a silent war with his now weak nerves. The final parting with the bodgie life happens when one day some of his old friends take him to the beach for a few drinks. The protagonist, having quit drinking on account of an ulcer in the stomach, now lucidly witnesses the brutality of the life he has led so far. As he defends a girl that is about to be gang-raped, he narrowly misses being assaulted by his old friends:

> "Well, Janice, it looks like yuh gonna turn it on for all of us, doesn't it?" said Harry as he took a swig from a bottle.
> "Bull-shit," she said in defiance. "Whadya bloody well think I am?"
> Without warning Harry [...] punched her in the face and she screamed out in pain and fell to the ground and lay there sobbing. [...]
> "Knock it off, Harry, there was no need to do that to her," I said. He never answered but just glared at me and drank again from the bottle. [...] All the boys were crowded around excitedly, talking; no one felt any pity for her. They only saw that here was a half naked woman ready for their use.
> [...]
> "What's wrong, Cookie, gone square again eh – mate?" [Ritchie] yelled with a sarcastic accent on the word "mate."
> "Give her back her clothes, Ritchie, and leave her alone, the poor bitch. Look at her – she's scared stiff." I said, and I thought of Carol and of my sister Joanie. (Dick 1984, 269-270)

The drunken boys, purely driven by instinct, act like a pack of wild animals. Terry, on the contrary, through love and commitment to another person, has recovered some moral values and is therefore compelled to condemn their behaviour. In one last struggle, as Terry holds Ritchie in a bear-hug, Harry is about to crash a bottle on his head: "I let Ritchie go and turned towards Harry and stared him straight in the eyes. He glared back at me, the bottle held high ready to crash me, but I stood my ground and wiped my mouth with the back of my shaking hand" (Dick 1984, 271). It is not fear that makes the protagonist's hands shake; as he demonstrated in previous fights he is not a "jell" (coward). On the contrary, it is his toughness that wears his nerves down. Being strong entails trying to be in control of a world that cannot possibly be tamed. After meeting Carol, the continuous tension of his previous life becomes unbearable and makes Terry sick. That night, as he manages to save himself and Janice from the crazed pack of boys, he also definitively abandons his criminal life forever and starts working his way out of his sickness.

After failing to cure his ulcer and his panic attacks with psychotropic drugs (phenobarbitone), Chinese medicine, homeopathic drugs and hypnosis, Terry is finally referred to an American psychologist. The treatment is a complete success; from the first session Terry begins to feel relieved and his hate definitively peters out. The therapy conducted by Dr. Huntington is indicative of the patient's disorder; during the first session he asks him to repeat over and over again, "I can't help it." The result is surprising:

> After a few minutes the words began to join into a cycle of words that were never ending [...]. I kept on repeating it. I began to grow angry and tensed up and I repeated the sentence through gritted teeth. I grew crazier but I kept it up. I'd forgotten Mr Huntington. I was yelling it loudly now and I punched the arm of the chair with my fist every time I said it. This went on for a period of a few minutes and then I began to get scared, real scared. [...] Tears started to [...] trickle down my face and the words were becoming jumbled with emotion and I could see my father as if I were dreaming. He had his bike turned upside down in the backyard and he was repairing the puncture in the back tyre. I could see myself and I was very young. I was standing there crying. I wanted to help my father fix the tyre but he wouldn't let me. I could hear him telling me that I couldn't help him. "I can't help it get fixed," I said aloud in the room as a tram went by. Tears poured down my face as my father gave me a backhander to stop me crying and I cried even more. (Dick 1984, 295)

Terry discovers that his nature would lead him to help others but somehow, from early on in his life, he has been taught by people and by circumstances that he cannot help anybody. Mr Huntington explains his frustration and rage to him interpreting the images he has seen during his rave and giving him a brief lesson in psychology:

4 The City: The Crumbling Bulwark   237

> There's a lot of significance in those pictures, because whether or not you know it, they are important to you. Some you hate, some you want, but they are always in your subconscious mind running havoc. We've just to get rid of them and stop them running havoc. The father picture represents the first time you really felt rejected and hurt, not allowed to be able to help. Everyone really wants to help everyone else. That's what life is, helping one another. That was the first time you got the basic idea you couldn't help people, and from then on 'couldn't' changed to 'don't care' to 'don't want to', and finally 'won't help them'. Then the hate followed. You know the rest, Terry. It's all just a pattern. (Dick 1984, 298)

This simple explanation of the origin of hate in youth subcultures solves the underlying riddle of the book: how can Terry and his associates be "good boys" and criminals at the same time? William Dick makes this clear all the time: in Goodway life is hard, at times horrible and unbearable, but people always retain their dignity and of course, in a way, their humanity. One brilliant example of this is when Ape, one of the toughest fighters in Terry's gang, steals money from the safe of his work place in order to buy himself toys and to help a friend's sick mother. Terry and his friends, under the hard shell they have developed during years of struggle, still have the potential to return to care for the rest of the world. What made the biggest difference for the protagonist and induced him to change was to meet someone that cared for him; this encouraged him to do things for someone else's sake. In fact, it is exactly at this point that his nerves completely break down. The need to do things for "Carol's sake" clashes with the subconscious principle ruling his existence: "don't care about anything / I hate everything."

The American psychologist's therapy aims at making this interior dilemma surface to the level of the conscious, in order to later follow it back to its origin. In one of the following sessions, Terry performs an exercise he calls "Wall of Reality." Terry is asked to walk from one side of the room to the other and to push with both hands against the perimeter walls. He is also asked to "feel how solid [each] wall is" and to try to imagine "the weight of the timber and mortar and the plasters and the nails that go into making the wall." Again the result is surprising, the patient's hands start shaking and his hanger grows until the moment he starts punching and screaming at the wall:

> I hated that rotten wall, I hated it and I wanted to push it over, right over. I hit it harder and harder till my hands hurt and I used every ounce of strength that was in my body as I tried desperately with a superhuman effort to push it over. "You rotten stinking bastard" I said softly, "get out of my bloody road, will yuh". (Dick 1984, 301)

Evidently the psychologist is trying to use the projective identification that induces Terry to so biliously assault the wall to access and treat the origin of that hate. In the next part of the exercise, the analysand, while still pushing against the wall, is asked to repeat to himself: "I can feel this wall, it is solid and hard" (Dick 1984, 301). After having unlocked the patient's most hunting anxiety Mr Huntington tries to teach Terry's unconscious to deal with its fear of being trapped in the despicable life of the suburbs. The protagonist's aggressiveness is sparked by a twofold distortion of reality. On one side, he is lead to care for and hate everyone. On the other side, this leads him to feel trapped by the innumerable objects targeted by his negative projective identifications. From this perspective, alone against the world, or worse, with the world turned against him, Terry had to fight for every inch of ground around him. The Wall of Reality forces the protagonist to confront the origin of his problem. Just as there is no reason to get in a fit of rage against a wall, there is no need to fight with one's father, bash immigrants and vandalize the city.

The psychological treatment is a success. As Terry learns to distinguish between things he has control on and things that he does not have control on, his anger subsides and he slowly recovers from his ulcer. During one of the last sessions of his treatment he realizes: "I didn't hate my father any more. I shouldn't have hated him ever. I shouldn't have hated the police or the dagoes. I shouldn't have hated the boys for what they did, because they didn't know what they were doing. I shouldn't hate anyone. I didn't hate anyone" (Dick 1984, 307). From that moment onwards, the protagonist is finally free of all the ghosts that haunted him for so long. The social despair experienced by the people living in Goodway (and in Melbourne's West) remains real, however, Terry Cookie learns that he is capable of helping himself out of that situation. The novel ends well for the main character who, having become a sales manager, moves out of Goodway and secures a happy and content life for himself and Carol. On the other hand, all the "boys" remain trapped in the rat-race of Goodway and lead dismal lives on the fringe of legality.

In the end, Terry's lack of sympathy for his old companions casts a doubt on his real comprehension of the dynamics from which he managed to escape. Talking to a youth from Goodway who is trying to work his way out of his situation he comments: "You're no snob, you're doing the right thing. You *are* higher" (Dick 1984, 320). William Dick, with this last comment and by making his main character say that he feels like helping *this* kid, and the ones *like him*, ultimately betrays what seems to be a kind of essentialism. After all, it is through his author's doing that Terry's life takes a different turn from that of most of his mates. Furthermore, it took both a bit of luck and lots of good will to manage to escape the desolate existence of his suburb. Certainly, this does not make him inherently "higher" than his old friends. In the end, with Terry's ascent to a comfortable middle class, *A Bunch of Ratbags* reinstates the system of social confinement and discrimination so far analyzed in this section. Terry's point of view reproposes Goodway as a hopeless breeding ground of moral debasement and criminality. As a matter of fact, when he hears that his old associates are still slowly and steadily sinking, he is neither surprised nor does he show any sympathy for their condition. Now that he belongs to a different area he can only discriminate against the past he once belonged to. Now that he has shifted to a new domain of reality, all he is capable of doing is wondering "what the past had all been about" (Dick 1984, 320).

4.6 Solving the Conflict

Starting from Christos Tsiolka's contemporary Melbourne and visiting 4 Australian capitals, this chapter returns to its origin while moving back fifty years in time. William Dick's Melbourne is not very different from the one described in *Loaded*; its main characteristic remains the fragmentation of the urban thread inducing social segregation. Chris Wallace-Crabbe, in his book *Melbourne or the Bush*, describes "Melbourne in 1963" (this is the title of a chapter) with a collection of different images ranging from the sun setting on the bay, the traffic of daily trippers heading home in the Eastern suburbs on the Nepean Highway of Heidelberg Road, and the dusty neon-lit CBD where shoppers seem to ghostly move around. Even when recalled with nostalgia, these images clearly evoke a sense of loneliness and alienation that all the characters of the novels analyzed seemed to share.

The 1963 Melbourne described by Wallace-Crabbe is also very reminiscent of the one described by Tsiolkas:

> One cannot focus on any place, any situation, and say, 'Here indeed is the true centre of Melbourne', for the city is not merely large, but to an extraordinary degree, sprawling and centreless. The mile-square grid of the city proper is somehow far less real, less permanent, than the hundreds of square miles of suburbia into which the population flees in the evening, draws down the puritan blinds and settles itself before the blue simmer of the television screen. (Wallace-Crabbe 1974, 66)

Again the emphasis falls on the overwhelming vastness of the suburban sprawl, on the anonymity granted by this structure, and on the resulting alienation of the residents. Television, the "soma"[20] of contemporary society, completes this picture by transforming each individual home into an impenetrable shelter where the citizens with-

---

[20] Soma is the wonder drug that, in the biotechnologically controlled society of *Brave New World*, by Aldous Huxley, rids the citizens of their troubling thoughts and guarantees a state of peace at every level of this futuristic society.

4 The City: The Crumbling Bulwark   241

draw from the surrounding reality. As demonstrated by each of the novels, inside or outside the walls of each home, within or beyond the boundaries of a neighbourhood, or anywhere in society anything could happen without anyone knowing or caring.

Wallace-Crabbe, confronting Melbourne's still unclear identity in the 1960's, calls into question the immaturity of Australian society and the resulting sense of Cultural Cringe theorised by his Melbourne colleague writer A. A. Phillips. In this case, the concept of Cultural Cringe is very aptly employed to evidence the un-severed link between the antipodes and the centre. Wallace-Crabbe observes that "Australian cities are still to some extent spiritual suburbs of London, Paris, and New York; in this, Melbourne is no exception" (Wallace-Crabbe 1974, 67). Forty years later the situation has changed, but only in a devious way. Australia has developed a profound sense of cultural independence, yet, this spawns from foundations which are still deeply entrenched in a culture alien to its land. Australianness, apart from the myths of the bushman with his ballads, yarns and good mates, is nowadays mostly identifiable with beach culture and western urban lifestyle. This, once again, indicates a profound failure of the attempt to create a sense of belonging to the continent where, as a result, cities remain the strongholds of western civilization, the scene. The metropolis becomes an independent microcosm where the infinite fragmentation of the urban structure becomes the recipient of a new arrangement of the concepts of inside and outside and therefore of scene and obscene space. Things and people, each with their passions and fears, can be moved from one side to the other of the cities, from one suburb to the other, but, in an infinite process of displacement, they can also be ostracized from society without being physically removed from it. The city has become covertly ob-scene. In this context, the protagonists of the novels here analyzed struggle to find their place in a culture that once again upholds its identity/integrity through the seclusion of otherness and the promotion of homologation.

The dynamics of this claustrophobic organization is comprehensible if we take into account the colonial influence in the process of socio-spatialization that shaped the modern Australian landscape. Germaine Greer, in her essay *Whitefella Jump Up*, very perceptively draws attention to this problematic situation:

> The settlers toiled like madmen to remove the scrub, bush and trees that stood in the way of cultivation. They no more realised that the newly denuded land would be vulnerable to extremes of heat and cold, drought and flood, than they realised that the rising of the water table would bring the stored salts to the surface, gradually poisoning the land cleared with so much blood sweat and tears. Nor did they realise that the willows they planted along the waterways [...] would spread through entire river systems, until the flows were clogged, or that their garden flowers would become a curse. The settlers imagined that they were redeeming a land the original inhabitants had failed to manage in any rational fashion, and that they could turn it into a new Canaan. [...]
>
> Ultimately, rural Australia ended up emptier than it was before it was "opened up". Australia has now become the most highly urbanised population of any country in the world. The whitefellas who tried to make a living in the bush soon fled from it, and wound up as far from the interior as they could get, on the continent's very edge, where they built themselves houses that faced outwards and away, across the ocean. Happiness is now a house in a seaside suburb with not a single native plant in sight. Most Australians would these days deny that they hate the land, but actions speak louder than words. (Greer 2003, 9, 11)

As a consequence, the Aborigine is still associated with that frightening empty space threatening to swallow the strongholds of civilization scattered around the immense Australian territory. Even if the threat does not exist any more, the paranoia remains and it causes the claustrophobic compartmental structuring of urban space. Michel Foucault argues that "a whole history remains to be written of *spaces* – which would at the same time be the history of *powers* (both of those terms in the plural) – from the great strategies of geopolitics to the little tactics of the habitat" (Foucault 1980, 149). This is exactly

4 The City: The Crumbling Bulwark 243

what the five texts here analyzed do; they are not history books, but very clearly they give a precise account of the failure of the current power-space management in Australia. The deep wound afflicting society can be explained in terms of a lack of acceptance of the "other." Minorities, on which the Dominant Discourse projects its negative drives, are still given neither space nor power. The sense of siege in white Australian culture remains: the boat people, the natives, the minorities integrated through multiculturalism and all minority groups are incarnations of the same ghosts that haunted the first settlers.

In his book *Edge of the Sacred* (1995), David Tacey analyzes this situation and suggests that in order to overcome this impasse Australia must first understand its origin:

> For two hundred years the majority of Australians have shielded themselves against the land, huddling together in European cities, pretending we are not in or part of Australia. But the landscape obtrudes, and often insinuates itself against our very will, as so much Australian writing testifies. The landscape in Australia is a mysteriously charged and magnificently alive archetypal presence. [...]
> The land is, or seems to be, the sacred which bursts in upon our lives, which demands to be recognised and valued. (Tacey 1995, 6,7)

Awakening to the existence of this problem, Tacey goes on to argue that "[t]he only way to develop a spiritually powerful culture in Australia is to enter more into the psychic field of nature; to 'shamanise' ourselves in the image of nature" (Tacey 1995, 7). There is therefore a precise need to reconcile with the land because it is the Australian land that has also been charged with images of otherness that confine white Australians in a state of fearful oppression leading to paranoia. Australia can be seen as an unhealthy subject whose pathology can be explained in psychoanalytical terms:

> As Freud and his followers discovered, the rigidly defensive ego-personality thrives on projective paranoia and dissociative strategies in order to force outside the self those disruptive elements that attack it from inside. Thus in nationalist Australia, negative projections,

scapegoating, acts of emotional or physical violence, attempts to subdue the other, are frequently indulged, while all the while the nationalist ego considers it is living in the worker's paradise, in the best possible of worlds. (Tacey 1995, 54)

For the "lucky country" the time has come to face its interior, the forests, the bush and, more in general, its unconscious. At the moment, captive as it is of its own internal fears, it only risks to collapse under the weight of its own super-ego. The dissociative strategies have already been individuated and the state paranoia is apparent in the Howard government's dealing with the asylum seekers, the terrorist threat and the Aboriginal people.

The five novels here considered precisely address this problem; all being written from an internal, but at the same time marginal, point of view (that of social minorities and underprivileged classes), they all address problems of integration, intolerance and belonging. In spite of multiculturalism, Anglo-Celtic Australia still keeps a hold onto the socio-cultural conformation of the continent, and it is this monopoly that Tsiolkas, Robb, Lucashenko, Weller and Dick seem to undermine. Their novels suggest that Anglo-Celtic and urban Australia, in the role of the moral bulwark of white civilization, have become a crippling inheritance for the multicultural society that has flourished in the vast land down under. However, as demonstrated by Tacey's argument, minorities are not alone in demanding a revision of the socio-cultural organization of space; mainstream Australia too asks to be freed from the constraints of an outdated legacy. In these novels Melbourne, Sydney, Brisbane, Perth, and the other cities that could not be considered, have turned into crumbling bulwarks of civilization due to their internal inadequacy to satisfy the needs of contemporary society. *Loaded, Pig's Blood, Steam Pigs, The Day of the Dog* and *A Bunch of Ratbags*, by disclosing this fault-line, instigate a change at the level of the Dominant Discourse. This process, if pursued, can lead to the healing of the wound created in Australian society by the Manichean tradition inherited from the old continent, and therefore to a better management of the socio-cultural structuring of space.

5 Back to the Outback

The socio-cultural rift imposed upon the Australian imaginative space evolved from a Discourse that – as illustrated in chapters 2 and 3 – gradually projected and rapidly relocated obscenity beyond the reach of its civilization. The cities, as radiating centres of this vision, remained entrapped in the function of scene, stages of a Discourse that gradually became more pathologically detached from its Other. The urban centres grew larger in size and, according to a cruel logic of internal marginalization, managed to harbour the vast majority of the Australian population. Cities, inevitably failing to remain the archetypical embodiment of purity, grew ever more cognitively detached from the interior. As small country towns vanished from the map and the bush became insistently marketed as an adventurous-spectacular destination, the real outback returned to being a largely un-intruded off-scene setting.

This chapter goes back to the outback in order to study the contemporary socio-topographic construction of a space that has once again managed to remove itself from the scene while, as if veiled by an immense backdrop, it also created the impression of an unobtrusive presence. Janette Turner Hospital's *Oyster* (1996) and Vivienne Cleven's *Her Sister's Eye* (2002) reveal two matching sides of this phenomenon; each in a different way, the novels explore this scenario and describe the collusion between the old colonial legacy and the continued desire for an everlasting secrecy. There are different reasons for wanting to impose such a suffocating silence. One can be the desire of escaping one's own past and, the other, the need to hide an inconvenient history. Ultimately, these are matching symptoms (projective paranoia and dissociative strategies) of the malaise that David Tacey diagnosed in nationalist Australia (cf. Tacey 1995, 54). The analysis of these novels is therefore intended to facilitate an examination of the contemporary imaginative construction of the off-scene Australian interior and to unveil its obscene side.

246 Obscene Spaces in Australian Narrative

5.1 An Ongoing Legacy

Janette Turner Hospital's apocalyptic novel *Oyster* is a perfect case study for the exploration of ob-scene spaces. For Outer Maroo, at the eve of the new millennium, to be an isolated town of Northern Queensland is not sufficient. After the work of cartographers had succeeded in taking hold of everything that could be traced on a map, the small village proceeded to escape authority by erasing itself from it. As if returned to the space beyond the old frontier, the village acquires the ambivalent freedom of in-between spaces. With no qualms, townspeople use this position to establish all sorts of illicit activities. Illegal opal mining and weapon smuggling are the principal businesses run in the village and it is therefore implicit that a deficiency of law is needed. Nevertheless, it is the population itself that seems to seek a repair from intrusive gazes, everybody seems to be running away from something and to be concealing some secret. Jess, who once was a surveyor cartographer of the state of Queensland and who has retreated to Outer Maroo to hide from guilt and justice, gives an illuminating account of what sort of setting the village has chosen for itself:

> In the very idea of 'breakaway country' there is an implication, purely verbal, of an event in time, of some particular incident that took place, before which there was a stable and appropriate state [...]. 'Breakaways', we surveyors labelled them, shading them in on government charts. [...] It is very personal, very judgmental, this language of the makers of maps. *Deviant landforms*, we say, and by implication: here are the moral boundary posts, running sometimes parallel, and sometimes not, with the dingo fence. (137)

Language imposes on this land a sense of instability and inaccessibility. In its topographic categorization this area is intrinsically confined to ob-scenity. Hence, Outer Maroo, being positioned in breakaway country, conceptually contains all the disruptiveness that in the end will literally flame out in a liberating catharsis. The citizens are all "breakaways" who seek to live out of the "moral boundary posts" of white Australia.

The "providential" encounter between breakaway subjects and territory, however, cannot provide a truly stable position because, as Jess points out, even the supposedly objective work of cartographers is only "judgmental." Therefore, the meaning inscribed into the territory, which is arbitrary and unstable, cannot provide a solid foothold to the inhabitants. Nevertheless, mapmaking is possibly the sole instrument through which this encounter between people and territory was rendered possible. As previously mentioned, Graham Huggan argues that maps and mapmaking interpret and enact the intentions of a certain Discourse by mimetically representing reality and imposing a Eurocentric perspective over the world (Huggan 1994, 126). As a result, the map is caught in between the tension of "its authoritative status and its approximate function, a discrepancy that marks out the 'recognizable totality' of the map as a manifestation of the desire for control rather than as an authenticating seal of coherence" (Huggan 1994, 127). Maps are western instruments of power that, responding to the Discourse's desire for control, frame the world in the attempt of creating the illusion of a coherent unity. Places, territories and entire continents are charted with the intention of creating spaces capable of welcoming people sharing the cultural values set on the chart. Australia, first in the process of erasure that contrived to represent it as a blank space (unknown = empty) and later, being seen as a coastal nation giving its back to an immense desert, is thus actively engendered as a rarefied space where just about anything can be done.

Outer Maroo, by losing itself in the vastness of the incandescent outback of Queensland and by effacing itself off the map, seeks to live outside the rules of common society. Yet, the ambiguous space that Jess identifies as breakaway country is also home to people seeking refuge from the civilized world. Thus, in spite of the sensational nature of the events recounted, the text also proves to be firmly grounded in contemporary western/Australian culture. As Bernadette Brennan notes, events such as Pauline Hanson's election in 1996

(Brennan 2004, 143) or the disastrous standoff between cult followers and US Federal Police in 1993 in Waco, Texas (Brennan 2004, 153), clearly frame this novel's position in the analysis of today's society. The Outer Marooans are the quintessence of the social discomfort fuelling these events and, in fact, their decision to retreat to the desert is motivated by a mixture of distrust at the government and a disillusion with the ethics of mainstream society. Therefore, in *Oyster* the desert is an "isolated and inhospitable" space offering "the exotic setting for fictional journeys of identity" (Müller 2000, 142), and at the same time, "a far cry from its potential as place of spiritual retreat or enlightenment, or the frontier of self-discovery and adventure as it is in Australian Literature" (Lovell 2004, 21). This contradictory situation is the inherent condition of breakaway country, a site that becomes a "metaphor of 'otherness': uncharted and uncertain, it represents the cultural margin where known values and norms cease to be in force, a site were past certainties are disrupted" (Müller 2000, 142). As Anja Müller points out – reminding of Jess' definition of this space – Outer Maroo seeks to disconnect itself both topographically and culturally from the rest of the world. Clutched in a state of paranoia, the community perceives the outside world as Other. For this reason they either seek refuge in religious fundamentalism or they start accumulating weapons because, as one of the opal miners declares, "the greenies, the Abos, the unions, [...] [n]ational parks, Land Rights, I tell you they are coming to take our land and we have to be ready" (Turner Hospital 1996, 243).

Outer Maroo, by severing its socio-cultural ties with the scene, becomes an off-scene scenario. However, it is only later on that, with the appearance of Oyster, this fertile ground becomes definitively obscene: the mysterious arrival of this character sets off a chain reaction resulting in the ultimate obliteration of the community. Oyster, posing as a messianic figure, has the capacity of bringing the community together and making everyone work to a common end. Unfortunately, as it is later revealed, he is only a puppeteer and the final goal serves only his purpose. This character gains an amazing influence upon an otherwise diffident society by appealing to each group's individual interests and by promising everybody earthly and spiritual compensation. As Müller points out, Oyster is simply a "mirage" (Müller 2000, 144) and, just like one, he almost miraculously appears in the midst of the drought-stricken community. He walks into town coming from the desert (Outer Maroo is off the map and more than a full tank of gas away from the closest settlement), and he enchants everybody with piercing blue eyes, a handful of stunning black opals, and a bible-inspired speech against the government prophesizing the end of the world:

> There were wars and rumours of wars everywhere, he would say, and who could disagree? There where fornications and perversions, there were men who were not men and women who were not women, and Australia should return to the way the world was meant to be. This was fertile ground. Governments were not trusted, he said, by the people they governed, and everyone passionately agreed. Politicians were as ravening wolves he said, and our governments, state and federal, spied on us and stole from us and squandered our hard earned cash. (Turner Hospital 1996, 301)

This is a clever strategy. Oyster audaciously switches between moral ("fornications and perversions") and materialist ("hard earned cash") arguments (Müller 2000, 146) while constantly appealing to the basic principle uniting and identifying an otherwise heterogeneous coacervate of people:

> both the godly and ungodly in outback towns distrust equally, the government, the coastal cities, the newspapers, the ABC, the Department of Education, the godless Other, the World, the Flesh, the Devil, all the people out there who are not in the crucible of pastoral us. (Turner Hospital 1996, 289)

Jess, who is also the narrator weaving the story together, tries to make sense of the way the stranger has instantaneously won the confidence of his first audience: the rough crowd of Bernie's pub. Even at the time of her writing, while fuel tanks explode underground and bushfires incinerate Outer Maroo, she still wonders how Oyster could get away with speaking like a Messiah to the "ungodly" at the pub. Reconstructing the scene, she almost seeks justification in "the rifle" he had on his back, "his bloodied foot," "the absence of any visible means of transportation," the "hours of mirages" and, of course, "the opals" (Turner Hospital 1996, 293). Oyster eases himself into the confidence range of these people by flaunting at them their own stereotypical self-image. He uses these clichés to approach them and let them imagine that they share the same background. He puts them at ease, makes an apology for the intrusion and then talks about oyster farming. With a speech that charms the audience with images of blue tropical waters and the alluring penetration of the soft mucous membranes of the bivalve mollusc, he suggests that "just as the oyster will after a certain period of time receive something of value for its discomfort, the community will reap material rewards from the uncomfortable stranger it has accepted in its midst" (Müller 2000, 147). As Müller suggests, however, Oyster is not the impurity introduced to make the pearl; he is the pearler (Müller 2000, 147).

Outer Maroo, dazzled by the images conjured by the false prophet, gives Oyster carte blanche in a space were restrictions do not exist in the first place. The most basic principle ruling this "ideal" off-stage situation is that "silence is golden" (Turner Hospital 1996, 193) – Jess, who is also known as Old Silence, exemplifies this by deliberately refraining herself from speaking – as a consequence the obscene becomes an intoxicating presence that deviously clutches the community and that eventually comes raging out of them in a definitive mayhem. Oyster sets off the spark. In a matter of weeks from his arrival young backpackers start flocking in town and congregate at Oyster's opal mine. There, he rapidly founds a new-age / fervent Christians religious community that lives in communal simplicity, ideally embraced by mother earth and adoring him as the new messiah. Clearly the cultural trope defining the outback and the desert as a mystical space is used to conceal a much different reality. After a period of short-lived harmony when even the local Aborigines join the community, the backpackers move in the shafts of the mine and live underground. This concealed space results to be the ultimate obscene space. The mysteries of Oyster's Reef, the opal mine that the kids dig under Oyster's guidance, are bound to remain buried under the collapsed mine. The numerous children given to Oyster by the girls, the fanatical religious life of the community, the long hours of work in the depth of the earth (something only comparable to slavery) and the kids themselves will all disappear in the blasting of the mine. At that moment Oyster disappears.

In spite of this, the ob-scenity of these events (both from a moral and topographic point of view) is counteracted by the nature of language itself. As Miss Rover says – she is the straight-talking schoolteacher whose cruel destiny is to be fed to pigs – words are shifty, they refuse to be seized and, more importantly, "words are maps and they'll get [people to Outer Maroo.]" (Turner Hospital 1996, 63) As J. U. Jacobs, in an essay on "Allegorical Spaces and Actual Places in Postcolonial Novels," argues, Janette Turner Hospital's novel takes full advantage of this aptitude of words and maps in order to construct a narration that is somehow reminiscent of the rhizomic structure proposed by Gilles Deleuze and Félix Guattari:

> Jess conceives of time as rhizomatic; […] consequently, the story of Oyster's reef to which she contributes, is based on a conception of narrative – the organization of time in words – as entering a spreading structure at any point. 'To put this another way', she says, 'stepping into a story or constructing a map are much the same thing; and both are like tossing a stone at a window: the cobwebby lines fan out from the point of impact in all directions' [43] (Jacobs 2000, 206)

Turner Hospital uses Jess' competence in cartography to construct her narration not simply as a straightforward account of past events but as a map of a psychic space (cf. Lovell 2004). Words and maps are intentionally interpolated in the narration. Jess' disconnected memories flow on paper as if charting the events with intertwining story-lines and intersecting time-planes. Only in this rhizomic fashion it is possible to reconstruct the full picture, the one comprising the censored. Past and present crimes suddenly emerge from in between the different story lines and Outer Maroo's obscenity, even the one preceding Oyster's arrival, is finally revealed.

Jacobs, quoting *Topographies* (1995) by J. Hillis Miller, explains that "every narrative [...] in the way it constructs an arrangement of specific places, provides an 'exercise of spatial mapping';" as a consequence, "the novel itself may also be seen in a larger sense as providing 'a figurative mapping'" (Jacobs 2000, 209). Thus, in *Oyster*, it is not only the small bush town that is being charted but also the wider Australian space that is roughly divided into costal cities and pastoral interior. Although this dichotomization does not do justice to the internal distinctions and shadings of the innumerable cases, it provides further evidence of the pattern of displacement moving the Other, the unconscious and the undesirable off the scene, in an ob-scene setting. Outer Maroo stands in opposition to the big cities, it is a necessary place; not a dumping ground for social waste anymore, but a place of voluntary exile where people can hide, depending on the point of view, either from their shame or the great shame the world has become. The centre-periphery opposition in the socio-topographic organization of space is still valid on every scale. On one level Oyster chooses the remoteness of Outer Maroo to put his plan into action, on another level this town has its own obscene spaces. Andrew Godwin has sex with Ethel, an Aboriginal girl, in the cover of his shed (Turner Hospital 1996, 63); Pete Burnett makes love to Andrew's wife in another isolated shed (Turner Hospital 1996, 248); the bodies of murdered people are fed to pigs living at the bottom of abandoned shafts (Turner Hospital 1996, 250); and Oyster's Reef itself is out of town and therefore doubly off-scene. This displacement is mostly related to the desire to forget and to cover up the obscene with silence. Jess, at the very start of the narration, explains that "in plain common sense, there are things it is better not to know because the knowing makes living too painful" (Turner Hospital 1996, 7). This new dimension of the bush presented in Turner Hospital's novel is thus exemplified in the collapsed mine were, during three years, kids worked like beasts, were sexually abused and, in certain cases, killed. All this happened under the indifferent and therefore complicit gaze of the inhabitants of Outer Maroo. The mine, with its buried bodies, represents the will not to face that truth ever again.

Susanna Rover refuses to respect this code of silence. So, when one day she confronts the drunken visitors of Bernie's pub with an insistent utterance of bare truths, she is savagely beaten to death. However, in her speech she points out a decisive fact – that silences can be very loud:

> There are letters and postcards being written and mailed every day. [...] You think you have stopped them getting out – Oh I know all about that; it took me a while but I know. [...] Only there's something I think you've all forgotten. [...] Because the people waiting for the letters that never arrive get a message, don't they? They get a very loud message. (Turner Hospital 1996, 60)

And this is exactly what happens; "words are like bushfires" and, as "you [can neither] stop them" nor "tell were they'll end up" (Turner Hospital 1996, 64), the parents of two kids arrive in Outer Maroo and start asking questions about their missing children. The arrival of Nick and Sarah marks the end of the community. Outer Maroo, strangled by guilt, cannot bear their inquisitive gazes. This demonstrates the way the censored – and the outback has effectively become the space of the censored – no matter how strictly guarded and far removed, inevitably becomes a silent but invasive presence in the community. However, things do not simply fall apart when questions start being asked – after all Susanna Rover was swiftly dealt with when she infringed the code of silence – it is more as if an equilibrium between silence and obscenity has been disrupted. The Old Fuckatoo, "a sort of mephitic fog, moistureless and invisible" (Turner Hospital 1996, 3), is the unremitting symptom of the disease weakening the community from inside:

"The Old Fuckatoo could brood, close and suffocating for days, [...] the stink of dead cattle would predominate; or else that particular rank sweetness of rotting sheep. On certain days, when hot currents shimmered off Oyster's Reef we could detect [...] the ghastly fug of the tunnels and shafts. Sometimes there was almost nothing, just the blankness of the outback heat, and this felt like a grace newly recognised. On other days – there was no escaping it – an already more disturbing trace would prevail, some terrible and indefinable emanation that suggested ... but no one wished to think what it suggested." (Turner Hospital 1996, 4)

The omnipresent smell of carbonized human corpses indicates the super-saturation of this ob-scene space with objects of the unconscious which are now overflowing into the space of the conscious: the scene. As it is clarified in the text, and as Müller explains: "nobody lives in a place like Outer Maroo unless he has things to hide" (Turner Hospital 1996, 275); which also means that those who have gone this far have the "desire to start again with a clean record on a geographical *tabula rasa*" (Müller 2000, 148). In its off-scene scenario, the town tries to create an appearance of normality and it proposes itself as an alternative/displaced scene. However, just like these people who have fled to an off-scene space, their secrets need a space where to be let out and securely contained; because "taboos [...] ferment, [...] insist in being broken; [...] people need to scream them in secret" (Turner Hospital 1996, 145), and rapidly "these hidden matters are so legion that they populate the desert spaces quite thickly" (Turner Hospital 1996, 275). In Outer Maroo the repressed saturates the outback until it literally explodes in flames and sets off stream of words. Just as the adolescent Mercy Given (a local girl who managed to flee from Oyster's Reef) drives Nick and Sarah towards Brisbane and "back on the map," the bushfire ignited by the burning of the Given's house (where Sarah, as a guest of the family, was supposed to be killed) obliterates the town. At that point Jess breaks her vow of silence – the one that compelled so many people to confess to her their unspeakable secrets (Turner Hospital 1996, 145) – and starts writing Outer Maroo's cruel story. The act of writing, as well as Nick's and Sarah's escape, put this self-censored space back on the map and, symbolically, they provide a safety-valve to the obscenity/unconscious bottled up in the desert.

As Homi Bhabha suggests, and as this text tragically demonstrates, the risk of not accomplishing this task is that of being perpetually haunted by *das Unheimliche* which, for Freud is "the name for everything that ought to have remained ... secret and hidden but has come to light (Freud, "The Uncanny"; qtd.in Bhabha 1994, 10). What comes to light in Outer Maroo is so powerful that in its sway it wipes out almost the entire community. What survives and is actually reinstated by this catharsis is an even older uncanny force. The bora rings, millenary Aboriginal sacred sites which, after being repeatedly desecrated by miners and graziers, remind of the violent usurpation of the Aboriginal land:

> [Ethel] has been putting the scattered rocks back where they belong, fillings gaps in the circles and centuries. They have been here, the bora rings, for over twenty thousand years [...]. From time to time Ethel grins at me, and her teeth flash in her black face like stark white lightning. [...]
> 'My mob chuckling up their sleeves,' she tells me. My mob been here all along. They been waiting for this.' [...] 'Whitefella Maroo been and gone once, and been and gone twice, and we're still here, my mob and me.' (Turner Hospital 1996, 40)

Although Maroo has burnt to the ground once before (the previous town was only a few kilometres away and called Inner Maroo), it is not necessary to imply, as Fiona Coyle does, that the Murris are responsible for the two arsons (cf. Coyle 2001, 125, 127); it is in the nature of taboos – which "insist on being broken" – to set things on fire. The bora rings represent one such taboo, "they brood in silence, [...] [a]bsences in their ghostly thousands thrum against the skin of red clay like a pulse" (Turner Hospital 1996, 137). It is a story that refuses to be forgotten and Ethel, by restoring the rocks of the bora rings to their legitimate places, symbolically reconnects the broken circles of her ancestors' lives: exterminated, absorbed, assimilated, stolen and reconciliated, the cyclic continuum of the dreamtime has been broken into segments that now, almost miraculously, fall back into place. Ultimately, in the place where "the First Ones speak to Ethel in lost tongues, [...] time does not run in a straight line" (Turner Hospital 1996, 42); on the contrary, it leaps forward from the past and returns spreading in unforeseeable directions. The secret buried in the outback is the dispossession of the natives. The consequences of this repression are evident in the unconscious of the nation. After centuries it still returns to haunt the consciousness of western society and, as it happens in *Oyster*, it eventually reclaims its legitimate space. Janette Turner Hospital concludes her novel with a hint of hope: "Gonna be rain" (Turner Hospital 1996, 399), Ethel says. Interrupting a drought that lasted several years, the rain will come to quench the thirst of the land but, most importantly, this means that "the Old Fuckatoo has fucked off." Along with the rain Ethel expects her tribe to come back. They have left after things turned sour at the reef, but they did not leave forever as they were only patiently waiting for history to run its course, for the obscene to become intolerable and for the uncanny to return.

Catharsis is therefore contemplated as the only possible way of purification. However, the price is high; as Jess reminds us, "it took the Great Fire of London in 1666 to wipe out the plague" (Turner Hospital 1996, 395). For an apocalyptic novel about a community that believes in millenarism and that, with the approach of the year 2000, prepares for the arrival of Armageddon and the new kingdom of God on earth, this is the appropriate conclusion. As in the case of the Great Fire of London the flames cauterize the "plague," leaving the numerologists to wonder whether it is the "footprint of the beast or act of God" (Turner Hospital 1996, 395). Of course, a continent-wide catharsis of this type is not a viable solution for the restructuring of the socio-topographic configuration of Australian space; Turner Hospital does not offer a solution to the problems exposed in *Oyster*, and therefore the *Unheimlich* remains a looming presence dangerously confined in the outback. The novel stands therefore as a powerful reminder of the urgent need of ceasing to turn one's back to the secrets buried in the outback. The author warns that, not in millenary but in sociological terms, Australia is close to that saturation point that would cause the unconscious to blazingly return with devastating consequences.

5.2 Tumbling Skeletons from the Closet

Australia is literally haunted by the persisting stain of colonial conquest and it is not surprising that ghosts return from the past to ask for attention in the present. Vivienne Cleven's most recent novel *Her Sister's Eye* addresses precisely this problem. In another typical small town of the outback of Queensland the willingly forgotten past inevitably catches up with the inhabitants of the village. In this novel Cleven presents a reality that closely resembles the one portrayed in Janette Turner Hospital's *Oyster*, although Mundra does not need to hide in uncharted territory because it finds shelter in its apparently blissful ordinariness and anonymity. Harmony and peace are used to disguise the tense equilibrium between scene and ob-scene, façade and taboo, and present and past. As in Outer Maroo's case, the community is held hostage by silences that insistently try to find a space where to liberate their voices. The return of the repressed is a theme common to both novels, however, it is interesting to notice the distinct approach each author uses and to consider the different perspectives offered by their stories. As a White Australian expatriate, Turner Hospital warns Australia against a pathology which threatens to seriously harm its society. Vivienne Cleven, as an Australian native, literally speaks from the other side that in *Oyster* is only cautiously hinted at as being the ultimate uncanny presence. Seen from this perspective, *Her Sister's Eye* works seamlessly as a continuation of the theme introduced by the previous novel. It explores the space of the outback starting where the white Australian author had to carefully forfeit her right to imagination.

The theme of white Australia being haunted by the ghosts of Aboriginal dispossession is in fact only eerily introduced in Outer Maroo; the voices arising from the Bora rings stand as reminders of a violent past, the particular story of which, needing to be recounted by an Aboriginal voice, remains undisclosed. Delving into this space, Cleven almost resumes and develops Turner Hospital's thematic exploration. With the slow unfolding of Mundra's violent history, the author brings the past back to life – in the form of ghosts and oral narrations – and, in the process, she exposes an intricate net of events outlining the socio-topographic configuration of the town. The river is the fulcrum of the story; it splits the town in two halves and it separates the Aborigines, on one side, from the white community, on the other. According to an old ban, natives were not allowed to enter the city but were compelled to remain on the other side of the river, where their camp was situated: "There would have been about six or seven of us fellahs in the town at that time. Not in town, but living on the edges, you see. The way things were back then was that blacks weren't welcome in town, white fellahs didn't want that" (Cleven 2002, 74). It was in the 1930s that this small group of natives, searching for work, gathered near Mundra and settled in the only place where they would be tolerated: "down there across from the old rubbish dump" (Cleven 2002, 73). Thus the topography of town roughly represents the split created by racial discrimination in the community: white on one neatly groomed side and Aboriginal on the other, dejected side. Although things have changed at the time of narration and the natives "enjoy" a certain level of formal tolerance, the old spatial configuration actually remains intact due to the mutually agreed code of silence covering the bloody deeds of the past. In the 1990s nobody lives in humpies built with rubbish recuperated from the dump anymore. However, that other side of the river remains an encumbering void in the present community because it is there that the past is buried. For this reason the later generations of natives feel deracinated:

> 'I need to know about our life in Mundra. I... I feel ...' She stops, casts a glance at Nana, then pushes on. 'I know this is gonna sound silly but I feel lost here. Like I don't belong.' She's always felt as if she doesn't belong, even though Mundra has been home to her since she was a child. There's an emptiness she can't explain and somewhere in the recesses of her mind she's always known it's to do with the town's history. (Cleven 2002, 72)

The emptiness Doris feels is a direct consequence of the unspoken legacy of the past. The old Aboriginal camp and, by association, all the space beyond the river have become the site where the community's unconscious – white and native – is actively confined. In this sense marginalization has never ended; the obscene past is ostracized from the scene so that the old hatreds may be carefully concealed from view. This does not mean that contrasts have ceased and that the village now lives in harmony; on the contrary, Mundra still endures the frictions caused by racism and by a forcedly silenced past. The river, a fluid boundary indicating the inevitable interaction between the opposite sides, is both materially and symbolically the point of encounter between these opposing forces. There, on its riverbanks, people got killed, and phantoms insistently reappear.

The type of haunting caused by the split in Mundra's psychic topography is also evident in two of the main characters, Archie Corella and Sofie Dove. Archie is an Aboriginal swagman who, having forgotten everything about his past, arrives in Mundra recognizing neither the place where he was born nor the son of the squatter who, by killing his sister, had ruined his family. His amnesia, the unmotivated blinding pain to which he periodically falls prey, and the unconscious circular journey are all forms of "haunting that in the end compel him to recall his true identity – he is really called Raymond Gee – and his past. Sofie Dove, a slightly retarded Aboriginal who quickly becomes Archie's best friend, has the faculty of speaking with the ghosts living in the river and, as Janine Little suggests in her review of the novel (Little 2002), by their voices she is instigated to metamorphose from victim into executioner. The past inevitably returns, and even after half a century the last descendant of the Drysdales still bullies the Aboriginal population. Sofie is one of Donald's victims – emblematically he abuses women in the concealment of a shed and not in the family house – but when she drowns him in the river she is capable of escaping the maddening force of violence by ascribing the actual killing to the voices that talk to her from the river. Thus, all the narrative threads, in a disconnected fashion which reminds of the rhizomic one exposed by Jess in *Oyster*, lead back to the river because "the final answer is down the dirt road" (Cleven 2002, 172), by the river were it all had begun.

It is in fact the crossing of this border that, in the early days of the community, prompts Edward Drysdale to kill the daughter of a headstrong Aboriginal woman whose only fault was to periodically visit town. Belle is the target of this revenge killing and, while playing by the river, she is murdered with a rifle shot. Her brother Raymond, who is with her at the moment, immediately tries to avenge himself, and only perchance fails in his intent. The very same day the Gee Family is dispersed and, in time, the young Raymond eventually forgets his sorrowful past and, suffering an amnesia, assumes his best friend's identity, Archie Corella, who had previously died in an accident with a horse. Led by the voices of his unconscious, which insist on trying to remind him who he really is, fifty years later Archie/Raymond is conducted back to his hometown at the discovery of his secret.

Although Archie's and Sofie's pathologies are clearly the product of the violence perpetrated by the white community, it is important to notice that the social landscape of the town is not rigidly described in terms of black and white; on the contrary, it is through a lifelike shading of the social texture that the story becomes more complex and credible. Caroline Drysdale is the principal white character who, not fitting in the mainstream society, is marginalized and bullied into submission. Her story – reminding of Bertha Mason's enforced condition of "madwoman in the attic" (Gilbert and Gubar 1979) as proposed in *Wide Sargasso Sea* (Rhys 1966) – is one of disempowerment and psychological persecution motivated by a perverse need for retribution against Caroline's parents. All this because, back in the 30s they were an illuminated family who sympathized with Lillian Gee (Belle and Raymond's mother), and, while publicly defending her against racism, they humiliated Edward Drysdale. Mundra is therefore not simply a racist town, but also a chauvinist community that joins together in discriminating against its opponents. This is also the case of Jenny Anne, a woman who gets locked up in her house after letting an Aboriginal woman hold her new-born baby (Cleven 2002, 152). Cleven's interest in feminist issues – also confirmed by the playful use made of *Wide Sargasso Sea* in her previous novel, *Bitin' Back*[21] (2000) – is mostly developed in Caroline, who, unjustly accused of being insane, is progressively driven mad by her husband's scheming. As a result, the type of haunting she suffers has to do with an obsessive desire to join the club of the Red Rose Ladies, a women's committee which, after the death of the last of the Drysdale bullies, has taken over the role of moral institution of town. Each year, Caroline renews her efforts in winning the approval of the committee by producing cakes and sophisticated dishes, however, the result is always the same. Polly Goodman, her deceased husband's lover, prevents her admission. Yet, Caroline's insistence has nothing to do with wanting to join forces with the tyrant ladies, on the contrary, as she explains to Sophie, she initially wanted to join the club because it would have been the only way to escape her tedious domesticity: "A wife was expected to look after a house and husband. Really there wasn't a great deal you could do outside the home. That's unless you joined a women's committee or the like" (Cleven 2002, 65). In later years, the yearly baking of cakes and the inevitable rejection becomes a ritual locked in a cyclic repetition of time.

---

[21] The Aboriginal male protagonist wakes up one day claiming to be Jean Rhys and starts dressing up like a woman. To the astonishment of his mother, it is later discovered that he is not a transsexual but a clever young author who is trying to experience gender discrimination in order to write about women with a better knowledge.

Ghosts will keep emerging from the past for as long as their stories will be held secret. The town's discretion is however motivated not solely by the threat posed by white people, it is also induced by grief. As Nana Vida tells her niece Doris: "there are people here that still hurt very badly about what I have to tell you" (Cleven 2002, 143). There is a complicity between the opposing sides, one tries to forget the pain endured in the past and the other tries to hide their guilt: "Mundra is full of fellahs that like to cover things over, especially certain ones that got something to hide" (Cleven 2002, 143). In a situation where the past is burdened with concealed traumas, ghosts eventually acquire agency and proceed to seek vengeance. This is the case of Donald's death, where Sofie becomes the agent of that otherworldly determination:

> Only one thing to do
> What that is
> Cut his water off
> How to
> Bring him this way […] Yeeeeaaaahhhh tha'll be a lesson for all bulls
> How Sofie do that
> Sshhhsssshh drop to the guts n crawl in
> Oh cold water
> *Shush now member what boo said they all blame the girl cos she got that thing n she a girl n girls dirty.* (Cleven 2002, 57)

As previously mentioned, these voices do not simply persuade Sofie to take action, they also become the agents of the killing. Later, they reassure Sofie by saying: "*He Jumped into us he did*" (Cleven 2002, 59). Just like in *Oyster*, there is a strong sense of predestination. Over time a secret will find its way out and will return in the most disruptive possible way.

With this warning Cleven is not actually threatening white Australia; conversely, the main lesson taught by the novel is that revenge cannot possibly unblock the situation. In fact, after the well deserved death of all the male Drysdales – Edward is accidentally shot during a raid to the Aboriginal camp, Reginald is killed by Caroline's tempering with his heart medication, and Donald is drowned by the river – the ghosts keep haunting and causing havoc throughout the city. Polly Goodman is the person to be targeted by the voices influencing Sofie. In retaliation against the pain viciously inflicted to Caroline Drysdale, Sofie urinates on the Polly's rose garden. After being caught, she tries to make up for it by mowing her lawn. In doing so, she accidentally sets her house on fire.

All considered, the risk posed by the unrelenting return of the repressed is reciprocal. Both Archie Corella and Sofie become helpless victims of Mundra's ghosts. Archie, having found his way towards the place where his sister was shot, re-lives the events of fifty years before and resumes his old identity. At that moment Sofie joins him on the riverbank with the local policeman at her back. In the confusion of the moment Archie does not see Sofie but mistakes her for his dead sister:

> He hears the low thwump, then sees the men trying to catch her.
> She is screaming, her white dress spotted with blood. Blood. Blood. A dead smell.
>
> She is trying to fight them. This time he can't let them do it. He knows there's a man across the river with a gun, pointing at him and Belle. [...] They've come back, they've come to get them all! They want him to pay the price for what his mother has done. (Cleven 2002, 219)

Thus, Archie/Raymond drags whom he thinks is his sister in the flooded river and they are swept away. The symbolic significance of the watercourse dividing the town becomes ultimately evident: the river could represent history itself and, through its haunting, the unnatural flow of psychic time caused by censorship and accumulated grief. As a further proof, the flooding of the river coincides with the convergence towards the river and the present of all the different threads of the story. Archie has found his true identity, and Sofie has avenged Caroline Drysdale by torching her enemy's house. At that moment the river comes washing the past away.

There is, however, a second thread of the story. While Archie retraces his true identity, and Sofie catches up on history by settling the score, Nana Vida, after many hesitations, recounts their stories to Doris, her niece. It is only after she has concluded her narration that the village seems to find its peace. The motivation seems to be implied in the words that the old woman tells her niece: "What I told you, pass on, girl. Keep this alive, tell em all. Funny thing is history. If you remember what others went through to get ya here then all is not lost. Some died for you, others fought for you. Always remember where you're from. There's hope. Always hope" (Cleven 2002, 229). This resolution suggests that, if only this story had been recounted earlier, Sofie, Archie and Polly Goodman – who gets severely burnt in the fire – could have possibly been spared their destiny. Instead, in an epilogue reminding Outer Maroo's blazing catharsis, the censored reaches its saturation point before the verbal disclosure of the obscene can deflate its accumulated pressure.

Significantly, after Nana finishes her account of the town history, the ground in Mundra becomes fertile and the roses that Archie was preparing to plant in his garden – flowers that "[would] never grow properly for him" (Cleven 2002, 2) – are placed in Caroline's garden:

> "The soil were always bad here, Caroline. You live at the dead end of the line." […]
>
> Caroline faces Murilla. "Well, what do you think? Do they have a chance here?
>
> Murilla studies the soil in her hands. "Yes, Yes, I think they do. […] [B]ut we have to keep an eye on things." (Cleven 2002, 231-232)

The chances the roses stand have more to do with Mundra's society rather than any botanical problem. All in all, Cleven's novel proposes a more positive perspective than Turner Hospital's *Oyster*. Although the outback is presently an obscene space dangerously populated by skeletons concealed in innumerable closets, it is also a space that can be returned to its people and transformed into a "fertile" space. In this project, as demonstrated by Murilla's and Caroline's friendship, Vivienne Cleven includes white Australians as well. This could be achieved through the careful reconfiguration of the socio-topographic function of the outback. From being the dumping ground of western present and past obscenity, it should be transformed into a space of mutual recognition. Just as in *Oyster*, for a drought-stricken land the prospect of a brighter future is foreshadowed by the coming of a storm: "Looks like a storm is coming from the east. [...] Good time to be plantin" (Cleven 2002, 232).

Bibliography

Allen Rogers, James (2000). "Darwinism and Social Darwinism." *Herbert Spencer: Critical Assessments*. Ed. John Offer. London: Routledge. 149-164.

Althusser, Louis (1994). "Ideology and Ideological State Apparatuses: Notes Towards an Investigation." *Mapping Ideology*. Ed. Slavoj Žižek. London: Verso. 100-140.

Arthur, Kateryna Olijnyk (1985). "Fiction and the Rewriting of History: A Reading of Colin Johnson." *Westerly* 30.1: 55-60.

Barrett, Donald (1982). "The Mythology of Pan and Picnic at Hanging Rock." *Southerly* 42.3: 299-308.

Barthes, Roland (1957). *Mythologies*. Paris: Editions du Seuil.

Baudrillard, Jean (1990). *Fatal Strategies*. Trans. Philip Beitchman and W.G. J. Niesluchowski. London: Pluto.

Baynton, Barbara (1993). *Bush Studies*. Sydney: Angus & Robertson.

Bessant, Judith and Sandy Cook (1997). *Women's Encounters with Violence: Australian Experiences*. Thousand Oaks: Sage Publications.

Bessant, Judith, and Rob Watts (1989). "Masculinity and Violence: An Ethnography of Exploration." *Gangs and Youth Subcultures: International Explorations*. Ed. Kayleen M. Hazelhurst and Cameron Hazelhurst. New Brunswick: Transaction Publishers. 189-220.

Beston, John (2003). "Will Voss Endure? Fifty Years Later." *Antipodes* 17.1: 50-54.

Bhabha, Homi K. (1994). *The Location of Culture*. London; New York: Routledge.

Blainey, Geoffrey A. (1993). "Balance Sheet on Our History." *Quadrant* 37.7-8: 10-15.

Bliss, Carolyn (2000). "Reimagining the Remembered: David Malouf and the Moral Implications of Myth." *World Literature Today* 74.4: 724-732.

Bliss, Carolyn (2005). "'Lies and Silences': Cultural Masterplots and Existential Authenticity in Peter Carey's True History of the Kelly Gang." *Fabulating Beauty: Perspectives on the Fiction of Peter Carey*. Ed. Andreas Gaile. Amsterdam: Rodopi. 275-300.

Bradley, Ian Campbell, ed. (1990). *The Penguin Book of Hymns*. London: Penguin.

Brady, Veronica (1974). "Of Castles and Censorship." *Westerly* 2: 45-50.

Brennan, Bernadette (2004). "Words of Water: Reading Otherness in Tourmaline and Oyster." *JASAL* 3. 143-157.

Brewster, Anne (March-May 2002) "Aboriginal Life Writing and Globalisation: Doris Pilkington's *Follow the Rabbit-Proof Fence*." Australian Humanities Review 25. <http://www.austra lianhumanitiesreview.org/archive/Issue-March-2002/brewster.ht ml> accessed Mar. 2005.

Brown, Jodie (1993). "Unlearning Dominant Modes of Representation: Mudrooroo's 'Doctor Wooreddy's Prescription for Enduring the Ending of the World' and Robert Drewe's 'The Savage Crows.'" *Westerly* 38.3: 71-78.

Brown, Michael P. (2000). *Closet Space: Geographies of Metaphor from the Body to the Globe*. London; New York: Routledge.

Buck, Joseph. (2001). "Trees That Belong Here: An Interview with Award Winning Author Kim Scott." *Boomtown Magazine*. <http://www.boomtownmag.com/articles/200101/benang.htm> accessed May 2004.

Burchill, Sandra (1993). "Katharine Susannah Prichard: `She Did What She Could.'" *The Time to Write: Australian Women Writers 1890-1930*. Ed. Kay Ferres. Ringwood, Victoria: Penguin. 139-161.

Carey, Peter (2000). *True History of the Kelly Gang*. St Lucia, Queensland: University of Queensland Press.

Clancy, Laurie (2004). "Selective History of the Kelly Gang." *Overland* 175: 53-58.

Clarke, Marcus Andrew Hislop (1970). *His Natural Life*. Harmondsworth: Penguin.
Clarke, Marcus Andrew Hislop (1992). *For the Term of His Natural Life*. Pymble, NSW: Angus & Robertson.
Cleven, Vivienne (2002). *Her Sister's Eye*. St Lucia, Queensland: University of Queensland Press.
Coetzee, J. M. (1996). *Giving Offense: Essays on Censorship*. Chicago, IL: University of Chicago Press.
Coetzee, J. M. (2003). *Elizabeth Costello: Eight Lessons*. Milsons Point, N.S.W.: Knopf.
Con Davis, Robert and Laurie Finke (1989). *Literary Criticism and Theory: The Greeks to the Present*. New York: Longman.
Corbould, Clare (1999). "Rereading Radical Texts: Coonardoo and the Politics of Fiction." *Australian Feminist Studies* 14: 415-424.
Coyle, Fiona (2001). "A Third Space? Postcolonial Australia and the Fractal Landscape in the Last Magician and Oyster." *Mapping the Sacred: Religion, Geography and Postcolonial Literatures*. Ed. Jamie S. Scott and Paul Simpson-Housley. Amsterdam, Netherlands: Rodopi. 111-130.
Crittenden, Anne (1976). "Picnic at Hanging Rock: A Myth and Its Symbols." *Meanjin Quarterly* 35.2: 167-181.
Dale, Leigh (1994). "'Coonardoo' and Truth." *Tilting at Matilda: Literature, Aborigines, Women and the Church in Contemporary Australia*. Ed. Dennis Haskell. South Fremantle, Western Australia: Fremantle Arts Centre Press. 129-140.
Daly, Sathyabhama (2000). "David Malouf's Remembering Babylon and the Wild Man of the European Cultural Consciousness." *LiNQ* 27.1: 9-19.
Darwin, Charles (2003). *The Origin of Species*. New York: Signet Classic.
Deleuze, Gilles and Félix Guattari (1987). *A Thousand Plateaus: Capitalism and Schizophrenia*. Minneapolis: University of Minnesota Press.
Dick, William (1984). *A Bunch of Ratbags*. Ringwood, Vic.: Penguin.

Eibl-Eibesfeldt, Irenaus (1979). *The Biology of Peace and War: Men, Animals, and Aggression*. New York: Viking Press.

Elliott, Brian Robinson (1958). *Marcus Clarke*. Oxford: Clarendon Press.

Ellis, Cath (1995). "A Tragic Convergence: A Reading of Katherine Susannah Prichard's 'Coonardoo.'" *Westerly* 40.2: 63-71.

Foucault, Michel (1967). *Madness and Civilization: A History of Insanity in the Age of Reason*. London, Sydney: Tavistock Publications.

Foucault, Michel (1979). *Discipline and Punish: The Birth of the Prison*. New York: Vintage Books.

Foucault, Michel (1980). *Power/Knowledge: Selected Interviews and Other Writings, 1972-1977*. New York: Pantheon Books.

Foucault, Michel (1984). *The History of* Sexuality. Vol. 1: An Introduction. Harmondsworth: Penguin.

Gaile, Andreas (2001). "Re-Mythologizing an Australian Legend: Peter Carey's True History of the Kelly Gang." *Antipodes* 15.1: 37-39.

Gilbert, Sandra M. and Susan Gubar (1979). *The Madwoman in the Attic: The Woman Writer and the Nineteenth-Century Literary Imagination*. New Haven: Yale University Press.

Glissant, Edouard (1996). *Introduction à une poetique du divers*. Paris: Gallimard.

Goldie, Terry (1989). *Fear and Temptation: The Image of the Indigene in Canadian, Australian and New Zealand Literatures*. Kingston Ont.: McGill-Queen's University Press.

Greer, Germaine (2003). *Whitefella Jump Up: The Shortest Way to Nationhood*. Melbourne: Black Inc.

Greet, Annie (1995). "Interview with Archie Weller." CR*NLE Reviews Journal* 1&2: 138-149.

Hall, Richard, selected and introd. (1993). *Banjo Paterson: His Poetry and Prose*. St Leonards, NSW: Allen & Unwin.

Harrison, Robert Pogue (1992). *Forests: The Shadow of Civilization*. Chicago: University of Chicago Press.

Haynes, R. D. (1998). *Seeking the Centre: The Australian Desert in Literature, Art and Film*. Cambridge; Melbourne: Cambridge University Press.

Henderson, Margaret (1998). "Subdivisions of Suburbia: The Politics of Place in Melissa Lucashenko's Steam Pigs and Amanda Lohrey's Camille's Bread." *Australian Literary Studies* 18: 72-86.

Herbert, Xavier (1969). *Capricornia*. Sydney: Pacific Books.

Herbert, Xavier (1975). *Poor Fellow My Country*. Sydney: William Collins Publisher.

Herbert, Xavier (1990). *Capricornia*. Introd. Mudrooroo Nyoongah. North Ryde, N.S.W.: Angus & Robertson.

Hergenhan, Laurie (1971). "The Contemporary Reception of His Natural Life." *Southerly* 31.1: 50-63.

Hergenhan, Laurie (1993). *Unnatural Lives: Studies in Australian Fiction About the Convicts, from James Tucker to Patrick White*. St Lucia, Queensland: University of Queensland Press.

Hodge, Bob, and Vijay C. Mishra (1991). *Dark Side of the Dream: Australian Literature and the Postcolonial Mind*. North Sydney, New South Wales: Allen and Unwin.

Huggan, Graham (1994). *Territorial Disputes: Maps and Mapping Strategies in Contemporary Canadian and Australian Fiction*. Toronto: University of Toronto Press.

Huggan, Graham (2002). "Cultural Memory in Postcolonial Fiction: The Uses and Abuses of Ned Kelly." *Australian Literary Studies* 20.3: 142-154.

Hughes, Robert (2003). *The Fatal Shore: A History of the Transportation of Convicts to Australia, 1787-1868*. London, England: Vintage.

Hutcheon, Linda (1988). *A Poetics of Postmodernism: History, Theory, Fiction*. New York: Routledge.

Hyam, Ronald (1990). *Empire and Sexuality: The British Experience*. Manchester: Manchester University Press.

Jacobs, Johan U. (2000). "Allegorical Spaces and Actual Places in Postcolonial Novels." *Spaces and Crossings: Essays on Literature and Culture in Africa and Beyond.* Ed. Wilson Rita and Carlotta von Maltzan. Frankfurt: Peter Lang.

JanMohamed, Abdul R. (Autumn 1985). "The Economy of Manichean Allegory: The Function of Racial Difference in Colonialist Literature." *Critical Inquiry* 12.1: 59-87.

Jebb, Mary Anne (2002). *Blood, Sweat and Welfare: A History of White Bosses and Aboriginal Pastoral Workers.* Nedlands, W.A.: University of Western Australia Press.

Kermode, Frank (1967). *The Sense of an Ending: Studies in the Theory of Fiction.* New York: Oxford University Press.

Kinsella, John (2002). "The Shifting City and the Shifting Bush." *Overland* 169: 23-34.

Kirkby, Joan (1998). "The Pursuit of Oblivion: In Flight from Suburbia." *Australian Literary Studies* 18.4: 1-19.

Lawson, Elizabeth (1987). "'Oh Don't You Remember Black Alice?' or How Many Mothers Had Norman Shillingsworth?" *Westerly* 32.3: 29-39.

Lawson, Henry (1896). *In the Days When the World Was High and Other Verses.* Sydney: Angus and Robertson.

Lawson, Henry (1927). *While the Billy Boils.* London: Cape.

Lefebvre, Henri (1991). The Production of Space. Oxford: Blackwell.

Lever, Susan (2000). "Realism and Socialism: Katharine Susannah Prichard's Coonardoo." *Real Relations: The Feminist Politics of Form in Australian Fiction.* Ed. Susan Lever. Rushcutters Bay, NSW: Association for the Study of Australian Literature, Halstead Press. 55-68, notes 154-155.

Lindsay, Joan Weigall (1975). *Picnic at Hanging Rock.* Adelaide: Rigby.

Lindsay, Joan Weigall, and Yvonne Rousseau (1987). *The Secret of Hanging Rock: Joan Lindsay's Final Chapter.* North Ryde, NSW: Angus & Robertson.

Little, Janine (2002). "Incantations of Grief and Memory." *Australian Women's Book Review* 14.2.
Lovell, Sue (2004). "The 'Psychic Space' of Queensland in the Work of Janette Turner Hospital." *Queensland Review* 11.2: 11-23.
Lucashenko, Melissa (1997). *Steam Pigs*. St Lucia, QLD: University of Queensland Press.
Lucashenko, Melissa (2002). "Many Prisons: Australian Aboriginal Women Face Racism." *Hecate* 28.1: 139-144.
Lucashenko, Melissa and O. Best (1995). "Women Bashing: An Urban Aboriginal Perspective." *Social Alternatives* 14.1: 19-23.
MacGregor, Justin (1992). "A Margin's History: Mudrooroo Narogin's "Doctor Wooreddy's Prescription for Enduring the Ending of the World"." *Antipodes* 6.2: 113-118.
Malouf, David (1993). *Remembering Babylon*. Sydney: Chatto & Windus.
Malouf, David (2000). "A Writing Life." *World Literature Today* 74.4: 701-705.
Martin, Susan K. (2004). "Dead White Male Heroes: Ludwig Leichhardt and Ned Kelly in Australian Fictions." *Imagining Australia: Literature and Culture in the New New World*. Ed. Judith Ryan and Chris Wallace-Crabbe. Cambridge: Harvard University, Committee on Australian Studies. 23-52.
McCredden, Lyn (1999). "Craft and Politics: Remembering Babylon's Postcolonial Responses." *Southerly* 59.2: 5-16.
McDonald, Avis G. (1986). "Rufus Dawes and Changing Narrative Perspectives in His Natural Life." *Australian Literary Studies* 12.3: 347-358.
McDougall, Russell (2000). "Collection of Two Articles on Xavier Herbert and His Work Capricornia." *Notes and Furphies* 43: 24-27.
Monahan, Sean (1985). "Xavier Herbert's Capricornia: In Praise of the Swagman Spirit." Westerly 30.4: 15-24.

Morley, Patricia A. (1972). *The Mistery of Unity: Theme and Technique in the Novels of Patrick White*. Montreal: McGill-Queen's University Press.

Morse, Ruth (1988). "Impossible Dreams: Miscegenation and Building Nations." *Southerly* 48.1: 80-96.

Mudrooroo (1983). *Doctor Wooreddy's Prescription for Enduring the Ending of the World*. Melbourne: Hyland House.

Mudrooroo (1990). *Writing from the Fringe: A Study of Modern Aboriginal Literature*. South Yarra, VIC: Hyland House.

Müller, Anja I. (2000). "Travels in No-Man's Land: Closure and Transgression in Janette Turner Hospital's Oyster." *Being/s in Transit: Travelling, Migration, Dislocation*. Ed. Liselotte Glage. Amsterdam, Netherlands: Rodopi. 141-153.

Nobel-Prize-Foundation. (1973). "Nobel Prize in Literature 1973." <http://nobelprize.org/nobel_prizes/literature/laureates/1973/> accessed 12 Jan. 2006.

O'Reilly, Nathanael (2002). "The Voice of the Teller: A Conversation with Peter Carey." *Antipodes* 16.2: 164-167.

OED Online. (Mar. 2004). <http://0-dictionary.oed.com.alpha2.latrobe.edu.au/cgi/entry/00329337> accessed 23 Aug. 2006.

Papastergiadis, Nikos (1994). "David Malouf and Languages for Landscape: An Interview." *Ariel* 25.3: 83-94.

Paterson, A. B. (1902). *The Man from Snowy River and Other Verses*. Sydney: Angus and Robertson.

Pease, Allison (2000). *Modernism, Mass Culture, and the Aesthetics of Obscenity*. Cambridge: Cambridge University Press.

Perera, Suvendrini (2000). "Futures Imperfect." *Alter/Asians: Asian-Australian Identities in Art, Media and Popular Culture*. Ed. Ien Ang et al. 3-24, 280-281, 289-313.

Povinelli, Elizabeth A. (1994). "Sexual Savages / Sexual Sovereignity: Australian Colonial Texts and the Postcolonial Politics of Nationalism." *Diacritics* 24.2/3: 122-150.

Prichard, Katharine Susannah (1956). *Coonardoo: The Well in the Shadow*. Sydney: Angus and Robertson.

Reynolds, Henry (1990). T*he Other Side of the Frontier: Aboriginal Resistance to the European Invasion of Australia.* Ringwood: Penguin.

Reynolds, Henry (2001). *An Indelible Stain? The Question of Genocide in Australia's History.* Ringwood, Vic.: Penguin.

Rhys, Jean (1966). *Wide Sargasso Sea.* New York: Norton.

Robb, Peter (1999). *Pig's Blood and Other Fluids.* Sydney: Duffy & Snellgrove.

Robinson, Jeffrey (1985). "The Aboriginal Enigma: 'Heart of Darkness,' 'Voss' and 'Palace of the Peacock.'" *Journal of Commonwealth Literature* 20.1: 148-155.

Robson, Leslie Lloyd (1963). "The Historical Basis of 'For the Term of His Natural Life.'" *Australian Literary Studies* 1.2: 104-121.

Rousseau, Yvonne (1980). *The Murders at Hanging Rock.* Fitzroy, VIC: Scribe.

Rowley, Sue (December 1989). "Inside the Deserted Hut: The Representation of Motherhood in Bush Mythology." *Westerly* 34.4. 76-95.

Ryan, Simon (1996). *The Cartographic Eye: How Explorers Saw Australia.* Cambridge: Cambridge University Press.

Said, Edward W. (1983). *The World, the Text, and the Critic.* Cambridge: Harvard University Press.

Savran, D. (1999). "The Sadomasochist in the Closet: White Masculinity and Culture of Victimization." *Differences: A Journal of Feminist Cultural Studies* 8: 127-152.

Schaffer, Kay (1983). "Barbara Baynton: Woman as 'The Chosen Vessel.'" *Australian Literary Studies* 11.1: 25-37.

Schaffer, Kay (1989). "Women and the Bush: Australian National Identity and Representations of the Feminine." *Antipodes* 3.1: 7-13.

Scott, Kim (1999). *Benang: From the Heart.* South Fremantle, W.A.: Fremantle Arts Centre Press.

Shields, Rob (1991). *Places on the Margin: Alternative Geographies of Modernity.* London: Routledge.

Shoemaker, Adam (1984). "Sex and Violence in the Black Australian Novel." *Westerly* 29.1: 45-57.

Shoemaker, Adam (1988). *Black Words, White Page: Aboriginal Literature 1929-1988*. St. Lucia, Qld.: University of Queensland Press.

Shoemaker, Adam (1993). *Mudrooroo: A Critical Study*. Pymble, New South Wales: Angus and Robertson.

Shoemaker, Adam (1998). "White on Black / Black on White." *The Oxford Literary History of Australia*. Ed. Bruce Bennett, Jennifer Strauss and Chris Wallace-Crabbe. Melbourne, Victoria: Oxford University Press. 9-20.

Slack, Michael (2002) "The 'Plains of Promise' Revisited: A Reassessment of the Frontier in North Western Queensland." *JAS, Australia's Public Intellectual Forum*, 71-83, 187-189 <http://search.informit.com.au/fullText;res=APAFT;dn=200302363> accessed 22 Feb. 2005.

Spinks, Lee (1995). "Allegory, Space, Colonialism: "Remembering Babylon" and the Production of Colonial History." *Australian Literary Studies* 17.2: 166-174.

Stallybrass, Peter, and Allon White (1986). *The Politics and Poetics of Transgression*. Cambridge: Cambridge University Press.

Stoler, Ann Laura (1995). *Race and the Education of Desire: Foucault's History of Sexuality and the Colonial Order of Things*. Durham: Duke University Press.

Tacey, David J. (1988). *Patrick White: Fiction and the Unconscious*. Melbourne: Oxford University Press.

Tacey, David J. (1995). *Edge of the Sacred: Transformation in Australia*. Blackburn North, Vic: HarperCollins.

Tatz, Colin (1999). *Genocide in Australia*. Canberra: AIATSIS.

The Oxford English Dictionary (1989). 2nd ed. Oxford: Oxford University Press.

Thieme, John (2001). *Postcolonial Con-Texts: Writing Back to the Canon*. London: Continuum.

Thomas, Sue (1987). "Interracial Encounters in Katharine Susannah Prichard's 'Coonardoo.'" *World Literature Written in English* 27.2: 234-244.

Tiffin, Chris, and Alan Lawson (1994). *De-Scribing Empire: Post-Colonialism and Textuality*. London: Routledge.

Tinkler, John (1982). "Canadian Cultural Norms and Australian Social Rules: Susanna Moodie's 'Roughing It in the Bush' and Marcus Clarke's 'His Natural Life.'" *Canadian Literature* 94: 10-22.

Todorov, Tzvetan (1984). *The Conquest of America: The Question of the Other*. New York: Harper & Row.

Treagus, Mandy (2000). "A Queer Kind of Belonging: Identity: Identity and Nation in Christos Tsiolkas's Loaded." *CRNLE Journal*: 219-227.

Tsiolkas, Christos (1995). *Loaded*. Milsons Point, NSW: Vintage.

Turcotte, Gerry (1998). "Australian Gothic." *The Handbook to Gothic Literature*. Ed. Marie Mulvey-Roberts. Basingstoke: Macmillan. 10-19.

Turcotte, Gerry (1999). "Colour My World: Fighting Free from the Virtual Prison of Race." *Sydney Morning Herald* (Spectrum): 9.

Turner Hospital, Janette (1996). *Oyster*. London, England: Virago.

Van Toorn, Penny (1992). "The Terrors Of 'Terra Nullius': Gothicising and De-Gothicising Aboriginality." *World Literature Written in English* 32-33.1: 87-97.

Vargas Llosa, Mario (1971). *García Márquez: Historia de un deicidio*. Barcelona: Barral Editores.

Vernon, John (1973). *The Garden and the Map: Schizophrenia in Twentieth-Century Literature and Culture*. Urbana: University of Illinois Press.

Wallace-Crabbe, Chris (1974). *Melbourne or the Bush: Essays on Australian Literature and Society*. Sydney: Angus and Robertson.

Weller, Archie (1981). *The Day of the Dog*. North Sydney: Allen & Unwin.

Wevers, Lydia (1995). "Terra Australis: Landscape as Medium in 'Capricornia' and 'Poor Fellow My Country.'" *Australian Literary Studies* 17.1: 38-48.

White, Hyden (1972). "The Forms of Wilderness: Archeology of an Idea." *The Wild Man Within: An Image in Western Thought from the Renaissance to Romanticism*. Ed. Edward Duddley and Maximillian E. Novak. Pittsburgh: University of Pittsburgh Press.

White, Patrick (1990). "The Prodigal Son." *Essays on Patrick White*. Ed. Peter Wolf. Boston: G. K. Hall. 21-24.

White, Patrick (1994). *Voss*. London: Vintage.

Whitlock, Gillian (1987). "'The Carceral Archipeligo': Marcus Clarke's *His Natural Life* and John Richardson's *Wacousta*." *Australian/Canadian Literatures in English: Comparative Perspectives*. Ed. Russell McDougall and Gillian Whitlock. North Ryde, New South Wales: Methuen Australia. 49-67.

Williams, Mark (1985). "Containing Continents: The Moralized Landscapes of Conrad, Greene, White and Harris." *Kunapipi* 7.1: 34-45.

Williams, Raymond (1973). *The Country and the City*. London: Chatto & Windus.

Windshuttle, Keith (2002). *Van Diemen's Land 1803-1847*. Sydney: Macley Press. Vol. 1 of *The Fabrication of Aboriginal History*.

Wright, Alexis (1997). *Plains of Promise*. St. Lucia, Qld: University of Queensland Press.

Wright, Alexis (1998) "Breaking Taboos: Alexis Wright at the Tasmanian Readers' and Writers' Festival, September 1998." *Australian Humanities Review* 11. <http://www.lib.latrobe.edu.au/AHR/archive/Issue-September-1998/wright.html> accessed 11 Sept. 2006.

Wright, Alexis (2002). "Politics of Writing." *Southerly* 62.2: 10-20.

STUDIES IN ENGLISH LITERATURES

Edited by Koray Melikoğlu

ISSN 1614-4651

1   Özden Sözalan
     The Staged Encounter
     Contemporary Feminism and Women's Drama
     2nd, revised editon
     ISBN 3-89821-367-6

2   Paul Fox (ed.)
     Decadences
     Morality and Aesthetics in British Literature
     ISBN 3-89821-573-3

3   Daniel M. Shea
     James Joyce and the Mythology of Modernism
     ISBN 3-89821-574-1

4   Paul Fox and Koray Melikoğlu (eds.)
     Formal Investigations
     Aesthetic Style in Late-Victorian and Edwardian Detective Fiction
     ISBN 978-3-89821-593-0

5   David Ellis
     Writing Home
     Black Writing in Britain Since the War
     ISBN 978-3-89821-591-6

6   Wei H. Kao
     The Formation of an Irish Literary Canon in the Mid-Twentieth Century
     ISBN 978-3-89821-545-9

7   Bianca Del Villano
     Ghostly Alterities
     Spectrality and Contemporary Literatures in English
     2nd, revised editon
     ISBN 978-3-89821-714-9

8   Melanie Ann Hanson
     Decapitation and Disgorgement
     The Female Body's Text in Early Modern English Drama and Poetry
     ISBN 978-3-89821-605-5

9   Shafquat Towheed (ed.)
     New Readings in the Literature of British India, c.1780-1947
     ISBN 978-3-89821-673-9

10   Paola Baseotto
     "Disdeining life, desiring leaue to die"
     Spenser and the Psychology of Despair
     ISBN 978-3-89821-567-1

11   *Annie Gagiano*
     Dealing with Evils
     Essays on Writing from Africa
     ISBN 978-3-89821-867-2

12   *Thomas F. Halloran*
     James Joyce: Developing Irish Identity
     A Study of the Development of Postcolonial Irish Identity in the Novels of James Joyce
     ISBN 978-3-89821-571-8

13   *Pablo Armellino*
     Ob-scene Spaces in Australian Narrative
     An Account of the Socio-topographic Construction of Space in Australian Literature
     ISBN 978-3-89821-873-3

FORTHCOMING (MANUSCRIPT WORKING TITLES)

Lance Weldy
Seeking a Felicitous Space
The Dialectics of Women and Frontier Space in *Giants in the Earth*, *Little House on the Prairie*, and *My Antonia*
ISBN 3-89821-535-0

Kevin Cole
Levity's Rainbow
Menippean Poetics in Swift, Fielding, and Sterne
ISBN 3-89821-654-3

Zeynep Z. Atayurt
'Excessive' Embodiment in Contemporary Women's Writing
ISBN 978-3-89821-978-5

Rana Tekcan
The Biographer and The Subject: A Study on Biographical Distance
ISBN 978-3-89821-995-2

Fatma Tuba Terci
Postmodern Goddesses in Contemporary Chicana Feminist Novel
Peel my Love Like an Onion, Caramelo, or, Puro Cuento: A Novel and Face of an Angel
ISBN 978-3-8382-0023-1

Series Subscription

Please enter my subscription to the series **Studies in English Literatures**, ISSN 1614-4651, as follows:

❏ complete series   OR   ❏ English-language titles
                              ❏ German-language titles

starting with
❏ volume # 1
❏ volume # ___
   ❏ please also include the following volumes: #___, ___, ___, ___, ___, ___,

❏ the next volume being published
   ❏ please also include the following volumes: #___, ___, ___, ___, ___, ___,

❏ 1 copy per volume   OR   ❏ ___ copies per volume

Subscription within Germany:

You will receive every title on 1st publication at the regular bookseller's price incl. s & h and VAT.

Payment:
❏ Please bill me for every volume.
❏ Lastschriftverfahren: Ich/wir ermächtige(n) Sie hiermit widerruflich, den Rechnungsbetrag je Band von meinem/unserem folgendem Konto einzuziehen.

Kontoinhaber: _____ Kreditinstitut: _____
Kontonummer: _____ Bankleitzahl: _____

International Subscription:

Payment (incl. s & h and VAT) in advance for
❏   10 volumes/copies (€ 319.80)   ❏ 20 volumes/copies (€ 599.80)
❏   40 volumes/copies (€ 1,099.80)
Please send my books to:

NAME_____ DEPARTMENT_____
ADDRESS _____
POST/ZIP CODE_____ COUNTRY _____
TELEPHONE _____ EMAIL_____

date/signature_____

Please fax to: **0511 / 262 2201 (+49 511 262 2201)**
or mail to: *ibidem*-Verlag, Julius-Leber-Weg 11, D-30457 Hannover, Germany
or send an e-mail: ibidem@ibidem-verlag.de

ibidem-Verlag
Melchiorstr. 15
D-70439 Stuttgart
info@ibidem-verlag.de

www.ibidem-verlag.de
www.ibidem.eu
www.edition-noema.de
www.autorenbetreuung.de

www.ingramcontent.com/pod-product-compliance
Lightning Source LLC
Chambersburg PA
CBHW072127290426
44111CB00012B/1808